"Inventive and filled with grace, *Hot Apple Cider* is just what its name implies: an open door, a warm invitation, a friend when needed and least expected, a gentle calling toward a generous life. From the shores of Australia and a woman's grief, to Romania and a choice we all must make, to the town of Stuckville anywhere in the world and a dozen other settings, in prose and poetry and non-fiction, these stories remind us that God draws us together and speaks to us uniquely and in community. If you're looking for inspiration, something to breathe in for reassurance that you're not alone, something to remind you to hear God's voice in acts of compassion, spend an afternoon with *Hot Apple Cider*. It could just change your life."

—**Jane Kirkpatrick**, award-winning author of *All Together in One Place*

"In the midst of our often-chilling nightly newscasts, the book *Hot Apple Cider* offers a tempting and 'toasty' reprieve. Filled with stories that will melt your heart, you'll want to keep it as handy as your favourite throw. This book is a wonderful way to feature the rich giftings of some of Canada's most talented writers. Let us encourage you to wrap your hands around this cup of creativity and drink in the warming words of these fine authors, many of whom we have been privileged to have as guests on our TV program. Go ahead... pour a cup!"

—**Ron and Ann Mainse**, hosts of *100 Huntley Street* television program

"In *Hot Apple Cider*, N. J. Lindquist and Wendy Elaine Nelles have assembled a vibrant compilation showcasing a diversity of styles and subjects. But what makes this such an appealing collection is the unique harmony of voices who are joined together by their individual—yet interconnected—journeys of faith. It's perfect reading for those days when we all are struggling with something."

—**Ben Heppner**, internationally acclaimed dramatic tenor, opera star and Grammy Award-winning recording artist; Officer of the Order of Canada and recipient of seven honorary doctorate degrees

"Much in the tradition of *Chicken Soup for the Soul*, these delightful readings are like a cozy cup of hot cider. Settle in for a moment of warmth and reflection. You will find *Hot Apple Cider* to be exactly what it promises. Enjoy!"

—**Brian C. Stiller**, President, Tyndale University College & Seminary

"Turning the pages of this collection, I have enjoyed reading pages from the lives of many other Canadian story-tellers—old friends, and many new writers. I found here stories that made me smile; stories that raised important questions, especially about the nature of prayer; and stories that challenged and sobered me. God is not explained or defended in these stories—but the experienced presence of 'Someone with us' is the common ground from which they spring. This is a book to sample, to savour and to share."
—**Maxine Hancock**, PhD, author and speaker; Professor of Interdisciplinary Studies & Spiritual Theology, Regent College

"One always appreciates a positive and encouraging word. *Hot Apple Cider* not only provides this, but does so in the format of real people sharing real experiences. I personally find that very helpful."
—**Thomas S. Caldwell**, Founder and Chairman of Caldwell Financial Ltd., known as one of the world's foremost investors in securities exchanges around the world; Member of the Order of Canada

"These are heart-warming accounts of everyday lives infiltrated by an anytime God. For the reader, these stories bring home the mysterious—yet practical—relationship available with One who is always close at hand. We are artfully reminded that hardship dispels the illusion of independence from God, and how He never fails to sustain us amidst suffering."
—**Sally Start**, National Director, Alpha Ministries Canada

"Every person has a story and I have learned so much from listening over the years. I now take more personal time to read, reflect and meditate. *Hot Apple Cider* is perfect for those quiet moments to slow down, to gain insight and to be refreshed. I often found myself smiling!"
—**Paul Henderson**, Director, LeaderImpact group; former NHL and Team Canada hockey player

"Whether you sip *Hot Apple Cider* slowly, one story at a time, or drink deeply and read it all in one sitting, these stories of fun, faith and fellowship by gifted Canadian writers will warm your heart."
—**Dave Toycen**, President and CEO, World Vision Canada

"Thoroughly enjoyable! *Hot Apple Cider* is a literary banquet table enticing the reader to explore, taste and ponder a diverse sampling of passions, experiences, intriguing personalities and life lessons. The compelling flavour is Canadian—a unique blend of personal history, culture and faith values. May this be the first of many compilations celebrating Canadian Christian writers."
—**Margaret Gibb**, President, Women Alive

"*Hot Apple Cider* is a fantastic read. Thirty Canadian authors fill the pages of this book with their unique insights and experiences. Although each author's contribution is different and distinct—reflecting our diverse nation—the book flows from one story into the next. All the writers share a bountiful supply of rich testimonies of a loving God's faithfulness and sufficiency. I'm thrilled that, finally, we all can be blessed by an anthology that depicts the voices of Canadians!"
—**Johanne Robertson**, Publisher, *Maranatha News*

"Imagine a group of Canadians circled around a campfire. They have two things in common: They're serious Christians and committed writers. 'Let me tell you my conversion story,' calls out Deborah Gyapong. Keith Clemons reads a short story and Brian Austin recites an original poem. Grace Fox shares a devotional piece. As the fire crackles and they sip their cider, all 30 speak from their hearts. That's the concept of *Hot Apple Cider*—and it's a good one."
—**Cecil Murphey**, author and co-author of more than 100 books, including *Gifted Hands: The Ben Carson Story* and the *New York Times* bestseller *90 Minutes in Heaven*

"*Hot Apple Cider* is a wonderful collection of stories of divine appointments, the awesomeness of God, and comfort in times of grief. Throughout my reading of these captivating short stories, I was compelled to reflect on my own life, my experiences, and my relationships with God, my family and others. This is an amazing book of encouragement. I loved it!"
—**Marlene O'Neill**, multi-award-winning Christian vocalist

Hot Apple Cider

Words to Stir the Heart
and Warm the Soul

Written by 30 Canadian Authors

Edited by
N. J. Lindquist
Wendy Elaine Nelles

That's Life! Communications

Hot Apple Cider

That's Life! Communications
Box 487, Markham, ON L3P 3R1, Canada
Call toll free 1-877-THATSLIFE
(in Toronto area, call 905-471-1447)
www.thatslifecommunications.com
thats-life@rogers.com

Cover design by Ingrid Paulson, Ingrid Paulson Design
Interior layout and design by Diane Roblin-Lee, byDesign Media

Library and Archives Canada Cataloguing in Publication

    Hot apple cider : words to stir the heart and warm the soul / edited by
N.J. Lindquist and Wendy Elaine Nelles.

ISBN 978-0-9784963-0-2

    1. Inspiration--Religious aspects--Christianity. 2. Spirituality.
3. Christian life--Anecdotes. 4. Authors, Canadian (English)--21st
century--Anecdotes. I. Lindquist, N. J. (Nancy J.), 1948- II. Nelles, Wendy E.

BV4515.3.H68 2008   242   C2008-900466-3

Contents

Foreword

by Janette Oke

*P*eople are always asking me why I write.

I suppose that is a question that every writer is asked many times over. The answer is not as simple as one might think, though we often respond with pat answers. "I write because I must," "That's who I am," "I like to write," or "I feel compelled to write."

There are other answers as well. "I write to discover who I am." "I write to express my thoughts, my feelings." "I find writing a great way to organize my own thinking." "I write to sort out my world." "I write in the hope that something I put on paper will help someone, somewhere, get a new perspective on who he or she is, or learn how to make the best of the world in which he or she finds him- or herself." "I write to share my worldview." "I write to express my faith journey in words that I hope will connect with a reader—somewhere."

There are many reasons for writing—and many ways to write. But in each case, the desire to communicate is what takes the writer to the stark, white page, or that blank computer screen, seeking to change that empty space into something that will reach another mind or another heart. It isn't just words—it is a message. It is a sharing of experiences—be they fact or fiction—that fuels the writer's passion.

Words are powerful. They are power-filled. They can encourage, direct, bring hope, empathize, instruct or empower. Put simply—yet honestly—words can change lives. As the wise man Solomon declared in Proverbs 25:11, "A word fitly spoken is like apples of gold in settings of silver." Solomon knew much about the worth of silver and gold. He saw more of it in his lifetime than most small countries do in our day. He is reminding us that words, used "fitly," are *treasures* each one of us should cherish. Thank God for words and for the ability to use them to communicate with one another.

Where do you find your inspiration?

This is another familiar question often posed to the writer. The answer: everywhere. All of life, all I know, all I seek to learn, all I find in others, all you share with me—all or any—can be the inspiration that I need to carry on. A writer never knows just what little spark might be the one to set off a raging fire or a gentle flame that will be the avenue of sharing a new story, a new thought or a new insight with a fellow-journeyer.

And so these stories are being presented to you—little "apples of gold"—and you may go ahead and make the apple cider if you so desire. Curl up before an open fire and sip the warm, inviting nectar. This is for you to treasure. Writers—many of them—are herein sharing their thoughts in new and various ways, to present to you, the reader, something that will stir your heart, awaken your thoughts, or focus your vision. My guess is that within these pages there is something that was meant just for *you*. God has exciting and miraculous ways of suiting a particular message to a particular person—at just the right time.

Jesus knew the power of stories and used them effectively in His earthly ministry of teaching the people. They understood the lesson of the sower, scattering his seed in the hopes of a good harvest, knowing that much depended on where the seed would fall. They had known of prodigals and the pain and longing of waiting, watching fathers. They understood how diligently a shepherd would search for his missing sheep.

Yes, stories connect hearts. Which story is the one that God has intended for your benefit? Perhaps there are a number that will touch your heart in deep personal ways.

As for me, I feel a bit proud in knowing that we, here in Canada, have so many skilled, inspirational writers who are able to present their work—their words—in this way. Ah—we have *treasures*, indeed!

Introduction

*A*s we searched for a title for this anthology that made us feel cozy, relaxed and, yes, Canadian, we kept coming back to *Hot Apple Cider*...

Someone told us that the title made him think of autumn. And, true, that's when fresh apple cider is first available—after the harvest. In fact, there's nothing better on a chilly autumn evening than a mug of hot apple cider. We curl up in a chair with a good book, stir the steaming beverage with a cinnamon stick, and sip nature's sweetness. Like chocolate, it has the magical ability to make us feel as though everything's okay. It's the most fun to buy cider at a farmers' market, but even the sight of a big plastic jug in the grocery store can make us feel warm all over.

But, when we think of apple cider, we also think of apple trees and the white and pink-tinted blossoms that burst forth in the spring. Without those sturdy apple trees, and their fragrant blossoms, you don't get apples. And without apples, there's no cider. Everything has a history. Apple cider doesn't just pop out of thin air. It's part of a long, intricate process that takes years.

First, you plant apple rootlings. Next, you graft a bud onto the rootling. As the tiny tree grows, you prune and train the branches so that each part of the tree gets the maximum amount of sunshine. After three or four years of training and pruning, you'll get your first apple blossoms and then your first apples—*if* there are other trees nearby so that honeybees can pollinate the flowers. A single apple tree can't bear fruit. It must be cross-pollinated by a neighbouring tree.

If you carefully tend your trees, protecting them from diseases, pests, and harsh weather; if you fertilize, spray and weed; and if there is just enough rain and sunshine—your trees will grow large enough to yield an excellent crop of apples.

The perfect apples are reserved for eating. The smaller ones, the ones with a few bruises or scars, or fruit blown to the ground by the wind, are used to make cider. The apples are washed, crushed, pressed and strained to get the juices out; and the liquids from sweet and tart apple varieties are blended to achieve just the right flavour.

Canadian Authors Who Are Christian Are a Lot Like Hot Apple Cider

In the same way that apple trees need to be cross-pollinated, writers need each other to produce rich work. In the past, individuals who belonged to the Group of Seven Canadian landscape painters or the Inklings (British writers including C. S. Lewis and J. R. R. Tolkien) thrived when they met together and helped each other. As members of The Word Guild, a coast-to-coast association of Canadian writers who are Christian, we validate each other's gifts and talents, but also spur each other on to produce even greater work.

Just as it takes years for apple cider to result from apple rootlings, great writing takes time and energy to develop. We owe a great deal to the trail-blazing Canadian Christian authors who have influenced many of the writers in this book, including Ontario's Grace Irwin, Margaret Avison, Margaret Clarkson and Les Tarr; Saskatchewan's Margaret Epp; and Alberta's Rudy Wiebe, Janette Oke and Maxine Hancock.

Today, many Canadian Christians are realizing that they'd like to read literature that reflects their own culture, values and experiences. At the same time, God is raising up writers and publishers who are passionate about helping Canadians to understand God's message from a uniquely Canadian point of view.

The inspirational stories by Canadian writers found in this anthology reflect our immense and diverse country. Although all write from a Christian worldview, they offer a full menu of styles and tastes based on their different experiences and outlooks.

Some are blossoming new writers discovering their passion, while others are mature writers who have polished their craft for many years. Some write sweet, encouraging words; others pen tart, challenging words. A few are well known; some haven't been discovered yet. But mixed together, they offer a uniquely Canadian flavour.

Whether non-fiction, poetry, or fiction, the stories in this book are thought-provoking and honest accounts about how faith affects real life.

Learn about a Canadian "Mother Teresa," a poor farmer's daughter who—against all odds—graduates as a doctor, goes to India, and helps thousands of impoverished villagers to gain better lives and better health. Discover what ensues after a young mother is forced to stay behind in Nepal as her newborn baby is rushed to the U.S. for emergency surgery; when a single woman experiences nervousness, disappointment—then elation—on yet another failed blind date; as a father worries that he will make the same parenting mistakes his father made; or after a missionary in Africa, dedicated to serving God, has a horrific car accident that leaves him brain-damaged.

There's no way to create apple cider except to bruise and crush the fruit. Our Canadian writers have the scars to prove they've experienced some of life's hard issues and grinding problems. They've been knocked to the ground by stormy winds… and learned that only experiences like these can create the character, insights and deepening of faith that produce rich, tangy writing. Drink deeply from the life-giving words in this book.

N. J. Lindquist
Wendy Elaine Nelles
Editors of *Hot Apple Cider*
Co-Founders of The Word Guild
www.thewordguild.com

It Was Then That I Carried You

Non-fiction
Angelina Fast-Vlaar

"*I*f you want to see it, come now!" Peter's whisper tickled my ear.

"Coming," I muttered. I slipped into my shorts and T-shirt and tip-toed behind him through Jim and Julie's house.

Peter gently shut the door. "There, we didn't wake the baby," he said with a grin.

He reached for my hand, and together we walked in the soft glow of early morning light, past houses on stilts and gardens green with tropical plants and flowering shrubs.

It was October, 1987, and we were in Palm Cove on Australia's east coast, just north of Cairns. We had come from Canada to visit our son, his beautiful Aussie wife, and their first-born child, our third grandson.

Through a row of palms, we stepped onto Palm Cove beach—a long solitary crescent stretching between water and forest. We sat down on the soft white sand and inhaled the peaceful morning scene, the music of the birds, the measured breathing of the water. The Coral Sea stretched out before us, its dark glistening water touching a far-off pink horizon. Spell-bound, we waited for God to make a morning.

Finally, a fiery arc appeared far across the water and Peter exclaimed, "There she is!"

Gradually, a blazing ball lifted out of the water and spread its light.

"Amazing," Peter whispered. "Did you know His glory is seen in the rising sun?"

"Yes, I know," I said, leaning against him. "How many sunrises have you seen here now?" I asked.

"I didn't miss many, so I guess about thirty. And each one was more spectacular than the one before." He turned to me, smiling. "Too bad you missed most of them."

The sun rose and we got up to saunter barefoot along the now sparkling aquamarine water, sand squishing between our toes. I noticed the footprints our feet left behind and decided to take some photos.

"I want a photo of just mine," I said.

"Why?" Peter asked.

"Just because," I answered, and waited until a wave had gently erased our prints. I walked alone and then clicked the shutter. I didn't know why, but something deep within compelled me to take this picture, to have a reminder of Margaret Fishback Powers's famous poem that contains the line, "When you saw only one set of footprints…"[1]

We strolled on and Peter remarked, "Hasn't it been great? Our holiday?"

"Much more than what I'd imagined," I replied.

"But you were so hesitant to come!" he commented.

"You're not in the best of health, you know," I returned. It was true. Although Peter was only fifty-five, he had had his ups and downs with a heart condition.

"I'm just fine. Didn't our family doctor *and* my heart specialist tell me to go and enjoy the trip?"

"Yes, Hon, they did," I said.

Excitedly, Peter continued, "And tomorrow we leave for our six-week *walk-about* to Adelaide!"

"Yes, but let's just remember the car we bought is old and has no air conditioning," I added cautiously.

"The car is just fine also! Didn't we take it for a test run?"

He turned to me and his grin changed to a chuckle, then to a belly laugh as we remembered our harrowing ride up to Cape Tribulation last week.

"We're all set to go," he said, and then added, "Through the outback."

Under my breath, I said, "That remains to be seen."

The next morning we set out, with our used Toyota Corolla pulling Jim and Julie's tent trailer. We promised we'd be back in time to celebrate Christmas together.

We headed south along the coast to Townsville, passing waving fields of sugar cane and acres of pineapples. We stopped at a road-side stand to sample one and, with juice running down our chins, exclaimed to the pineapple pickers how sweet the fruit was.

"You don't grow pineapples in Canada?" they queried.

"No," we replied, "but we do grow peaches!"

We spent the next day exploring Townsville, including the astonishing walk-through aquarium. After a swim in the public pool, I settled in the shade of the ornate bathing house and studied our map once more. Going through the outback, the *Never, Never,* seemed risky to me. Jim had said, "You'd better think it over, Dad. That desert is hot and it's a long, long way to Adelaide." But Peter had insisted that anyone in his right mind would not want to pass up an opportunity to see the mysterious outback first-hand. I still had my reservations and would have preferred to drive further south along the coast, maybe as far as Sydney, and this way skirt most of the desert-like country. Observing our map, I decided to tally the kilometres of each route and excitedly discovered the coastal route to be shorter by a bit.

When Peter approached, I called out, "Look, Hon, the coastal route is shorter!" thinking this would convince him.

It didn't. He held my eyes and I read the sadness he was feeling. He quietly said he'd shop for some groceries. I knew that enough had been said. I'd leave the decision to fulfill his long-held cherished dream up to him.

When we left the campground the following morning, I waited with bated breath. At the gate Peter slowly, ceremoniously, turned the wheel to swerve the car onto the highway that would lead us directly into *the back of beyond.* He turned to me, grinning mischievously, the familiar twinkle in his blue eyes. Despite my misgivings, I returned his smile. I loved this handsome, grey-bearded, fun-loving man. I loved him for his strength and his brave, courageous spirit. We'd share this adventure together.

As we drove out of town, the outback scene slowly became a reality: skinny cows, thirsty stunted trees, anthills several meters high standing like grave monuments on the cinnamon sand. As the fiery sun climbed higher, the interior of the car heated up like an oven. Around noon, the road led up to a rocky height. We stopped and in awe observed our 360-degree horizon. The outback stretched around us without end. We felt very small, two tiny specks in this vast heated wilderness. I gained a deeper understanding of the term *Never, Never*.

In the late afternoon, we turned into a lonely campground, set up our gear and cooked our supper. Peter went for a walk. "I saw graves back there," he said when he returned. "It must have been lonely—probably no doctor."

I didn't want to comment, so kept myself buried in my novel.

The sun set and a soft orange veil stretched over us, enveloped us, wrapped us in what seemed like God's protective love. The shrubs and spheres of spinifex grass on the red earth glowed as if on fire. Darkness gradually fell and the sky became a black velvet dome punctured with brilliant lights. A poet saw the stars as "altar fires."

Early in the morning we continued on. We drove through towns that were no more than a cluster of dust-covered buildings; we stood in line at service stations to have a cool shower; we found a patch of skinny shade to sit and make a sandwich. Our car and clothes began to blend into the red landscape.

The further we drove into the outback, the quieter we became. We felt lonely, fragile, vulnerable on the hot empty plains. But it was more than that. The isolated stillness around us, around me, amplified the "noise" within. Desert journeys tend to do that. With outward, surface distractions virtually absent, we encounter our inner selves. That night I lay awake and confronted my fear.

Two mornings later, I woke very early. As my eyes feasted on the desert bathed in pre-dawn pink, I realized how much more my heart, now quieter, blended with the stillness around me. My heart was still, because God is God.

Later that day, we arrived in the middle of the outback, in the small oasis-like town of Alice Springs nestled in the curve of a red rocky mountain range. A spring in the desert. We set up camp in a lovely shaded campground at the edge of town and spent three beautiful, joy-filled days in Alice.

We ended our first day of happy sight-seeing with a drive up Anzac Hill to watch the sun complete its daily round. We sat close together on a west-facing bench and marvelled as colour seeped into the sky and turned the red hills into shades of purple.

When it was almost dark, I said, "It's over, let's go."

"No, it's not over," Peter said, "Turn around."

I turned my head and, amazed, saw Alice twinkling with light. As the world in front of us had darkened, the town behind us had begun to shine like a precious jewel.

"Look, the City of Light!" Peter whispered, his voice breaking with emotion.

We sat spell-bound and drank in the beauty of the evening laden with meaning.

The next day, Sunday, we attended an Aboriginal evening service. Peter was asked to bring a greeting from overseas, which he happily and movingly did. The leader of the group invited us to come and visit the Aboriginal community where he lived. We set out the next morning and spent an enjoyable time meeting the friendly native people and admiring the craft items they designed to be sold in town.

Back in Alice, we decided to get our roll of film developed. One photo of Peter and me was especially lovely, and we ordered several prints to send to our children back home. It would take some time.

Peter said, "I'll go to the grocery store while you wait."

I sat on a bench in front of the photo shop and opened the envelope of prints once more. The footprints photo I had taken was captivating. The grey, red-rimmed clouds in the sky were reflected in sheets of water spread on the beach by the rising tide. Alongside foamy froth was a lonely set of footprints. I planned to enlarge the photo and frame it.

But where was Peter? He'd looked tired after our adventure. I was relieved to see him emerge from the store. We drove back to the campground and went for a swim in the pool. Peter pulled himself out rather quickly.

"I forgot my nitro pills, so I'm going to lie down," he said.

I followed him a little later and found him sleeping. I showered and changed and lay down to have a nap. It was 6 o'clock in the evening. I fell into a deep sleep and woke at midnight. Peter's breathing was deep and even. I decided to just go back to sleep.

When I woke at 6:00 a.m., Peter was sitting up. He told me he'd had a bad night. True to character, he turned everything into a joke by telling me a funny story. Laughter filled our camper. It was too early to rise and we decided to doze off again.

Suddenly I sensed a shiver pass through Peter's body. I turned with a start and asked, "Hon, are you okay?" He didn't respond. I jumped up. Leaning over him, I stroked his hair and asked again whether he was all right. His face was pale, almost grey; his breathing shallow; his eyes shut. My mind began to race— *Help! I need help!*

I ran to a silver RV parked a few spots over to our left. No one answered my frantic knocking. I ran to another RV parked on the other side. Again, no one answered. Running back to our camper, I noticed a pup-tent set up just behind us. I desperately called out, "Is there someone here who can help me? My husband is very ill!"

The tent jiggled and a young man crawled out while trying to pull on a pair of jeans. Without saying a word, he ran like a leopard toward the office.

I rushed back into our camper. Peter was the same—short, shallow breaths. I stroked his hair, his cheek, while tears filled my eyes. "Oh, Hon, what is it? What can I do?"

The shallow breathing suddenly stopped. Then one long breath escaped his lips and everything became eerily still except for the pounding of my heart.

Moments later, I heard vehicles squeal to a stop. Two uniformed women rushed into the camper, one carrying paddles, the other a mouthpiece for oxygen.

"How long has he been this way?" one asked urgently.

"A few moments."

"Please wait outside."

My feet were frozen in place.

"Please wait outside!"

I managed to obey the command and stumbled to the large tree that sheltered our camper. I leaned against its sturdy trunk. A terrible trembling now wracked my body from head to toe as it began to sink in what was happening. Peter likely had had the dreaded heart attack. Jim was 3,000 kilometres away on the east coast; our four other children were back in Canada; I was alone in a town where I didn't know a soul. A desperate cry escaped my lips, "Lord, what am I going to do? What am I going to do?"

Just then, I became aware that I was not alone. I lifted my head. Something glistened in the rising sun. I blinked away my tears to see a man in a bright white shirt. I noticed his kind brown eyes, his neatly trimmed dark beard.

"Is it your husband who is ill?" he said gently. I nodded and he said, "I have come to look after you."

I struggled to grasp the meaning of what he'd said, his comforting, calming words. He had come to look after me? Where had he come from? Was he an angel?

He touched my elbow and I felt my trembling ease. Softly, he said, "Let's sit in my car." I hadn't heard a car drive up, but there was a dust-covered vehicle parked behind the ambulances. He opened the door for me, walked around and slid into the driver's seat. I sat, tears now streaming, on the passenger side.

"Tell me what happened," he said.

I haltingly told him about Peter and what had just occurred. He listened. He nodded with understanding. He *was* an "angel."

"I'll go check on your husband," he said, and walked to the ambulances. He returned and told me they were taking some time to stabilize Peter before transporting him.

"I'll take you to the hospital now," he said. "There will be a *sister* waiting for you."

He slowly drove along a few quiet streets. The hospital was close by. The two-storied rectangular building had a long sidewalk leading to glass doors. Two nurses, dressed in white uniforms, opened the doors and welcomed me by name! They took me across a shiny floor to a long counter where I answered questions to fill out a registration form.

I turned, wanting to thank the kind man, but he had gone. I stared at the long sidewalk—how could he have walked that length so quickly…?

A nurse invited me to follow her to a small room. A young lady, with a kind, open face and shoulder-length straight hair, stood as I entered. She reached for my hand. "Angie? I'm Michelle. I'm here to be with you. Would you like a cup of tea, some toast?"

I wondered who she was. She didn't have a nurse's uniform on and she didn't seem like office personnel. She set the tea tray on a low table and sat down beside me.

"Tell me what happened," she invited.

She listened to all I needed to say, and an hour later held my sobbing body when the doctor came to tell us their attempts to save Peter's life had failed.

Shortly afterwards, a social worker stepped into the room. Her kind blue eyes held mine as she said, "I'm Margaret. I'm here to be with you and to help you with everything that needs to be done. Let's go up to my office."

She led me up a staircase. As I entered her bright, sun-lit office, a poster hanging on the wall faced me directly. On the left side was a little koala hopelessly entangled in a shrub. On the right side was a soft curve of light suggesting the Shepherd might appear at any moment. The caption read, "Relax, I AM in charge."

First, the heart-rending call to my son Jim. We decided it was best for me to go to Peter's niece in Adelaide as planned. Jim and Julie would fly down, and other family members traveling in Australia could gather there. I kept glancing at the poster.

Margaret had some difficulty getting an overseas telephone connection, but finally handed me the receiver. Standing behind me, she let her hand simply rest on my shoulder as I tried to voice the devastating news to our four other children. It was the most difficult task I'd ever done. I felt drained and let my tears flow onto Margaret's desk. When I looked up, my eyes again fell on the poster. *Relax, I AM....*

Gently, Margaret said, "I'll now take you to an undertaker to make all the arrangements." I followed her obediently into this strange new world. On the way back, she stopped at a travel agency for me to buy a ticket to Adelaide.

When we returned to her office, she arranged for tea and sandwiches to be brought up. In between glances at the poster above her desk, I munched on the sandwiches and expressed my thanks again for everything she was doing. I wondered about the amount of time she was able to spend with me.

Pushing back her greying hair, she smiled, and softly said, "Angie, today my work is to help you. And if that takes all day, I have all day."

I saw the loving sincerity in her eyes.

She telephoned a pastor to meet us at the campground to help pack our gear. I went through the motions, as if on autopilot, and calmly decided what needed to go where and guided them in how to fold up the tent trailer. The pastor led the way to the train station for me to ship the car and trailer to Adelaide. Margaret took some of Peter's clothes to the undertaker.

When we met back at her office, there was a call from Jim. In a voice hoarse and heavy with emotion, he said, "Mom, we have our flights booked. We'll see you tomorrow at 6:00 p.m. in Adelaide. Please take care. I love you."

Margaret tucked a bar of soap and a towel into my hands and said, "You have time to take a shower before I take you to the airport."

The warm water mixed with my hot tears, but could not wash them away. Nor could the water rouse me from my dream-like state, or open my numbed mind to absorb reality. Peter gone? How could that be? We laughed when he woke this morning...

Margaret drove me to the airport in time to catch my flight. Over the roar of the engines, I hugged her and thanked her again and again. We promised to keep in touch.

A kind stewardess, seeing my tear-crumpled face, whispered, "Would you like a private seat in the back of the carrier?"

I gratefully accepted.

The airplane lifted, banked, and I glimpsed Alice Springs below, cradled in the mountain range. She had indeed held a spring for me. I reeled to think what this day had brought. Yet, everything was done. I had been cared for; I had been carried.

One set of footprints in the red sand...

1. "Footprints in the Sand," copyright © 1964 by Margaret Fishback Powers. Used by permission.

This selection is adapted with permission from the publisher from *Seven Angels for Seven Days*, copyright © 2005 by Angelina Fast-Vlaar (Castle Quay Books Canada / *www.castlequaybooks.com*).

Faith of Our Mothers —Holy Faith

Non-fiction
Keith Clemons

*H*e was born with a smile on his face, so they called him "Sunny." Though on paper they officially dubbed him Walter, Sunny was the name he would go by all his life. I can't say I blame him. What child in his right mind would want to be called Walter?

His wife would be Norma Jean, though he certainly didn't know it at the time, nor did he care; but that was God's plan, and a good one too. How can you fail with a name like Norma Jean? Having the same birth name as Marilyn Monroe practically made her a star.

Sunny's mother heard the call of God as a young adult. She'd gone forward and been baptized by Aimee Semple McPherson herself, and if that didn't make her Christian, well, what did? At least she thought so. But her faith was sincere, so even though Sunny's father refused to go, whenever Dad was out of town, Mom would bundle the kids up and hustle them off to church. So it was that at age 12, Sunny made that all-important decision to follow Christ. But that was pretty much the sum of his religious training. He grew up believing God was somewhere out there in the cosmos and figured that was pretty much all he needed to know.

Sunny was 19 when World War II broke out, so he enlisted in the U.S. Air Corps to become a pilot. His first week on base in California, he was assigned responsibility for more than 300 men as a squadron leader, which was pretty heady stuff for a young cadet. He was so full of himself, the buttons nearly popped off his uniform.

Norma Jean's life was somewhat different, though not in a good way. Her parents didn't know God. Their idea of being filled with the spirit was drinking 90-proof liquor from a bottle.

But they were a close family. Being good parents, they wouldn't think of leaving their kids home when they went out for the evening. Instead, they'd lock the children in the car and leave them shivering in the parking lot while they went into the dance hall and partied till the wee hours of morning. It was a marriage doomed to destruction.

In spite of their parents' ongoing verbal abuse and periods of heavy fighting, Norma and her brother did have moments of respite. During tumultuous times when their parents wanted to be alone so they could fight in private, the children stayed with their grandparents, who were Christians. I guess, in some weird way, you could call her parents beating on each other a blessing. And there was a short two-year period of grace when her folks more or less got along.

The interludes gave Norma and her brother an opportunity to go to church, but not with their parents—the Holy Spirit invited them, so they went with Him. It wasn't long before these two dear children of God went forward to accept Jesus. The only bad thing about church was they eventually had to go home. It was next to impossible for their faith to grow in a house where there weren't any Bibles and the only time they heard the Lord's name was when it was taken in vain.

One Saturday night, a busload of girls arrived at Sunny's army base for a dance. Having decided not to go, Sunny stayed in his barracks listening to the sound of the band wafting across the parade grounds. But as the evening lagged on and loneliness set in, he changed his mind. He walked into that gymnasium down past all the gals and guys seated along the wall until he spotted the prettiest girl on the floor, the one with the most effervescent smile and hair that just wouldn't stop bouncing.

He cut in on the dancing couple and it was what you might call love at first sight. Boy meets girl. Sunny meets Norma.

Norma was living in a town 50 miles[1] away, but that didn't stop Sunny from hitchhiking every Saturday night for the next few weeks to see her. On their eighth date, Sunny asked Norma to be his wife, on their ninth they got a wedding licence, and the tenth time they saw each other, they got married. You had to act fast in those days; there was a war going on and Sunny was bound for overseas.

Sunny's parents couldn't make it to the ceremony, though Norma's mother did. There were, in fact, only 12 people there. But just before he shipped out, Sunny's mother gave him something that proved to be of more value than any wedding present she might have bought; she snuck a New Testament into his duffel bag.

Sunny wound up being stationed in Chabua, India, flying cargo ships over the Himalayan Mountains (affectionately called "the Hump") into China to assist Chiang Kai-shek, who was fighting the Japanese. It was some of the most dangerous flying in the Pacific theatre. Pilots had to negotiate 45,000 pounds of loaded weight over the highest mountain range in the world through thunderstorms, gale force winds, snow, ice, sleet and hail. The cabins weren't pressurized or heated. The crew wore two pairs of almost everything just to keep warm, and had oxygen masks glued to their faces from takeoff to landing. They lost about a plane a week. Good thing Sunny had a praying mom.

One evening, as they were preparing to fly out of Kumming, China, for some strange reason (let's just call it what it was—*God*), Sunny decided he needed more fuel. Gas was scarce in China. Each plane was allotted 750 gallons, no more. But on this trip Sunny refused to go unless they gave him 1,000 gallons. To this day, he doesn't know why he was so stubborn. He didn't have any particular reason for wanting extra fuel; he simply butted heads with the operations officer, and pride made him insist on getting his way. Pilots had the right to refuse to fly if conditions were deemed unsafe for the plane or crew. The operations officer was furious and, while he did give Sunny the extra gas just to get him off the tarmac, he swore he'd have his hide nailed to the wall when he got back.

The three-man crew—pilot, co-pilot and navigator—took off without getting a compass reading from the base. The nearest check-point at Yu-Nan-Ye was only 10 miles out, so they figured they could always get a bearing there. But they flew that ship way beyond where Yu-Nan-Ye should have been and never saw it.

Radioing back to base, they were told Yu-Nan-Ye was off the air, which was not good news. They were flying in the pitch black of night without a bearing, and they had no idea how to navigate home. To make matters worse, it wasn't long before the sky erupted with thunderheads, creating an electrical discharge that played havoc with their radio directional finder. The lightning kept attracting the loop antenna which caused the needle to spin around the dial. They didn't know if they were heading west straight into a mountain or east into the jungle. They were simply flying blind.

The thing about gas is (if you drive an SUV, you know) the further you go, the more you burn. And this wasn't a Toyota they were flying (Japan wasn't even our friend then); this was a Curtis-Wright freight train in the sky. One by one, the fuel gauges read *empty*: front tanks—*empty*; rear tanks—*empty*. Good thing Sunny asked for that extra gas. They were almost through their last remaining tank when he finally had to swallow his pride and admit they were lost.

Hailing "Mayday" was reserved for extreme emergencies. It just wasn't done unless absolutely necessary. But in this case they had no choice. So the navigator dropped a long-range antenna out the bottom of the ship and sent the distress call.

Their only hope was that the base would pick up the transmission and give them a heading. There were three possible answers: they could get a Class A: "We have you, here's where you are;" or a Class B: "We think you're approximately here, use Pilot's discretion;" or, the least desirable, a Class C: "Sorry, Charlie, we can't locate you. You're on your own." Did I say least desirable? Hardly. In this case they couldn't even get a Class C heading. They simply got no response, which could only mean they were way off course and out of range.

On they went, watching the blackness slide by the window, still not knowing whether they were heading into a mountain, or into the drink, burning gas with each passing mile. Bailing out was an option, but very few who bailed out ever got back alive. The likelihood was that they were somewhere over the jungles of Burma. You had to go through the trees before you hit ground, which meant the possibility of getting caught in a treetop and not being able to get down, or suffering broken bones from crashing into tree limbs and therefore not being able to walk. And the jungles were full of tribal headhunters seeking trophies for the game rooms in their grass huts. And if that wasn't enough, the place was crawling with unfriendly Japanese. They decided to ride it out. The navigator was still hailing Mayday on the long-range radio, but to no avail.

Right now, I want you to imagine Sunny's dear sweet mother down on her knees back home praying for her son at that very moment—after all, this is a story about faith.

All of a sudden, Sunny got the crazy idea to try his command set. That was the radio he used for landing. It only had a 75-mile range and was primarily employed on approach with the base in sight. He hailed a Mayday and, wouldn't you know, got an immediate response. The voice was unmistakably British. "This is George King. We read you R5-S5, what's your problem?"

R5-S5 was the British code for "loud and clear." In fact, the transmission was so clear, Sunny assumed the base was somewhere beneath them. He explained the situation, gave the man a count, and received a bearing. That gave everyone pause to take a breath, but when he pulled out his chart to fix their position and determine exactly where they were, there was no George King on the map.

They knew how many hours they'd been flying and regardless of how far off course they might be, they could only be so far from their base in China, and his radio had a maximum range of 75 miles so they kept searching but... nothing. He got out another set of charts expanding the distance, and then another and, what do you know, there it was, George King, right there on the map. On a radio with only a 75-mile range they were talking R5-S5 to a base 1,000 miles away in Calcutta. Go figure.

They have a technical term for what happened. In the parlance of communications, the phenomenon is known as "radio skip distance," but let's just call it what it was—a miracle. Sunny's mother always did say she prayed him through the war.

The base at George King gave them a bearing, but that didn't mean they were home free. They were still off course, flying on fumes, and 40 miles over Japanese lines. They turned north toward Mount Everest and headed for the base at Chabua on a wing and a prayer. As soon as they were within radio distance, Sunny requested a straight-in approach.

By now, every gas gauge was reading zero and they were coming in too low to bail out. The crew knew if the plane ran out of fuel before they hit the runway they'd have to ditch it in the jungle, and they knew what that meant. Soon after he had arrived on base, Sunny had been assigned to be a pallbearer for a crew member of a plane that had overshot the runway. The jungle just opened up, swallowed that flying bucket of bolts, and bounced back without leaving a trace. It took two months to find the plane and its crew, and by the time they did, jungle ants had eaten nearly all the flesh off the bodies.

By the grace of God, they touched down and taxied in. Sunny dismissed his co-pilot and navigator, but he stayed behind, curious. The ground crew came out and did their post flight inspection and when all was said and done they found the plane had about two gallons of gas in it, just enough to fill the lines and sumps in the carburetors. The Curtis Commando C-46 sported two of the biggest engines ever made. With the gas-guzzling size of those 2,000-horsepower motors, the weight of that bird (30,000 pounds, even when empty), and that thimbleful of fuel, they couldn't have stayed in the air even a few minutes more.

At that time, pilots usually were encouraged to take a shot of brandy upon landing to calm their nerves and help them sleep, but Sunny didn't take the elixir that night. He went straight to his tent. There was always someone to talk to in the tents, but when he arrived, he found the place unusually quiet—which was good, because if someone else had been there, he probably wouldn't have done what he ended up doing. He was, after all, a whiskey-drinking, cigar-smoking, hell-raising pilot with an image to protect.

But he was alone, and it occurred to him that none of this had happened by accident. Stubbornly demanding extra gas for no reason, not taking a routine tail bearing, having the weather knock out their navigation systems, receiving help from a base a thousand miles away on a short range radio, and landing with only the fuel in the lines— too much coincidence to be a coincidence. Someone was trying to get his attention.

He remembered the New Testament his mother had put in his duffel bag and went to see if it was still there. It was. He lit a kerosene lamp, sat down in a wicker rocker and began to read. Before long, a supernatural peace came over him, the likes of which he'd never known. He dropped to his knees and, not really knowing how to pray, called out to God using a few expletives and said, "God, if You get me out of this *blankity-blank* war alive, I'll serve You the rest of my life."

It may not have been the usual response to the preaching of Billy Graham, or a waltz down the aisle with George Beverly Shea singing "Just as I Am," but surely the angels sang out a new name in heaven as this sinner came home.

Sunny crawled into the sack and slept like a baby. He eventually made a hundred trips over the Hump, earning a Distinguished Flying Cross, two Air Medals and a Citation from Chiang Kai-shek himself, and he never had to ditch a plane. That in itself was a miracle. Thank God for praying moms.

Sunny got home determined to honour his commitment. He returned battle-weary, a different man than when he left, to Norma, a woman he hardly knew.

But God had uniquely placed these two together. Both had accepted the Lord at a young age, and both came from unchurched backgrounds, so they had that in common, and God promises never to leave or forsake His own. Sunny and Norma never discussed religion before they got married, but now, the two of them set out on a journey to find God together.

The command to be fruitful and multiply was observed after the war as parents everywhere sought to replenish that which was lost. It wasn't long before they had three lovely children, Kathleen, followed by Keith (that's me) and then Christine. They were the perfect church-going, Bible-believing, Christ-centered family. Sunny, with his engineering background, worked in aerospace as the world raced for the moon, and Norma set up housekeeping in suburbia where it seemed new inventions to make life easier were being invented every day—a television with color pictures, can you imagine? About the biggest concern they had was that they might miss an episode of Bonanza on a Sunday night—when Christine suddenly fell ill.

The entire family was about to be given a glimpse of how God imparts faith to mothers.

For two days, Christine lay curled up in her bed holding her stomach. Sunny and Norma took her to the doctor, but she was only three years old, just a bitty thing, and couldn't explain what ailed her. All they knew was that she was listless and wouldn't eat. The doctor sent them home with medicine for the flu.

They waited another two days before they insisted on seeing the doctor again. He opened his office to them on a Saturday, but 50 years ago they didn't have the tests we have today, so he had no way of determining what was wrong. Nonetheless, since Christine hadn't eaten anything in several days, the doctor admitted her to the hospital. He knew the problem was internal. There was nothing he could do but go in and take a look, and what he found was that her appendix had burst and she was filled with gangrene. Sunny had lost a sister to appendicitis when he was a young boy; now he faced losing his daughter. Back then, appendicitis was the number two killer of women. And the complication of gangrene made it worse.

They removed Christine's appendix, but her vital signs were weak, and infection had spread throughout her body. The doctor gave her as many penicillin injections as possible (so many her bum looked like a little red pincushion) but it had no effect. Nothing they tried seemed to work.

The doctor counselled the couple to go home and prepare for the worst, but they refused. They stayed at Christine's bedside for two days praying as her health continued to deteriorate. By the third day, they'd all but abandoned hope.

Sunny had walked every hall in the hospital and couldn't take it anymore. He decided to go into his office and make a few calls, just to get his mind on something else, and he convinced Norma she needed to rest. After dropping her at home, Sunny went on into work, but he was too distracted to get anything done. It wasn't long before Norma called and, with the anxiety of a worried mother, insisted they return to the hospital.

Now, they'd both prayed the whole time they were with Christine, but for some reason God chose this moment to assure Norma everything would be all right. As she knelt by her bed waiting for Sunny to drive back from the office, you could almost hear the angels sing, "When peace like a river attendeth my way, when sorrow like sea billows roll..."2 Norma opened her Bible to a passage where Christ was healing the sick, and all of a sudden she rose to her feet filled with what she describes as "perfect peace" (the same thing Sunny felt that night in his tent thanks to another praying mom). Somehow, Norma knew everything would be all right. She started doing the laundry.

Sunny arrived home to find his wife singing and hanging clothes on the line in the back yard. To say he was unnerved by her calm would be an understatement. She should be weeping, or praying, or *something*. She'd called *him*, for crying out loud. Shouldn't she be insisting they return to the hospital at once? He was confused and angry, but Norma just kept singing and putting clothespins on those socks, content to wait until the laundry was done.

Today when they tell this story, Sunny is honest enough to admit his wife's faith tested the limits of his patience. What made her so sure everything was okay?

But when they entered Christine's room, they found the oxygen tent had been removed and the nurse was gushing with excitement. "Your daughter's eating again," she exclaimed, and when they looked into the crib, Christine reached up and wiggled her fingers, begging to be held.

Don't you just love happy endings? By the way, when asked what time she'd first noticed signs of improvement, the nurse gave the exact hour Norma had risen from her knees and felt that perfect peace.

How about that?

And those are only two of many stories I could tell.

I'm reminded of that grand old hymn, "Faith of Our Fathers,"[3] in which the refrain rings out, "Faith of our fathers, holy faith!" It's a great song with a fantastic message, but I can't help feeling it leaves our mothers a bit short-changed. Anyone with a praying mom knows the faith of our mothers is a "holy" faith as well.

1. Rough metric equivalents for U.S. measures used in the story:
   1 mile = 1.6 kilometres
   1 gallon (32 ounces) = 3.8 litres
   1 pound = 454 grams or .454 kilogram
2. Hymn "It Is Well with My Soul," Horatio G. Spafford, 1828-1888. Public Domain.
3. Hymn "Faith of Our Fathers," Frederick W. Faber, 1814-1863. Public Domain.

The Diamond Ring

Non-fiction
N. J. Lindquist

The other guests at the birthday party appeared to be having a wonderful time. I was counting the minutes until I could go home and read a book or design more clothes for my paper dolls. As soon as we'd eaten the birthday cake, I said I had to leave early. Dressed in my best party dress and wearing my white sandals, carrying a little basket of candy and trinkets, I fought to hold back the tears that started the moment I closed the door.

Our house was on the outskirts of town, and to reach it I had to cross a set of railway tracks. I stopped and walked along the rails. By now, I was sobbing in earnest, and I didn't want my parents to see—didn't want them to worry. I also was trying to figure out why I wasn't like other people. For a moment, I thought it might be a huge relief if a train would come along and erase the pain.

It was 1955, and I was seven years old.

I had two loving parents, a dog and a cat, a nice home, no worries about getting enough food, no fear of being abused in any way. I was a child who apparently had everything a child might want—and yet loneliness was my constant companion.

I spent whole days reading books and making up stories with my paper dolls. I perplexed my mother because her only daughter wanted toy six-guns instead of a new dress. I lived in another world, spending hours staring out a window daydreaming, having to be called 10 times to come set the table for supper because I was engrossed in a book and hadn't heard my parents calling. And even when I responded, I might go to the kitchen and forget what I'd been asked to do. Or set the table with a book in one hand. I rarely spoke, especially to people I didn't know well; and when I did, I was inclined to say exactly what I thought instead of making small talk; too much like *Little Women*'s Jo and Amy, with none of the gentler attributes of Meg or Beth.

And because I was adopted, my parents had no frame of reference to understand me. They couldn't say, "She's just like your sister," or "I know exactly how she feels because I've felt that way, too."

When I got home that day after the birthday party, my mother was coming out the door to look for me. My classmate's mother had phoned.

I told Mom I was fine. Hadn't felt good. Hadn't had much fun. And, as usual, my mother worried about me. But neither she nor I knew what to do.

Fortunately, God did. And He sent exactly what I needed to see me through the coming years.

Seven months after the party, my mother, my dad and I were in the kitchen of our two-storey frame house in the village of Crystal City, Manitoba. We'd finished eating supper and were about to have home-canned peaches for dessert.

When the phone rang, Mom jumped up to answer it. At first she sounded confused. Then she furrowed her brow and looked over at us. Her tone grew higher as she became excited. Finally, she picked up a pen and paper from the nearby counter and wrote something down.

My dad and I kept looking at each other. Mom's side of the conversation made no sense to us.

"That was my Aunt Olive's widower, Frank Miksell," Mom said when she finally hung up. "He must be 80 years old, but he's coming all the way from San Francisco to give me a diamond ring!"

My mother's wedding ring was a simple silver band. Although they'd been married 18 years, my dad had never been able to give her an engagement ring. While Mom didn't complain, clothes and appearance were very important to her. She was thrilled at the thought of having a diamond ring.

The events leading up to that phone call were actually set in motion decades earlier in Orillia, Ontario, in the late 1800s.

A boy named William Bruce MacDonald had a sister, Olive Margaret. The two were very close. But while Bruce and Olive were still young, their parents separated. The mother took Olive with her to the United States; the father took Bruce to Manitoba to be raised by his grandparents.

Bruce grew up and became a barber in Rossburn, Manitoba. He and his wife Alice had seven children, the oldest of whom was named Olive Margaret after her aunt. Bruce died from a heart attack when he was 55.

Bruce's sister Olive wrote now and then over the years from her home in California. After her first husband died, she married a man named Frank Miksell. When Olive's health became poor, Frank began to keep in touch with her relatives, especially Olive's sister-in-law Alice. Because Olive never had children, when she died, Frank decided that he wanted to give the engagement ring he'd bought for her to her eldest niece and namesake, my mother. Hence, the unexpected long distance telephone call.

As we drove across the border to meet the train from San Francisco at Rugby, North Dakota, I wasn't exactly looking forward to the next couple of weeks. What does an eight-year-old say to an eighty-year-old stranger? Besides, I'd have to sit next to this visitor in the back seat on the long drive home. I dreaded the moment when his train would pull into the station. But the train arrived, only a few minutes late.

At first glance, he looked just as I'd anticipated—old and wrinkled. A small, thinnish man with snow white hair, he was dressed formally in a black suit and white shirt and a tie. He looked as if a small shove would knock him over.

But in spite of his fragile appearance, he held himself erect and firm, and his sharp, bird-like eyes seemed to see everything. Eyes that held an unexpected twinkle. Thin lips that smiled.

Sitting beside him on the trip home, I quickly discovered that Uncle Frank was unlike any adult I'd ever known. Unfazed by his long train ride, he took a newspaper he'd read on the train, made a sailor hat out of it, and put it on his head. When I asked him how he'd done that, he made one for me—gleefully, as if he was having the time of his life. At the same time, he talked about California and his train ride, and his words brought both to life. My shyness disappeared. I'd known adults who expected me to answer all manner of questions that I didn't think were any of their business, adults who didn't know what to say to me any more than I knew what to say to them, and adults whose attempts to joke with me had made me feel awkward. But this man didn't fit any category—he almost seemed to be a child himself.

I can still picture him sitting on the green carpet in our living room, surrounded by scraps of newspaper, making his pièce de resistance—a newspaper ladder. And I can still remember the excitement I felt. We had no television, no videos, only the odd film at the town's theatre, so this was first-class entertainment—and it was happening right in my own living room!

Of course, he hadn't come to entertain me. He'd barely known of my existence. He'd come to make sure my mother got her aunt's engagement ring. As he presented her with the large diamond on a platinum band, my mother was ecstatic. The ring was far beyond anything my father could ever give her. And it also had a connection to her beloved father's only sister.

Diamond rings are nice, of course. But Uncle Frank gave me something far more valuable. Though we were worlds apart in age and experience, we were bound together because of who we were. Like me, he was "different." Simply by being who he was, he gave me permission to be the person I was. He made me feel, for the first time in my life, that I wasn't alone. I now knew there was at least one other person in this world who was "different" like me.

When he returned to California after a couple of weeks, he left something to take his place. Knowing that Olive's niece had a young child, he'd brought along a copy of *A Child's Garden of Verses*. Over the following months, I read the book over and over until I had most of the poems memorized.

I can still feel the emotions I experienced as I read Robert Louis Stevenson's poem "The Little Land."

> When at home alone I sit
> And am very tired of it,
> I have just to shut my eyes
> To go sailing through the skies...[1]

It was as if Uncle Frank had given me permission to dream.

For Christmas, Uncle Frank sent me *Peter Pan* and I learned to fly. The next summer, when school was over, *Alice in Wonderland* arrived. I decided to learn how to play chess. Neuberger's *The Royal Canadian Mounted Police* appeared the next Christmas. I remember thinking how funny it was to get a book about Canada from an American. The banister around our porch became a horse, and I rode it all over the Prairies.

The summer I was ten, Uncle Frank came to visit us again in Souris, Manitoba, where we now lived. This time, he made the journey without the excuse of a ring. But he brought both Hans Christian Andersen's and the Grimm Brothers' books of fairy tales. He hadn't changed, except he was more wrinkled and even more frail. Inside, however, he was still more alive than anyone else I knew.

When he left, the fairy tales mesmerized me. I particularly loved the story of the ugly duckling, since it gave me hope that no matter how different I felt from other people, in the end a swan might yet emerge.

I read those books over and over until I probably could have told the stories from start to finish without missing any details. They were my retreat, my textbooks on creativity, and my doorway into another world. Like Robert Louis Stevenson, I soared on magic wings beyond the tangible world to a place where I could be anyone I wanted to be.

Uncle Frank sent me a few other books, and several puzzles. And then we learned that he was gone.

It wasn't until second-year university, when we did a raft of tests for our experimental psychology labs, that I began to understand why I had always felt so different. My results showed me—for the first time—that I tested in the top percentiles for IQ and creativity.

I know we did IQ tests while I was in both elementary and high school, but no one ever told me, or my parents, that I was gifted, and that this might make me emotionally sensitive. That it might cause trouble relating to my peers. That I might feel isolated.

Today, I sometimes wear the diamond ring that never left my mother's finger while she was alive. And I still have the books Uncle Frank gave me. Each one is inscribed "To my little sweetheart," or "To Nancy Jane Shaw, who I love very much." To me, they are treasures of far more value than mere diamonds.

My four gifted sons have read these books and many, many more. And they, more easily than I, have learned to unfurl their wings and delight in who they are.

I've been back in Manitoba a few times in recent years, taping television interviews, teaching workshops, and talking to booksellers who carry my books. On one of my trips, I decided to drive to Crystal City. It's still there, a small village nestled in the midst of fields of sunflowers, rye and canola. Our house is gone; there's only an overgrown field where it once stood. But the railway track is still there.

I parked my rented car, walked along the rails, and remembered that day long ago when I had felt so very much alone. I thanked God that He had made it all work out for good—that the ugly duckling had become a swan after all.

I don't know what compelled Uncle Frank to make that long trip by train from San Francisco instead of sending the ring by courier, but I know Who was behind it. And I know that the only reason I can write the books I write, and speak on the topics I speak about, is that I once was a lonely little girl walking on the railway tracks wanting the pain to go away.

1. Poem "The Little Land" by Robert Louis Stevenson. Copyright 1913, Public Domain.

This selection is adapted from the forthcoming book *LoveChild*, copyright © 2008 by N. J. Lindquist (That's Life! Communications/*www.lovechildministries.com*).

An Almost Silent Friendship

Non-fiction
Marcia Lee Laycock

The bitter Yukon wind tried to bite through our parkas as we stood on the tarmac of a small airport, waiting to board a plane to Alaska. But my friends and I were so excited, the cold couldn't dampen our enthusiasm. We smiled and chatted with one another as our luggage was loaded. We were on our way to a women's retreat.

I was a brand-new Christian and these women were new friends, so I stood back a little and just listened as the conversation flowed. I was still going through a bit of an identity crisis as I adjusted to the idea of being a Christian and tried to fit into the new culture to which I now belonged. At times I felt more than a little out of place and alone.

As the plane bounced over the frozen terrain and lifted into the air, I let my mind speculate on what the weekend would be like. I'd been asked to give my testimony, but I wasn't worried. I expected the gathering to be small, as most were in our tiny northern town. Since I had been raised in a tradition where "retreat" meant deny yourself, examine yourself, and don't dare say a word, I expected we would meet in silence. I expected the meals would be meagre. And I expected to be somehow changed. The last one was the only expectation that became a reality.

When we arrived at our destination we were picked up and driven to a school. All the sessions, we learned, would be held in the gym. When I walked into that building, I'm sure my shock was evident. Almost 300 women were there, many of them native women from all over Alaska and the Yukon Territory. And they were all talking at once. Strike expectations one and two. Then we were ushered into a dining area. Strike expectation number three. The tables were laden with steaming main dishes and tantalizing desserts.

After the meal, the first session was announced. I started to shake. Could I tell my story in front of them all? I wondered if it would be a sin to run out the back door.

Then I saw her. She was taller than most of the other native women there, with a long greying braid and chiselled, weathered features. Our eyes met across the room, and something connected between us. With that one look, I was somehow given courage and my knees stopped shaking. A moment later, it was time for me to speak. I don't remember exactly what I said, although I know I praised God for changing my life and for bringing me into a fellowship of believers who had reached out to me and my husband during a difficult time in our lives.

Afterward, a few women came over to talk to me. As I was engaged in conversation with them, I felt someone's hands on my shoulders and heard a soft mumble of prayer. When I was finally able to turn around, the woman was moving away. I saw the back of her tall statuesque form and the long greying braid as she melted into the crowd.

Throughout that weekend we "met" several more times, without a word being spoken between us. Just when I was feeling like the clichéd fish out of water, I'd look up and there she would be, with a look, a smile, a nod—always from a distance. I tried to seek her out a few times, but I was never able to find her when I had a free moment to talk.

Then it was time to pack up and head home. I tried to find her as we got ready to leave, and was disappointed that I had to climb into the bus and head out to the airport without seeing her one more time. But God had arranged a meeting. I found her sitting in the airport.

Almost expecting that she would melt away before I could speak with her, I approached her hesitantly. Her smile beamed like a beacon when she saw me, and she motioned for me to sit beside her. Our conversation was brief, but I felt another immediate bond as the woman, whose name was Lorna, told me she lived in a remote village on the Yukon River. I lived on the Klondike, which feeds into the Yukon. When I told her that, she smiled again, nodded, and said that every morning she would wake up and look at the mighty Yukon and think about Jesus. The simplicity of that image touched me deeply. She said she knew I would speak often about what God was doing in my life and she pledged to pray for me as He used me in that way. As I remained seated, she rose and laid her hand on my head, closing her eyes in silent blessing. Then she was gone.

There have been many times over the years, especially when I stand in front of an audience, that I have thought of that dear woman. I see her eyes and am given courage. I see her smile and feel the assurance that I am among family. I have sensed, most of all, the whisper of her prayers. I believe she was a divine appointment. I believe she was part of the circle of friends that God had arranged for me as I moved out of my lonely, dysfunctional world into the family of God.

I look forward to the day I will meet Lorna again. I envision being able to sit together by the banks of the mighty river of life and talk about Jesus.

Blind Date

Fiction
Paul H. Boge

Maybe this would be the one.

Snow drifted down on Vancouver Island as Alexis Carter pulled off the quiet highway into the parking lot of the Masthead Restaurant. The wood frame and frosting on the edge of the windows gave it a warm, cabin-like feel and brightened up an otherwise dark stretch of road. She parked near the entrance and glanced at her dashboard clock, then checked her makeup and hair in the rear-view mirror.

Opening the door of her red sports car, she was about to step out when she second-guessed whether her black leather jacket was the right choice or if she should go with the classical look of her light blue jean jacket in the back seat. The getting-out-of-the-car part was supposed to be quick and easy, the result of everything having been planned out. But with so much riding on those oh-so-important initial three seconds of a first impression, it was tempting to question what small advantage one option might have over the other. It made her wonder how she would feel later this evening when she would be driving home.

Go with the leather. She stepped out into ankle-deep snow, closed the door and clicked the lock button. If she hadn't been concentrating so hard on staying calm, she would have taken the time to stand under the only light in the parking lot and stare up at those huge flakes of white snow that seemed to stay suspended in air. She stole a quick look up, more to say a prayer than to look at the snow, and in that moment remembered what it was like when her dad was still with her and they would make snow angels and wait for those flakes to land on their noses, all the while pretending that the snow was in fact standing still and it was the two of them who were traveling through space and time together.

When she opened the door to the Masthead she felt an immediate sense of calm. Ambience. It was as if she had been given a transfusion of peace. She looked around the restaurant and had the strangest feeling that she had been here before. As if she was returning to a place she had been dreaming about for years.

A man in his seventies played "Moon River" at the piano off to her right. Wooden tables and chairs were spread out around the restaurant. A teenage boy and his father ate a mound of shrimp at a table in the centre. A crowd in the corner erupted in laughter. A man with short hair wearing a blue, oil-stained mechanic's jacket passed by her on the way out. A red-haired woman approached. By the way she broke from a nearby table to greet her new guest, Alexis assumed she was not only the host but also the owner. She had a smile and a vibrancy that people have when they are doing what they are designed to do.

"For two. Reservation for—"

"Alexis Carter," the woman responded, making Alexis wonder if *he* was already here. Early is good. Punctuality says so much. Though if her clock in the car was any indication, she was 14 minutes early.

Alexis was shown to a table with three porthole windows that offered a view of the harbour. She glanced out at the ocean, which dissolved into blackness in the distance. Three seconds. *Why is it that we are so fast to determine whether we think someone might be a match?*

Another gorgeous evening. Another prospect. Heaven knows she'd been here enough times before. Well, not here, as in the Masthead, *per se*. This place was a first. But she was no stranger to blind dates. Twelve, last she counted. Fun when you're in your twenties and the clock is some object that hangs on a wall. Not so fun when you're in your mid-thirties and things that were supposed to have worked out by now haven't, and that clock has become more like a drum banging away inside your brain, as if you need any help remembering that you are still single. The busyness of life—career, church involvement, nieces and nephews—normally kept her mind from noticing that time was marching on; but at times like these—late at night, the drive home from work, or staring out at a snowfall—she felt alone, and in spite of all her attempts to the contrary, wondered if perhaps there was something she wasn't hearing from God.

The door opened. *Don't look. Don't appear too anxious. Just relax and—This should feel more natural than it is. This is just like Grade Eight, when the phone rings and you wait there dying, knowing it's him calling, but you have to give it the obligatory three rings because every girl in your class does that.*

She did glance. Tall, coke-bottle glasses, trench coat. Like someone out of a bad CIA movie. Her heart skipped a beat, but for all the wrong reasons. He sat down at a booth off to her left. She exhaled and later felt bad for being relieved that it wasn't him. Glancing back at the harbour, she wondered what it would be like to sail out into the ocean.

Will he, the real he, be interested in sailing? What is he like? Will we have that initial spark? Her date this evening had been set up by a common friend who assured Alexis that this would, at the very least, be fun, and, at the very most, be the start of a relationship with the person she had been searching for all this time. "You guys are perfect for each other. What's the harm in a little dinner? It's not pressure. You're a pro at this." (That part didn't help.) "You meet, have a few laughs and then decide from there. There's nothing—"

"Alexis?"

A jolt of adrenaline shot through her. *It's him. He has a really cool voice. I could get used to that voice. There's something reassuring in the tone. Something natural. Something fitting. Okay, get that deer-in-the-head-lights look out of your eyes. Smile. And be genuine. Be natural. What you see is what you get.* As she turned to look at him, in that moment when her gaze changed from the harbour to her blind date, she had the nervous excitement that culminates in three words: This is it.

"Michael."

Brown eyes. Dark hair. Comforting smile. She reached out to shake his hand. One second. He grasped her hand firmly, yet not too tight.

She returned the smile. Eye contact. Real eye contact. Not just looking at him, but looking into him, studying him for any hint as to whether the connection was really there. Two seconds. There it was. This was new. This was different. Wow.

Kiss those 12 previous blind dates good bye. There was more here in three seconds than all the others combined.

He sat down opposite her. They exchanged introductions and then talked about the things people talk about when they are breaking the ice and testing the waters for that all too elusive bond. She told him she had studied business at Providence in Rhode Island and followed that with a Master's in Health Administration; had been on three short-term missionary projects, most recently in Africa; had taught Sunday School to four-year-olds; and loved hockey, especially the Canadian Women's National team.

He was a lawyer, served on his church's finance committee, and enjoyed rock-climbing. They laughed. They shared. Cautious at first, the way people are when they're being careful not to send the wrong message with a misinterpreted comment or gesture. But then the ice did melt. He was the kind of person she felt she had known her whole life.

Two hours went by so fast that Alexis had to do a double take to realize that three groups of patrons had sat at the table beside her since she had sat down. She was gathering up the courage to ask him if he wanted to join her for lunch next week when he interrupted her thought.

"Alexis…?"

Okay, here it comes. The moment. He's starting off by saying my name. What does that lean towards? Yes? No?

"I'm not sure this is going to work."

She held her breath. *No.* Where does all the blood go when it drains out of your face?

Michael spoke in a quiet, even tone, but to Alexis it seemed he was shouting. It was as if the piano had stopped playing, the room had suddenly gone quiet, and everyone in the restaurant was now focused on her, listening to her indictment. As often as she had been through this before, both on the receiving and the giving end, she hadn't gotten used to the feeling of optimism slipping out of her life.

Any chance you could have said "no" later in an e-mail? I would have really liked to have one evening where I could drive home to my empty apartment and think to myself that maybe, just maybe, I've met the guy of my dreams, that maybe you're the one, that maybe things are finally starting to fall into place, that maybe…

Her date felt like Hollywood. The town of the quick hello and the slow goodbye. Weeks from now she would look back and be thankful for his honesty. Still, here, in this moment, it was hard to hear his explanation. She nodded, but she wasn't listening. She heard the words, but it seemed as though she was in a fog. *Stay upbeat. Stay friendly. Don't show any disappointment. Maybe he's right. Better to know now than to get the "Dear Jane" e-mail later.*

He finished. She thanked him for coming. They talked about nothing, as though doing so could somehow ease the pain. Her pain. As he stood up, she heard the piano again. No one had been listening, of course. The people in the restaurant were just as oblivious to her now as they had been before.

She watched him leave. It was a vain attempt at hanging on to whatever semblance of hope was left. *Strange*, she thought. *Why is it that one person can feel so right about a relationship while the other person feels nothing? Why is it that sometimes the connection only goes one way?*

She found herself wishing she was back at her apartment, sitting on her couch, in her pyjamas, watching a movie with a big bowl of popcorn and a cup of herbal tea, instead of sitting here in the restaurant, with only the sting of disappointment to keep her company. Whoever said "nothing ventured, nothing gained" had never been turned down at a harbour during a beautiful snowfall.

"Can I get you anything else?" the red-haired lady asked.

"Just the cheque," Alexis replied, being careful to make eye contact while trying hard to find a way to pretend that this was anything but a blind date that hadn't turned out in her favour.

"It's already been covered," the owner said as she left.

Even worse. Getting dumped wouldn't be nearly so hard if the guy had stiffed her with the bill. At least that way she would have had some comfort on the ride home knowing that he was a cheap, self-centered, egotistical.... But he wasn't. He was Prince Charming. And the slipper, alas, did not fit.

She remembered one of her father's favourite sayings: "The next business deal is only a phone call away." She could have used a call from him right about now.

The walk to the car felt longer than it was. Her feet felt heavier than they were. There seemed to be more snow on the car than what was there. After she swept it off, she sat behind the wheel of her car. Thinking. Wondering. Wishing. She glanced at the clock. *Any chance we could turn life back two hours and redo this?* She didn't check the mirror this time.

The drive home was darker than she expected. The snow that had seemed to be highlighting the way to the Masthead on her drive there now felt like a blinding maze that prevented her from seeing the curves in the road.

A semi passed and sprayed her windshield. She touched the brakes and reached for the wiper control to change from slow to fast. Somewhere between taking her left hand off the steering wheel and releasing her foot from the brake she lost control of the vehicle.

At first it felt like a skid that she could steer against to regain her position. But when the back end swerved out from her, she got that sick feeling of knowing that she was at the mercy, or lack thereof, of the laws of physics. *How close am I to the edge?*

The car spun forcibly around, jerking Alexis in an unpredictable manner. She drilled the brakes and clutched the steering wheel, bracing herself for impact. *Dear God. Dear God. Dear God.*

There was a loud bang, and then the scraping sound of snow against the bottom of her car before it came to a stop. She breathed in slightly through her mouth. Her throat throbbed. Her muscles were tensed. She waited to confirm she wasn't hurt, then put the car in park and tried the ignition. No response. *What if I'm sitting in the wrong lane of traffic?* She pulled on the handle, but the door didn't open. She pushed against it, but it barely budged against the packed snow.

Alexis crawled over to the passenger side. She pulled the handle and half expected to see headlights bearing down towards her.

Instead, the door opened to reveal an embankment. Alexis stepped out and saw that the front of her car on the passenger side was smashed in. She looked down the highway in both directions and determined that she had crossed over into the other lane and spun around into the ditch. *You could have been killed.*

She took a deep breath and tried to get herself under control. Closing her eyes, she brought her pointer finger and thumb to the bridge of her nose. *It's just stress. Breathe. You're fine. Just relax. Think. Get some help.*

She reached back into the car for her purse. Digging out her cell phone, she hit the power button. Nothing. She hit it again. Still nothing. Hadn't she charged it last night? *Great timing, Alexis.*

The inevitable decision. Risk waiting in the car all night or take a chance walking down the highway? How long had she been driving? Had she passed any vehicles on the road? That one semi. Any others? Would anyone else be coming by this way? *Jesus, what do I do?*

Alexis got into the passenger seat and closed the door. She couldn't recall whether she had seen a gas station or a hotel since she left. She estimated that she had been driving about 10 minutes, which she figured put her about a two-hour walk back to the Masthead. *That's doable. Isn't it?*

Mid-thirties. Single and looking. Broken down car. Dead cell phone. Stuck in a snow storm.

Had it come to this?

Better to wait in the car. No telling how cold it might get. Plus, if an unwanted person stopped by she could always make the excuse that help was just about to arrive.

Tomorrow, while relaying the story to inquisitive coworkers, she would look back on this evening and provide the obligatory laugh, the kind of laugh that comes from the outside, not the inside. She rubbed her eyes, and, anticipating a long wait, took off her leather jacket and reached behind for the blue one to put on underneath. She wrestled her arms into her jean jacket and was about to reach for the leather one when she saw headlights in the distance.

She waited those anxious moments until the vehicle stopped in front of her. Squinting from the glare, she managed to see the outline of a tow truck. A man wearing a blue jacket stepped out. Alexis had the strange feeling that she knew him. As he approached, she opened the passenger door just enough to hear him.

"You alright?" he asked.

"I'm okay." Where had she seen him?

"Mind if I take a look?" he asked, gesturing to the front end of the car partially buried into the snow.

"Okay."

The man pulled out his flashlight and bent down. She heard him clearing away snow around the front tires. Moments later he reappeared.

"Bad luck. The quarter panel is pushed back into the tire. I can tow you into town if you like?"

She looked closer at his eyes. Of course. The man she had passed as she was walking into the Masthead. "That'd be great."

She climbed into the passenger side of the truck and took him up on his offer to use his cell phone to let someone know she was all right. As she was listening to her friend's attempt at encouragement ("It'll be fine, there are other fish in the sea, nothing ventured, nothing…") her mind trailed off from the conversation and was diverted to a small Gideon Bible on the seat beside her. She ended the conversation as the man got in the cab.

"Quite the snowfall, isn't it?"

"It's incredible," she replied, glancing behind to see that the red light he had put on top of her car was flashing.

"You know, it's coming down so heavy that if you'd lie down and look straight up, it would seem like the snow is standing still and that it'd be you who was moving." As if suddenly becoming aware of how odd that must have sounded, he turned away, put the truck in gear and began to drive.

"I know what you mean."

"You've looked at a snowfall like that before?"

Alexis nodded. She glanced up at the falling snow. "You have great timing. That you happened to be coming down this road just after I spun out of control…"

"We almost didn't have anyone working this evening. My uncle runs this company, but he got sick tonight and his partner is out of town. So he phoned me up to ask if I could take a call for him. I drove all the way out, but no one was there. I was just on my way back when I saw you."

"You always work the evening shift?"

"Not any more. It's been years since I drove a tow truck. I used to drive while I was in med school. I just came back from a year in Africa where I was working at an orphanage for street children."

"Your family must be proud."

"My parents were sad and happy to see me go, if you know what I mean. My brothers and sisters all have their own families so… Say, did you get through to your family? They know you're okay?"

She caught him trying to look at her left hand for a ring. "I left a message with a friend from church."

"Good."

He took off his toque and put on a cap. Alexis caught the reflection of the Vancouver Canucks hockey team logo in the rear-view mirror. She turned to confirm what she saw. "You a Canucks fan?"

He smiled. "Diehard. All the way back to when they had the yellow, orange and black jerseys."

"Those were cool. Remember Stan Smyl?"

"Absolutely. Richard Brodeur?"

"Great goalie."

"You still go to the games?"

"When I get a chance."

He paused just long enough for Alexis to realize that he was evaluating the options. *Is he interested? How much does he really know about me?* Nothing ventured, nothing—

"As it turns out, my uncle and I were planning on going to the game tomorrow night, but I don't think he'll be in any shape to go."

"Are you sure? He might be better by then."

"If he found out that he was taking your place, he'd never forgive me."

For no apparent reason she laughed. It filled the entire cab of the truck. She hadn't heard herself laugh like that in a long time.

He laughed, too.

Alexis made eye contact with him. There was a cool, calm glisten in those pools of blue. One second. "Thanks, that'd be great."

"I'm David."

Two seconds. He stretched out his hand.

"Alexis."

She grasped his hand and sensed his assurance that she didn't need to concentrate on making an impression, that she could talk and feel the way that came naturally with being Alexis Carter.

Three.

The further they drove and the more they talked, the more the evening's previous events were erased from her mind, and replaced with the time she was spending with him.

"This snow is really something," he said. "I have to drive slower. Hope you don't have anything you're late for."

Alexis looked over at him and shrugged her shoulders to indicate she didn't mind.

The slower the better.

Romance Amid Reality

Non-fiction
Sheila Wray Gregoire

*E*very Valentine's Day, many of us are plagued with questions in the romance department. Will he send flowers? Will she say yes? My question last year was a bit different: Why can't he ever bang up his car?

I would feel significantly better about myself if just every now and then my husband would back into a tree, or rear-end the car in front of him, or hit a fire hydrant. I've done all of those things (I've actually hit a fire hydrant twice), and I don't see why I should be the only one.

The latest accident happened a few weeks ago when the roads were really icy. I was only going about 20 kilometres an hour when the truck ahead of me stopped. I had plenty of room, but I hit an icy patch and just couldn't get the brakes to respond. My front bumper hit his trailer hitch. Guess who won?

In retrospect, I can't see anything I could have done differently. It was just one of those things. But here's my problem. If it truly wasn't my fault, then why aren't all our accidents divided equally between the two of us? Why is it only ever me?

Of course, Keith did the proper husbandly thing and said, "All that matters is that no one was hurt." And he treated me perfectly well all day long, which of course made me suspect that he was harbouring some horrid thought like: "Why can't she just learn to drive?" And for the next few days, no matter what he said to me, I snapped. I couldn't shake the feeling that he was thinking I was incompetent. And I had to punish him for thinking that.

The biggest barrier to romance, in my opinion, isn't necessarily the failure to remember flowers on Valentine's Day (though chocolate couldn't hurt). It's this tendency we all have to build walls between us because basically we're all insecure. We know what we hate about ourselves, and one of our worst fears is that those we love will notice these flaws, too.

Men and women experience this differently. John Gray, author of *Men Are from Mars, Women Are from Venus*, posits that men read guilt trips into everything. "Come to the table! Dinner's ready!" for instance, means "Why couldn't you get off that couch earlier and help me make it?" Women, on the other hand, nurse the suspicion that deep inside our men may know we're less than perfect.

Since I can speak to the female side of that equation better, here's a primer for men. If she asks you if you think she's gaining weight, the answer is always "No." If she asks if you think she's becoming boring because the kids have taken over her life, the answer isn't just "No;" it's "No" plus a reassuring hug, and an offer to change the next dirty diaper. And if she ever asks you if you would find her more exciting if she looked more like model Rebecca Romijn, the correct answer is "Who's she?" These things go to the heart of her self-esteem, and it's very important to get them right.

We women need to remember the other side of the coin. When he says, "Wow, that's quite a hole in the bumper," take him at his word. He may not mean "It's a wonder they ever gave you a license in the first place." That may simply be the voice in your head working overtime. Likewise, if he says, "Wow, this place is a mess," put down that frying pan. He may not be blaming you. He may just be commenting on the need to teach all residents of this house who are over the age of six to stop living like pigs.

Sometimes men need to read between the lines a little bit more to hear what she's really saying. And sometimes women need to stop reading between the lines and just read his lips. Kissing them is probably a good idea, too. As are chocolate truffles. That's what made my Valentine's Day, and I hope you enjoy your next one, too.

Sheila has more advice on romance in her book *Honey, I Don't Have a Headache Tonight: Help for Women Who Want to Feel More in the Mood* (Kregel Publications).

A Prairie Storm

Non-fiction
Carolyn Arends

$\mathcal{T}$he relatives on my father's side were farmers: hard-working, plain-spoken people who understood and loved the earth and harnessed its power through sweat and skill and faith. At least that is how I imagine them. I am prone to remember them in fits of romantic contemplation, during which I suspect something of their noble, earthy spirit lives on in me. In my more lucid moments I see, clearly, it does not. I must confess that I am the poster girl for comfort-craving suburbanites everywhere. When I get close to the earth I so profess to love, it seems, well... dirty.

I was not without promise in my early childhood. No Fisher-Price farm set was ever as beloved as mine, and for six futile birthdays in a row I asked passionately and expectantly for a pony, whom I planned to call "Black Beauty" and keep in my bedroom. I see further evidence of my proud ancestry in my son, who as a toddler was so enamoured with cows that he reached heights of near-ecstasy in the dairy section of our local supermarket. "Moo!" he would cry, oblivious to the chill, pointing to the pastoral scenes that adorned each and every milk carton with a fervour that would have made his great, great-Grandma Bittner most pleased.

I met my great-grandmother Bittner only once, when I was very young. My parents, in a sudden spasm of suburban guilt (at least we know where I get it from), decided it was time to embark on a pilgrimage to the family homestead. And so, in the summer of 1972, my brother Chris and I spent a wide-eyed week on the Bittner wheat farm in Yorkton, Saskatchewan.

A four-year-old possesses a mind's eye like a fun house mirror; the shapes of everyone and everything are stretched to larger-than-life proportions. To this day I can play back my memories like scratchy pieces of stop-motion film.

The wheat is militant, standing at attention in uniform rows until a prairie wind spots me in the distance and decides to put on a show. Stalks higher than the Empire State Building become Motown dancers, bending and swaying, swaying and bending for an awestruck audience of one. My great-uncles are benevolent Goliaths with wide grins and huge, leathery hands. At the end of the day they smell a little like ripe fruit. Their own children are no longer children, and yet when they enter the farmhouse they are once more the dutiful sons of Grandma Bittner, who is all one could hope for in a family matriarch. Eighty-five laborious years have compromised her mobility (I picture her in a wheel chair—my parents tell me it was really just a kitchen chair from which she seldom moved), but she is still a dominant figure. I am a little afraid in her presence, but there is a softness beneath her severe strength. The Saskatchewan sun has turned her a golden brown, and she is as kneaded and plump as the fragrant loaves of bread cooling on her counters.

The Bittner wheat farm is pure magic, but I am not purely happy. Even a four-year-old can tell when something is amiss, and I am troubled when my uncles' open faces cloud over. I strain to overhear and understand their conversations. *The crops are in trouble. No rain for months.* We hoist Grandma Bittner into the car for a drive, and each field we pass elicits the same response. *Too dry, too dry.* My heart sinks further with every mournful shake of her heavy head. I've never heard the word "drought" before, but I'm sure it's not good.

In the cool of the evening my great-aunts and uncles gather in the kitchen and bring my parents up to date on the latest family gossip. Chris and I grow restless, so one night we are permitted to sit by ourselves on the front porch. We are sleepy and warm and somewhat intoxicated with our freedom, until all at once the universe begins to go horribly wrong.

A cloud of mosquitoes attacks my brother. The air is thick with them, and they only want Chris. We are mutually hysterical, and the grown-ups come running in the kind of panic that leaves spilt teacups and crushed pastries in its wake. The family surrounds my brother, and he is as frightened by their flailing attempts to beat off the insects as he is by the mosquitoes themselves. Eventually they manage to get him inside, and the surviving mosquitoes fly off in a well-fed stupor. With the resiliency only a two-year-old can possess, Chris is happy once again, consoled by some chocolate and an ancient set of building blocks.

Now I am alone on the porch, still sweaty and jittery from my brother's ordeal. Before my heart rate can return to normal, a new onslaught is launched. But this time it is not mosquitoes.

The world is suddenly lit in a ghoulish white flash that scorches my eyes. A second later, all is consumed in darkness. The wind begins to howl, enraged to be losing a shouting match with thunder that is more terrifying than anything I've ever heard or imagined. The rain the heavens have been hoarding is released with a savage vengeance, pelting the roof and slashing at the windows, drenching me instantly. Even the sturdy old farmhouse has turned against me, violently banging the screen door open and shut behind me. The lightning strikes again and again and again, illuminating the holy terror that is my first prairie storm.

My parents find me inside the farmhouse, sitting on the cellar stairs, my hands clamped over my ears in an effort to drown out the rattle of the rain crashing into the huge metal rain-water cistern next to me. I am nearly doubled over by my sobs. My father scoops me up and carries me into the safety of the kitchen. A flash of hot light illuminates my relatives for a moment—inexplicably, they are sitting together staring out the farmhouse windows with strangely calm smiles. "It's just a storm," they murmur. There is even some quiet, gentle laughter. I only cry harder. "Sweetheart," pleads my mom, "don't be afraid." I shake my head. I am afraid, but more than that I am sick with a guilt so crushing I can't speak under the weight of it. The family—both immediate and extended—is sympathetic, patient. They don't understand that the chaos outside is *all my fault.* "What is it? What is it?" they chorus. Several minutes pass before I summon the courage to confess my terrible secret.

"I... prayed... for... rain."

Now the laughter is not so quiet. There is even a little applause. "Oh, Honey, the rain is wonderful," someone says. Before I can catch my breath the uncles are teasing me. Someone brings me some warm milk, and soon I can't keep my heavy eyes open, not even to watch the storm. "Hey Sweetheart," calls an uncle as my daddy carries me off to my room, "could you pray for some cash?"

In the morning I awake to the sounds of my uncles' hammers. They are repairing wind-damaged fences, and they are still laughing, jubilant in the mud. The crops will make it after all.

The storm and the terror, the giddy relief and elation, the instinctual and unwavering belief that my prayer had saved the Bittner family farm—these are among my earliest memories. And I consider them now with a sense of both wonder and dread that has only deepened over the years. The night the Prairie Drought of 1972 came to an end was the night I began to understand that there are forces even towering great-uncles cannot tame, forces so ferocious in their power that—even if they bring you exactly what you need (*especially* if they bring you exactly what you need)—they are likely to scare you silly. I had already heard much about God in my young life—already, I think, learned to love Him. But hearing the heavens thunder, I had my first taste of what it is to fear Him, my first encounter with what a quarter of a century later I am learning to call the *mysterium tremendum et fascinans*—the tremendous and fascinating mystery of God. On the front steps of that Yorkton farmhouse, a holy secret was whispered into my soul: *Prayer is the point of access, the place where the finite and the infinite intersect and converse. To pray is to enter at least a little ways into the mystery, or—and this is even more dangerous—to invite the mystery to come to you.*

And so, these days, I pray. Whether I am on a front porch in Saskatchewan or a back deck in British Columbia, whether I am praying from a surrendered or a stubborn heart, I speak with the God of Creation. I am ushered—sometimes reverent, sometimes willful, never worthy—into His presence, and when the language is beyond me it is spoken on my behalf. I pray for the wisdom to learn more about prayer, and for the courage to pray the prayers that will change me. And in my best and bravest moments, when I ache to know more of the tremendous and fascinating mystery of God, I pray for rain.

The Neatness Wars

Non-fiction
Eric E. Wright

Can marriage survive the neatness wars? My life-partner, Mary Helen, feels called to organize our household space so it is open, understated and immaculate. In my office, however, piles of magazines and papers suit me fine. They might come in handy for my research some day. I need pens, paper clips, sticky notes, yellow markers and coffee cups near at hand. I'm insecure unless I can plaster several bulletin boards with notes on things I might get to. I believe space is to be utilized—fully.

The day of the garlic affair I thought I finally had ammunition to curb Mary Helen's passion to tidy up. Earlier in the day, while making everything shipshape, Mary Helen arrived at the laundry room where I lay out garlic and sundry other items to dry. Most of the useable garlic had already flavoured curries and soups. A few wizened bulbs of garlic remained—which she trashed. Then she turned her attention to a dish full of much firmer bulbs. Slicing them up, she dumped them into the pot for supper.

That night when we sat down to enjoy our stew, I noticed these pale bits scattered through the dish. I made no comment at their rather bland flavor. The next day, however, when I went into the laundry room I noticed that my gladiola bulbs were missing. After inquiry, I discovered that—yes—she had mistaken the gladiola bulbs for garlic! Through hoots of laughter I dimly perceived a weapon to use in my attempts to curb her penchant for neatness.

Not that I can use this tale much: she denies it ever happened! Fortunately, I don't need to use it as leverage. Years of good-natured sparring have mellowed us to the point where we give each other a lot of leeway.

Experience has taught us that the very differences that attracted us to each other can easily spark disagreements. Rather than argue, it's much better to agree on a compromise. Mary Helen lets me do just about what I want in my office—as long as I vacuum regularly and dust occasionally. I give her free reign in the kitchen, the dining room and even the bedroom. She grants me freedom in the garage.

The Bible has a lot of great advice for getting along with others. "Accept one another, then, just as Christ accepted you" (Romans 15:7). "Be completely humble and gentle; be patient, bearing with one another in love" (Ephesians 4:2).

If I try to curb Mary Helen's fondness for a tidy house, we'll both end up unhappy. Better to accept her and celebrate her marvellous personality. What a boring marriage it would be if we were the same! I must admit I'm rather proud of what she's done in the living room. And she does come to me when she needs something from one of my files or wants me to fix a broken appliance.

Every relationship, not just the marital union, requires a lot of give and take and tons of humour. In business, in the family, among our neighbours, with our relatives—and certainly on the national and international scene, learning to be forbearing is more valuable than learning how to win arguments. "Love is patient... It is not self-seeking, it is not easily angered, it keeps no record of wrongs" (1 Corinthians 13:4-5). Love, which includes forbearance, is the oil that keeps relationships from squeaking and squealing worse than the hinges on a rusty garden gate.

Of course, no relationship is perfect. In spite of our negotiated treaty on spheres of influence, Mary Helen will occasionally frown and say, "Honey, can you tidy up the garage? The kids are coming for the weekend and it's really looking messy."

She's probably right, but if my defences are down I may respond, "Hey, I'm organized. I know exactly where everything is! Just relax. Your problem is, you're compulsive."

Those are fighting words, best left unsaid. Time to say, "I'm sorry," and make up. "Bear with each other and forgive whatever grievances you may have against one another. Forgive as the Lord forgave you" (Colossians 3:13).

Heavenly Father, we're all so different. Husbands and wives. Neighbours. Colleagues. Relatives. We like different colours and foods and clothing. We vote for different people. Help me to accept those differences—even when they seem so strange. Enable me to be a patient, loving and encouraging person who is quick to overlook personal quirks and foibles. After all, you have accepted me through Jesus Christ.

This selection is an excerpt from the book *Down a Country Road*, copyright © 2008 by Eric E. Wright (Day One Publishers / *www.dayone.co.uk* or *www.countrywindow.ca*).

What Your Sock Drawer Says About You

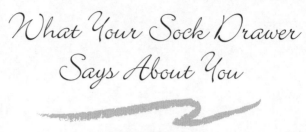

Non-fiction
Sheila Wray Gregoire

While walking through the mall last week I saw something inspiring. A man was pushing a baby carriage, inside of which was a baby wearing two different socks! One was pink, one was yellow, and they obviously did not come from the same pair.

Now, perhaps this man is just clothing-challenged when it comes to little girls. My husband, for instance, lives by the credo "girls' buttons always go at the back," which led to some very odd placement of bows and front collars on the rare occasions I actually allowed him to dress our daughters. He now lets them dress themselves, which is a whole other horror story.

I prefer to think that this stranger was not creating an inadvertent fashion faux pas, but was instead being deliberate. I think he was trying to liberate himself from the stupidity of some of the customs we cling to. I currently have (I just checked) four pairs of socks in my drawer, three in each of the girls' drawers, eight in my husband's, and 62 single socks in my stray sock drawer. If we were to mix and match, think of the money and frustration we could save!

That's not the only silly thing we do in our homes, though. Ironing has to rate high on that list, too. I stopped ironing a few years ago, as anyone who has ever seen my husband in dress shirts knows. (If we have to go somewhere fancy, it's Keith who works that dreaded small appliance.) When it comes to clothes shopping, I only buy knits, and in the process save plenty of aggravation.

Then there's dusting. Dusting does not actually take very much time if you have little to dust. Wiping a cloth over a clear surface is a breeze. Dusting around 30 trophies that you won in Grade Four for some softball championship during which you spent seven innings on the bench takes much more effort. So does dusting all those knick knacks your in-laws bought you, the ones that cause you to wonder whether you have truly been accepted in the family yet or whether they're still trying to test you.

In fact, we could apply this principle to almost everything in our homes: stuff is your enemy. The more stuff you have, the less room you have for all the new stuff you're bringing into the house. Stuff piles up on your kitchen counter, your dining room table, your front stairs, and soon you have stuff everywhere and you don't even know where to start cleaning. Throw stuff out and you have room for the important things in your life.

Much of the problem with wasted effort around our homes really stems from the fact that we're aiming for the wrong thing. We want to have a perfect house to prove something to people. In the process, we end up compulsively dusting a living room no one ever sits in, to save it for company who, when they arrive, hang out in the kitchen anyway. Let's reclaim that space and aim for a comfortable home instead. Don't feel guilty if it's not perfect. Your house, after all, is meant to be lived in. And besides, there's no point getting stressed over housework that will never truly be finished anyway.

I keep telling my kids that they can turn those matchless socks into sock puppets as soon as I've done all the laundry and made sure there are no stray socks in hiding. But we all know that laundry is never actually finished. So if those sock puppets are going to see the light of day before my kids are too old to enjoy them, I had better loosen up. Maybe if we all relaxed a little, our homes would be much more comfortable, even if that means our socks don't match.

For more of Sheila's advice on household organization, read her book *To Love Honor and Vacuum: When You Feel More Like a Maid than a Wife and Mother* (Kregel Publications).

Faith, Hope and Love: Give Them a Chance to Improve Your Health!

Non-fiction
Denyse O'Leary

The apostle Paul once wrote that only three things were of ultimate importance for humankind: "And now these three remain: faith, hope and love" (1 Corinthians 13:13).

I'm sure we've all read that verse and shrugged our shoulders and gone our way, accepting it as truth, but not really understanding what it means in terms of our practical lives. However, while working with Montreal neuroscientist Mario Beauregard on our recently published book, *The Spiritual Brain: A Neuroscientist's Case for the Existence of the Soul* (HarperOne, 2007), I had an unexpected side-benefit: I learned more about the practical effects of faith, hope and love. I also learned that our minds—our mental states—influence our health far more intimately than I had ever realized.

As a woman in my fifties who wonders about the future health of my loved ones and myself, I was pretty glad to learn what I did. And as a journalist, I am happy to pass this useful information on to you.

Now, I am *not* referring to any New Age claims about mysterious healing powers, adorned with exclamation marks, on the back covers of dodgy magazines. I mean cold sober research done in laboratories and published in scientific journals. On the contrary, if there is any mystery, it is that we so often ignore research findings, when greater awareness would help our families and ourselves.

Three areas that caught my attention are:

- The role that our expectations play in how well treatments work.

- The ways in which our minds—our immaterial selves—can change our brains (by "our brains," I mean those physical organs that relate our minds to the world around us).
- The role spirituality plays in helping us to better health.

Here are some things I learned from exciting new findings in these areas...

The Difference Faith Makes

You probably aren't waiting for science to come up with "the perfect pill for every ill," but if you know anyone who is, he or she likely will be waiting a long time. Not because dramatic science discoveries will fail, but because the effect of many medical treatments depends at least in part on the patient's expectation. Doctors know this by experience, of course, but research has shed new light on how powerful the patient's expectation is.

In 2004, University of Michigan researchers reported on a study of pain experienced by healthy young male volunteers. To induce pain, they injected saltwater into their volunteers' jaws and measured the impact by positron emission tomography (PET). They then gave the volunteers a substance described as pain relief. Not only did the volunteers report feeling better thereafter, but a number of brain regions that activate when we experience pain showed a reduced response. In other words, there was external evidence that the volunteers' subjective belief that they felt better corresponded to the reality of pain signals in their brains.

However—and this is the key point—no pain relief drug had actually been used in the study! The volunteers felt less pain simply because they believed they had received a powerful drug. The researchers commented that their study demonstrates how our perceptions truly affect the amount of pain we experience. This study, along with many others, showed that the effect of what we believe is real and measurable in scientific terms.

This effect is usually called the placebo effect, after a Latin word meaning "I will please." Some researchers prefer to call it the "meaning effect" or the "remembered wellness" effect. Whatever its name, the meaning you attach to a treatment helps determine how effective that treatment will be for you.

For example, anthropologist Daniel Moerman of the University of Michigan notes that various studies have shown that large pills work better than medium-sized pills and four pills work better than two, even when all the pills are sugar. And culture can make a difference in the relief we experience too. North Americans tend to believe that injections are more powerful than pills, so injections of sterile water may provide us more relief than a sugar pill (even though both are placebos). But that does not work for Europeans who do not think that injections are more powerful than pills. Blue sleeping pills work better than other colours—except when given to male Italian soccer fans whose team colour is blue.

Even sham surgery works. Sylvester Colligan of Beaumont, Texas, could barely walk before his 1994 knee operation. He was mobile and free of pain six years later. But, as he later learned, he was actually in the control group. Yes, he received three knee incisions, but he was just sewn up again afterward; no conventional arthroscopy was done. But his body did not know that, because his mind did not.

Similarly, a 2004 study compared 30 patients who received controversial embryonic stem-cell implants for Parkinson's disease to patients who received only sham surgery. The patients who thought they had received the stem cells reported better quality of life a year later than those who thought they had received the sham surgery—regardless of which surgery patients had actually received. Ratings by medical personnel tended to concur with the patients' own views. That last point is significant. The more your doctor believes in a treatment, the more likely you are to experience relief from it.

At one time, doctors suspected that more emotionally expressive people responded more strongly than stolid souls, but that does not seem to be the case. Our minds are real, and what we expect to happen is important.

Still, there are limitations on the power of our minds. Placebos do not help to treat cancer (though they help cancer patients with appetite and pain control). Also, only a person who is intellectually capable of believing that a medication provides relief can experience the effect of faith. One study found that Alzheimer patients whose cognitive deficits interfered with their ability to expect relief did not experience it.

Still, looking at the big picture, the effect—call it "placebo" or "meaning" or whatever you like—is pretty powerful. All drugs are tested against it—not because it doesn't work but precisely because it *does*. A medication must work five percent better than a placebo to be licensed for use. That makes sense. You certainly would not want to pay $159.95 for a prescription that worked only one percent better than faith that you will get well. The money would be much better spent on a day at the spa.

So... throw out the medications? By no means! They already have been tested and found to be more useful than placebos, or they would not be on the pharmacist's shelf. But, as Moerman says, the power of expected healing shows that *meaning*—our interpretation of what is happening to us—can make a huge difference to how effectively medications work. He sums it up: "Meaning can make your immune system work better and it can make your aspirin work better too." Whether medications are intended to help us with physical or psychological problems, we must actively cooperate with them to make them work their best for us.

The Difference Hope Makes

Many years ago, doctors believed that the brain was an inflexible organ. You got a certain number of brain cells as a baby, the cells laid down communications networks with each other, and that was that. Neurons (nerve cells) did not regenerate. If your brain was damaged, you lost a function. In other words, your brain was no more likely to get fixed without intervention than your TV would be.

In the 1990s, all that changed. New investigation techniques enabled doctors to learn that the brain is highly plastic. Semi-liquid and always in motion, it is more like an ocean than a machine. (The idea of brain waves is highly suggestive...) But in one important way our brains are unlike oceans. No sailor can alter the currents of the oceans, but our minds can and do change our brains.

Mario Beauregard is one of the neuroscientists who study changes that our minds can induce in our brains. In addition to the landmark studies of spiritual experiences that form the core of *The Spiritual Brain*, Mario and some of his students at the Université de Montréal studied Quebec women who were terrified of spiders. They studied these women as they slowly got over their fear—with a bit of help from the team, of course—and *changed their brains* in the process.

People who have never had a phobia—an irrational fear—should count their blessings. An irrational fear generates the same panic as a rational one. But there is no rational way to counter it. Some people think that telling the phobic to just "get over" her fear is helpful. Actually, that's about as helpful as a police officer would be if, when you phoned to report an intruder, she scoffed, "Oh, just *relax*! We're busy here, and there is only a small statistical chance he will assault you." The officer may be right about the crime statistics, but to be of any help, she must address the caller's emotional experience of fear and violation as well.

Spider phobia is a common fear. It is common not only in regions where poisonous spiders present a threat, but also in Canada where they rarely do. That's because the fear doesn't stem from the actual risks spiders present. Spiders' natural habits— lowering themselves by a strand of silk and hanging in midair, or spinning a web right across a path and sitting motionless in the middle—may create the false impression that they are stalking a human. In a susceptible child, such an encounter may trigger the beginning of a phobia. Unfortunately, the more we behave as if the irrational fear is normal, the more it dominates our lives and begins to seem normal.

How does that happen? The phobic has built up a large number of dedicated brain circuits around an irrational fear. Overcoming the irrational fear means *un*building a large structure in the brain. It is not an easy job, and not completed quickly. Many phobics are afraid to even start.

And what if they don't? As we recount in *The Spiritual Brain*, people who fear spiders may avoid going barefoot and may be especially alert when taking showers or getting into and out of bed. They have been known to pour bleach onto the floor between their kitchen appliances each night, put masking tape over tiny holes that they fear spiders might use to enter their home, and inspect every inch of their bedrooms before sleeping. Many come to believe that spiders work in teams to watch them and follow them around. One woman told Britain's *Daily Telegraph* that she once ran outside completely naked because she spotted two huge spiders on the wall of her shower. She hid in the garden until her husband came home. Lucky for her, it was warm that day.

The good news is that phobias like hers can be cured. Cognitive behaviour therapy (CBT) is especially effective. CBT consists of two parts. In the case of spiderphobes, they gradually desensitize themselves to the presence of spiders and they also learn to accept natural facts about spiders that resolve fears. (For example, they learn that spiders do not work in teams, and that they never stalk humans.)

Using CBT, Mario's team helped 12 women, mostly in their late teens or twenties, get over spider phobia. The neuroscience researchers' objective was to scan the women's brains using functional magnetic resonance imaging (fMRI) to see what physical changes were taking place while they were unlearning their fear. (Brain scans do not read our minds, but they can often tell us what effect our thoughts are having on our brains.)

The team began by advertising in a Montreal newspaper for women who admitted that they dreaded spiders. After excluding from the study anyone who had a neurological or psychiatric disorder apart from the phobia, they administered standard questionnaires about phobias in general, and spider phobias in particular, to ensure that the subjects truly feared spiders. The researchers also simulated part of the experiment, showing film excerpts of spiders to the phobic women inside a mock fMRI scanner, to make sure that the study subjects could tolerate enough contact with spiders (and scanners) to actually complete the study.

Meanwhile, the researchers scanned 13 psychologically healthy women of a similar age who claimed not to fear spiders, showing them the same film excerpts. These women (the control group) were used for comparison to the study group (spiderphobes) because the scans showed that they did not experience fear while viewing films of spiders.

During the study, the participants were scanned while they viewed film excerpts of living spiders and of living butterflies. Butterflies are generally considered harmless, so the brain state while viewing butterflies could be compared with the brain state while viewing spiders.

Then, the spiderphobes were given therapy to correct mistaken beliefs about spiders. The phobics met for four weekly three-hour intensive group sessions. The first week, participants were asked to look at an exercise book containing 50 color pictures of spiders. The second week, they were gradually exposed to film excerpts of living spiders. They also were assigned homework, and asked to continue to look at the printed pictures and watch the videotape at home between sessions. The third week, they were asked to stay in a room that contained living spiders. Finally, during the fourth and last session, they were asked to touch a huge, live tarantula.

And they all did.

So we could say that they had graduated from "Take Charge Academy." Indeed, as Canadian science writer Michael Smith later reported in *Peer Review*, "Valerie Bouchard has a pet tarantula. That is, of course, unusual in itself, but for Bouchard, the choice is particularly odd: until recently, even thinking about spiders could trigger absolute terror. For years, an irrational fear of spiders—arachnophobia—controlled Bouchard. The mere thought of a spider could rule out anything from swimming to camping, even mundane activities like cutting the grass. While Bouchard's conscious mind knew there was nothing to dread, something in her brain kept overriding her better judgment. But, as her hairy housemate proves, Bouchard is phobic no more."

The mind's gradual reshaping of the brain was actually captured in this study, as in other recent studies where participants' brains are scanned before and after. So there is indeed such a thing as "mind over matter." And hope over fear. As philosopher Nicolas Berdyaev has said, "Fear is never a good counsellor and victory over fear is the first spiritual duty of man." And perfect love casts out fear (1 John 4:18).

The Difference Love Makes

Have you noticed the huge number of "anti-God" books published in recent years, with titles such as *Breaking the Spell: Religion as a Natural Phenomenon* (Daniel Dennett); *The God Delusion* (Richard Dawkins); *God: The Failed Hypothesis—How Science Shows that God Does Not Exist* (Victor J. Stenger); *God Is Not Great: How Religion Poisons Everything* (Christopher Hitchens); *Letters to a Christian Nation and End of Faith* (both by Sam Harris)?

Here are two things you need to know about the anti-God books: First, not one of them offers a single new idea. All their anti-God arguments have been around since the 18th century, and they are no more convincing now than they were then. If anything, they have become much less convincing in recent years. Modern science is showing more and more clearly that we live in a universe that shows clear evidence of intelligent design.

On that basis alone and without any religious experience, one of the world's most famous atheists, Antony Flew—who authored many books promoting godlessness—recently abandoned atheism and wrote a new book titled, *There is a God* (Harper One, 2007). However, other atheists have chosen a different path. Insisting that science supports atheism, they have rushed into print enough books to fill a shelf. Essentially, they are hoping to convince you to be an atheist now, before you get a chance to learn about all the evidence that shows why they are simply, completely wrong.

The second thing to know is that, contrary to the general assumption underlying the anti-God books, spirituality (love for God and others) is good for us. We will be worse off if we abandon it. Fifty years of medical research has established that people who follow a spiritual tradition usually have better mental and physical health. Bottom line: People who love the Lord live longer and are happier.

Now let's think about that for a moment. If the atheists are right, spirituality should be bad for us. After all, delusions are generally destructive. So people who love the Lord should all be sadder and sicker than people who do not. But we aren't! And why aren't we?

The current crop of atheists says that spirituality is a very special case where evolution has accidentally guaranteed that our delusion is good for us. Well... it's a free country, and you can believe that if you want. But my advice would be to assume, as I do, that spirituality is good for us because it reflects *the way things really are* in our universe. It's good for us for the same reason that water is good for us, because it's part of a healthy human life.

We know that God is a loving Father. Faced with the challenge of illness, we must ask, if our Father asks us to walk this path rather than another, what blessing does He have in mind for us? Perhaps it is a blessing that He very much wants to give us now, but cannot... until we have walked through this suffering with Jesus. And if He wants us to be well, He will ensure that we achieve that goal.

And what if this challenge—achieving our complete humanity— should take us beyond the grave? We need not fear because our guide is Jesus who loved us so much that he destroyed death in the very act of enduring it. Our victory is assured, and all we need do is press on to claim the crown awaiting us.

Faith, hope and love... a familiar triad to be sure, for they are the principal Christian virtues. And—this should be no surprise—they play a key role in maintaining our health and happiness.

This selection includes material adapted from *The Spiritual Brain: A Neuroscientist's Case for the Existence of the Soul*, copyright © 2007 by Mario Beauregard and Denyse O'Leary (San Francisco: Harper One/*www.harpercollins.com*).

Nitroglycerin

Brian Austin

I've got a bottle of nitro
    in the pocket of my jeans.
I can't find any answers
    on just what a fall might mean.

I'd rather not make headlines
    as a "suicide" attack,
but what happens if I stumble
    and this bottle takes a smack?

I've got a bottle of nitro
    in the pocket of my pants.
It's s'posed to help my heart out
    but what will be my chance…

If it blows me into orbit
    and sets the house on fire?
A man-sized hole through the roof
    might stir my spouse's ire.

I've got a bottle of nitro,
    so I'm walking dynamite,
but every time I stumble
    it gives me quite a fright.

I'm shaking and I'm trembling.
    High risk for a heart attack,
'cause I've got this nitroglycerin
    and I want to give it back.

This selection is adapted from *Laughter & Tears*, book and audio CD, copyright © 2005 Brian Austin (LittleBoxStudios/Word Alive).

Our Kids: Enemies, Allies, or What?

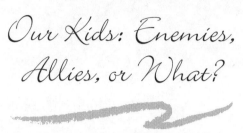

Non-fiction
Ron Wyse

The day my older brother came home with his hair cut short is deeply imbedded in my memory. At 17 years old, Charlie had been butting heads with Dad for quite a few years, and his formerly long hair was only one of many contentious issues. I just happened to be standing near Dad, who was sitting in his living room chair, when I heard the click of the front door opening. Turning my head, I was shocked. There was my brother—The Cool One—quietly closing the door, looking over towards us, hair cropped *very* close.

Dad didn't look up from his newspaper, so my brother, still standing beside the door, shifted his feet ever so slightly and cleared his throat.

Dad finally looked up, flipped down the corner of the paper for a moment, then went back to his reading. There was no acknowledgement of this amazing haircut concession, of how my brother had tried, of how he had waited specifically as if to re-connect with Dad.

Just one caustic comment came from my father's lips as the paper was flipped back up for reading: "You know what I think."

Dismissed!

My brother's face registered shock, and he turned to go downstairs—down to his very loud music, down to his way of dealing with the pain.

There was enmity, sure enough. But—*who* was the enemy?

Fast-forward a few decades.

Now, I have my own teenagers. We're at the dinner table.

How did our casual conversation suddenly touch on something life-threatening? Honestly, I can't recall. All I know is that suddenly my daughter's face turns to stone; a frozen, hard expression that reminds me so painfully of the one my brother used to wear. Her tone likewise turns harsh. She's fighting—no!—she's storming the castle gates, flinging out words like rocks and fiery ice.

I'm in deep shock, at a loss for words. *What did I ever do to deserve this?* I wonder to myself. My wife, looking unusually flustered, desperate, reacts with words that fight fire with fire.

On another occasion, my son surprises me with an uncharacteristic, out-of-the-blue tone of rebellion. We're just passing by each other in the living room, something that happens 20 times a day. What I say, I don't know. But instead of his usual humorous reply, his voice suddenly has a hard edge to it. In my head, I register that he's just been talking to his sister in the kitchen. Swayed by her fast-talking cynicism, he's taken up her cause.

Shocked again, except this time I'm the one who reacts with fire. "*Excuse me?*" I start, with rising tone, "*What* did you say?" I keep my reaction short. A few brief statements and I'm off for my own time-out.

I grew up with tension. Looking back, I can feel it rolled up tight in the pit of my stomach. From time to time, the silence would grow deeper. I'd hear the giant stirring, pacing, muttering in a nearby room. Barely breathing, I'd wonder, *With all that pressure building, when will the volcano explode... with hot words flying everywhere—scorching, shredding—with thunder that shakes the very foundations?*

The parent loses it. The child loses it. There's fallout everywhere.

What about my own reactions? "Really," I say to my wife, "It wouldn't happen if she didn't put on that stone face... if he hadn't shocked me with that rebellious tone... if she didn't cut so deep with that insolent voice!"

Sometimes such scenes are rare, as with my son. Sometimes, it's distressingly all too common, as it was between my dad and brother. Come to think of it, these scenes of conflict between parent and child have been repeated time without number, in every part of our country, in apartments, townhouses, condos, and mansions. Sometimes it feels like there's some kind of war going on, right within the home front. It almost seems as if it's unavoidable.

So then the question becomes, how do we respond to these inevitable conflicts at home? If we can't avoid the occasional skirmishes, can we find a way to defuse them? When conflicts suddenly erupt, and our kids go on the attack, are they suddenly our enemy, or—what?

We certainly don't feel kids are an enemy when babies are born. Don't we long for the kind of family we see in commercials and on family-oriented TV shows, where children are a long-awaited blessing? How nice it must be to delight in our infants, children, and even teenagers! Wouldn't it be amazing if our life with kids—from our own offspring to our grandchildren and great-grandchildren—was one long process of joy?

A friend I've known since our church youth group seems to be wired like this. Beth eventually married another friend I'd known since Grade Six! Together they've not only had four kids, but cared for dozens of babies awaiting adoption. Once, when my wife and I were visiting them, we were amazed to hear Beth say with a glowing face, "I *love* being pregnant!" Wow. Such people are rare jewels!

But unfortunately, for most of us, kids are more of a "mixed blessing." Sometimes life is sunshine and happiness reigns, but at other times clouds descend from nowhere—and suddenly we're living in a war zone.

We dream of a home that's safe and secure, but in reality it's all so fragile. Safe and secure from what? Downsizing? Job uncertainty? Illness? Family conflict?

Thanks to TV, DVDs and the Internet, our ability to control what our kids see and hear is more difficult every day. Soon after toddlerhood, kids can do it all—from mastering the next generation of computer games to conversing with strangers around the world. And how many parents can keep up? I sure can't! It's possible to live in homes where the family members inhabit different worlds, only occasionally crossing paths as they get food or rides. In the midst of all of this, an "in your face" attitude sometimes surfaces among the young towards anybody older who doesn't inhabit their brave new world, or doesn't quite understand it.

In our heart of hearts, how do we feel about our kids? We still remember their first steps, changing diapers, playing hide-'n'-seek, holding their hand to cross the street, the trust they had in us… But suddenly, they're older. Are they still a blessing, or do they occasionally—or even constantly—seem more like "the enemy within the gates?"

I know how my Dad seemed to answer this question. Following the incident I depicted in the opening of my story, Dad and my brother never seemed to get beyond a "cold war" kind of relationship during the decade before my father died. The hostilities and conflicts were buried deep. It seemed to me that they probably did see each other as enemies.

But is that the best way to understand what was going on in such family conflicts? Who, or what, is the real enemy?

In the heat of the moment, it would be easy to point to your teen and answer this question with the obvious answer: "Right now, my enemy is that completely irritating person over there!" The words—expressed or repressed—come easily to mind. *It's her fault, I didn't do anything! If only he'd stop attacking me like that! If only she didn't sound so bossy!*

In striking contrast to these reactions to conflict, the apostle Paul once penned these astounding words: "our struggle is not against flesh and blood" (Ephesians 6:12).

Full stop. What's he saying? That my struggle about my daughter's "stone face" expression isn't really about her? That my shock over my son's sudden rebellious tone isn't about him? That my outrage about my daughter's insolent tone of voice isn't *her* problem?

In my reactive moments, I would beg to differ! But despite my reaction, I turn back to take a second look at what Paul is getting at. Paul is indeed quite serious. He's actually saying that contrary to all appearances, our heartrending and frustrating struggles are not against people.

Now how could Paul, of all people, say such a thing? Few people have suffered at the hands of others more than he did. Listen to how he put it: "I have been... flogged... Five times I received from the Jews the forty lashes minus one. Three times I was beaten with rods, once I was stoned... I have been in danger... from bandits... from my own countrymen... from Gentiles... from false brothers" (2 Corinthians 11:23-28).

Despite all this human opposition, Paul saw that our real conflict was not with people. He went on to say that our struggle is "against the rulers, against the authorities, against the powers of this dark world and against the spiritual forces of evil in the heavenly realms" (Ephesians 6:12).

Stop and think about it. This applies to our relationship with our teenagers. It means that our kids are not our enemy. Our real warfare, our "struggle," is *spiritual*.

Blaming our kids for all our relational difficulties is the same as saying, "It's not my fault—it's *them*. If they didn't exist, I'd be OK, I'd be sane, I'd be able to cope. They bring out the worst in me. It's *their* problem." When we say that, we're back in the Garden of Eden with Adam blaming Eve for all his problems.

Paul turns our attention from the people involved in our struggles, even the in-your-face conflicts with our kids, to the *spiritual* nature of such struggles. But we need to turn to another writer to unpack what's really going on, and to get help in dealing with it.

James put his finger on the root of inner struggles when he asked his readers "What causes fights and quarrels among you? Don't they come from your desires that battle within you?" (James 4:1).

What does this have to do with conflicts with our teens? James speaks of the root, and the fruit, of both our highest ideals and our worst reactions.

Let's consider the ideal for a moment. James asks, "Who is wise and understanding among you? Let him show it by his good life, by deeds done in the humility that comes from wisdom" (James 3:13). Doesn't this sound like the perfect parent—wise, understanding, responding with humility? I'd sure love to be like that!

We read on to discover both the root, or source, and the "fruit," of this admirable character: "the wisdom that comes from heaven is first of all pure; then peace-loving, considerate, submissive, full of mercy and good fruit, impartial and sincere. Peacemakers who sow in peace raise a harvest of righteousness" (James 3:17-18).

Wouldn't every Christian parent love to be described that way! The term "righteousness" is about living in right relationships with others, yes—including difficult-at-times teenagers.

Unfortunately, we all occasionally slip—however momentarily—into a less than ideal behaviour when reacting to our kids. Why is this? James shines the light deep into our hearts, clarifying the root of the problem: "But if you harbour bitter envy and selfish ambition in your hearts, do not boast about it or deny the truth. Such "wisdom" does not come down from heaven but is *earthly, unspiritual, of the devil*" (James 3:14-15; emphasis added). James goes on to tell us what this leads to: "For where you have envy and selfish ambition, there you find disorder and every evil practice" (3:16).

There are only two ultimate sources influencing and empowering our relationships. One source is from above, "*from heaven*," the work of the Spirit. The other may seem everyday and ordinary ("*earthly*," "*unspiritual*"), but its roots actually are "*of the devil*."

So we need to check ourselves. In our moments of conflict, where are we rooted? Is God our source when we're reacting to stressful people, or are we being affected by the only other spiritual source—the devil? In other words, are we behaving as children of light, or as those who live in spiritual darkness?

James admitted that he himself was a mixture of good and bad. When writing about those who use their mouths to both bless and curse others, he included himself as an offender (James 3:9-10). Like James, we are a mix of both the heavenly and the earthly. We're rooted in both light and darkness, and in our relationships we bear both sorts of fruit.

Hence, our struggle.

We've moved a significant distance to understand that the real enemy is not "that irritating person" right in front of you. So what do we do? How can we move from reactions based on earthly wisdom, to the Christ-like character that flows from heavenly wisdom?

The key is choosing the source from which our inner life flows, particularly in those difficult times of conflict. James describes the pathway back to God as a pathway of humility. "God opposes the proud but gives grace to the humble" (James 4:6). After expanding on what's involved in this, in a later verse he returns to this crucial point: "Humble yourselves" (4:10). Humility and antagonism cannot live in the same heart.

In humility we can progress towards the very root of our problem, which is our relationship with God in the heat of the battle. James says to "Purify your hearts, you *double-minded*" (4:8). Here he is echoing some of his earlier comments, which deal with our constant need to continue to believe, or trust, in God: "If any of you lacks wisdom, he should ask God... But when he asks, he must *believe* and not doubt, because he who doubts is... a *double-minded* man, unstable in all he does" (1:5-8 *emphasis added*). To purify our double-mindedness, we need to become single-minded; we need to become utterly wholehearted in our faith at all times—*especially* in the midst of times of conflict.

To trust, or not to trust—this is such a crucial question in our Christian lives. It is fundamental to how we react in our closest relationships. If I draw back from trusting God fully, then I will—however momentarily or occasionally—function like those who have no faith, like those who have no God. I'll become "unstable" (1:8); in my inner world "disorder and every evil practice" (3:16) will arise. In my reactions to others in difficult times, I will respond like those who operate out of selfish ambition or act out of jealousy (3:16). In other words, I'm going to mess up my relationships.

James notes a number of things that we are to do in the midst of our struggles (see 4:7-8), but there is one item in this list that has astounding implications. James would have us be as emotional about repentance and change as we are about anything we earnestly desire. "Grieve, mourn and wail. Change your laughter to mourning and your joy to gloom" (4:9).

I suspect this call to "sackcloth and ashes"—common enough in the Old Testament—is pretty foreign to most of us today. I almost missed seeing this verse, it resonates so little with my personal and cultural experience.

Why would we mourn and grieve? Look at the implications of not walking in faith. Any time we are rooted in and reacting out of darkness, we ruin our relationships! We destroy the very peace and joy we long for. We experience chaos instead of the taste of paradise we so earnestly desire. Marriages, families, and entire societies have been ruined because of the relentless pursuit of selfish pleasure, ambition and pride.

When we are injured physically, we instinctively groan in pain. Grieving for broken relationships and emotional pain are just as natural. No family on earth has escaped the ravages of relational sin caused by spiritual darkness. There is much cause for mourning!

The good news is that genuine sorrow about our brokenness can turn us toward God's light. We don't have to pass on to our children whatever darkness has pervaded our own hearts. And even though our children may at times painfully expose some of our deficiencies—our lack of love, purity, peace, patience, and goodness—this doesn't make them our enemy. They can, in fact, be used by God to remind us of our need for Him, and of our need to be more rooted in the true source of all goodness and light.

So what is the outcome if the parent has this new mindset of inner grieving towards God? This new attitude can revolutionize the relation-ship between parent and child! Humbled people don't tend to be antagonistic. They don't fight fire with fire. Bad attitudes and sudden flare-ups will not evoke the same reaction in kind. A humble and tender heart is able to judge a situation; it knows when to back off, and when to stand firm.

When I pondered my daughter's stone face, I realized that I needed to refocus. I needed to ensure that I was rooted in God. Alone, I could draw near to God again and grieve; grieve over the distance that could so easily spring up between parent and child. The kind of distance that grows whenever someone taps into darkness in his or her relationships. The kind of distance that suddenly develops when an unexpected rebellion flares, or when we receive a barrage of insolent and hurtful comments.

In drawing near to God, I found myself tapping into "wisdom from above." I moved away from reacting angrily to my daughter's hard expression, and moved closer to single-mindedness—with God at the center. As I reflected on how to resolve this situation, I decided that this harsh countenance should not be allowed to create discord in our family. So, when it happened the next time, I responded in a calm voice and simply said, "No stone face."

Amazingly—she softened up. Ah, how James 3:17-18 arose before my very eyes: what relational peace, what mercy, what a good result in our relationship. How I savoured being at peace with my girl. Now, I hardly ever see a "stone face." Incredible! Likewise, if she speaks in an abrasive, grating voice, I ask her to please repeat it "in a softer, gentler voice." Again, it works! This is progress.

Now if the kids aren't the enemy, how do they fit into the battle scene?

We may forget that our kids have the very same struggles we do. They too are under attack, by the world and its godless perspectives and values, by their own developing sinful nature, and by the devil and his spiritual forces (all of which James touches on in 4:4-8). Like us, they need to learn how to combat evil and darkness.

Parents and kids are actually co-combatants. Although we are *over* our children in care and authority, we are *together* with them in learning from God, and in needing grace. Each of our kids struggles, as we do, against spiritual forces that seek to undo his or her trust in and obedience to God. What often seems like a battle between parents and kids is actually a battle within our own inner darkness. If we simply call this a battle of egos, we'll miss the spiritual basis of it all. The real battle takes place within our hearts and souls, as both parent and child struggle to trust God in our individual journeys.

If we can learn to see all such parent-child conflict—not in terms of the people involved, but in terms of each party either battling against or going along with "the world, the flesh, or the devil"—we will be better equipped to deal with, and to resolve, our conflicts.

Oh yes, there still are times when the pain of family conflict cuts so deep I'd rather run away and do without the relationship. But at the same time, each member of my family is one of the chief blessings I have known!

It clarifies the issues and helps us cope if we remember who the enemy is, and that we—husband, wife, children—can band together and be united against our common foes. "The weapons we fight with are not the weapons of the world. On the contrary, they have divine power to demolish strongholds" (2 Corinthians 10:4).

Our kids are not "the enemy within the gates." Our enemy is the spiritual force of darkness; darkness within, and darkness without. Through trust and humility, we can resist evil, draw near to God, and grow in the grace of His wisdom. And with our kids, we can face our common foe.

This selection is adapted from material in *Beyond Survival: Marriage and the Quest for Paradise,* copyright © 2005 by Ron Wyse (VMI Publishers/*www.vmipublishers.com*).

Perspective

Non-fiction
Mark Buchanan

*I*n a church I recently visited, this item, from an unknown source, was reprinted on the back of the bulletin:

> Stu Clark belongs to what is believed to be the smallest small group in America: himself. "I meet at my house every week in the living room," he says. "I bring snacks and my Bible, and after some chit-chat I get down to discussing that week's reading, sharing my burdens, my praise reports. Then I pray for myself."
>
> He enjoys the intimacy he has gained with himself over the weeks. "There was a lot about me I didn't know," he says. "The small group setting brings out those personal details you might not otherwise share." He has tried larger groups, but doesn't get as much from them.
>
> "When you have to be social, it detracts from your real heart issues," he says. "Having other people in the picture complicates things. But I can deepen my relationship with myself much better if it's only me. There's a level of closeness you have when it's just one of you."
>
> Stu's pastor has seen a marked difference in the man. "He's definitely matured in his faith since starting the group," the pastor says. "I guess it's not the group size that matters, but the quality of the people in it."

This comes as huge relief. It explains nearly everything. This accounts—finally, and thank goodness—for something that's stumped me nearly lifelong: why I'm having such a hard time growing up.

It's your fault.

If I had only to deal with me, talk to me, pray about me, get close to me, be honest with me—if only the groups I associated with had my kind of people in them, namely, me—I might have long ago reached a state of sinless perfection.

But as Stu so keenly observes, "Having other people in the picture complicates things."

Indeed. Stu's singularly singular Bible study may be news, but his insight hardly is. Having other people in the picture *does* complicate things. We've known this since the garden. One day we behold our companion with wonder and gratitude: *Ah, look—bone of my bone, flesh of my flesh!* We sense a kinship here so rich that, at long last and forevermore, we can be naked and feel no shame.

The next day, we find ourselves seething with blame: "This person you gave me ruined everything!"

Many friendships are only one hard bite away from breakdown. They shift from thanksgiving to resentment, praise to reviling, openness to hiddenness, with breathtaking abruptness. One rogue gesture can turn trust to suspicion in mere days. A subtle slight, a slight curtness, a hint of slander—these can damage intimacy and lead quickly to estrangement.

It's happened to me. More than once, I'm afraid to say. I look back on all the "best" friends I have had in my life and most now are only a rubble of fading memories. What went wrong? In some cases, nothing. One of us moved, and we were both too lazy to write. It was a season of life, and the season changed. One or the other fell in love, and a deeper call took hold. But there are other cases. Fights never resolved. Accusations never cleared up. Jealousies never dealt with. Rivalries never confessed.

Joel[1], for instance. For close to two years you couldn't part us. We both had young brides we loved, no children yet to consume our daylight energies. At the height of life's summertime, we discovered the extra richness of good manly companionship. It seemed we could talk about anything: music, marriage, our fears, our doubts, our deepest convictions, our madcap ambitions. We talked about God, not in some smarmy, pious way, but in a way I think Paul and Silas, trudging from town to town, or shackled side by side in a prison cell, or bent over together in a common task, talked about him: earthy and urgent and real, wrestling theological truth into the messiness of the everyday.

For almost two years it was like that. Deep calling to deep. Iron sharpening iron. I could drop in on Joel anytime, he on me. There was nothing between us.

And then, suddenly, there was. To this day, I still don't know exactly what. But both of us started being less open with the other. Little irritations, always there, flared into major annoyances, and then into unsolvable grievances. I started complaining to my wife a lot about Joel. I think he might have been doing likewise with his wife. Goodwill and shared respect had reinforced each other, up and up and up. Now ill-will and mutual wariness pushed each other, down and down and down. Within a few months one of the richest friendships I've ever known was effectively over. Though we never had a clear falling-out— one stark, terrible moment in time when our friendship died hard—the end result is the same: we have not spoken in years, and I only have the vaguest notion where he is, what he does, who he's become.

I wish this wasn't part of my story, but it is. I wish this wasn't such a common story, but it is.

The good news is that God already knows, and has given us, at the very least, a rich cache of scriptures that address this very thing: the fragility of our friendships, the tentative, rickety, makeshift nature of all human community. Repeatedly, the Bible calls us to bear with each other, to forgive each other, to go the extra mile and turn the other cheek. It commands us to make every effort to keep the unity that Jesus died to create. It warns us not to be outwitted by the devil, whose main ploy is to have us nurse wounds and bear grudges.

We're to love our neighbour as ourselves.

But there's something else, something more: we're to see our neighbour as a new creation.

We're to see her, not just as she is, but as one day she will be.

We're to see her from the perspective of heaven.

There are two women in scripture who needed that perspective. They have funny names, but common enough back then: Euodia—*Sweet Fragrance*—and Syntyche—*Lucky Chance*. They were once, it appears, close, companions in life, partners in ministry. Some speculate that one of them was none other than Lydia, the first convert in Philippi.

But something went awry. Who knows what: a lunch that one hosted and didn't invite the other to, an admonishment that was ill-delivered or ill-received, a disagreement over Sunday School curriculum.

Whatever.

The result is that two women who once contended at Paul's side in the ministry of reconciliation were now contending with each other and in need of reconciliation. Paul calls them to that. He invites one of the leaders of the church to help them in it.

But Paul also, just before he addresses Euodia and Syntyche and their situation, addresses the whole church in Philippi on another matter, seemingly unrelated to their fracas. Related or not, what Paul says provides a rich clue in how to keep our relationships from breaking, and how to restore them when they do.

What Paul says is this: View everything through the window of eternity. Stop fixing your eyes on *what is*, and start fixing them on *what is to be*. Quit your fruitless preoccupation with things seen, and foster an obsession with Things Unseen.

Have the right perspective.

Here's the actual passage:

> But our citizenship is in heaven. And we eagerly await a Saviour from there, the Lord Jesus Christ, who, by the power that enables him to bring everything under his control, will transform our lowly bodies so that they will be like his glorious body. (Philippians 3:20-21)

You're a citizen of heaven, and you're not finished yet.

Right now, not one thing on earth is as it should be. Everything's tainted. Everything is, at best, provisional. Nothing quite works. This should not surprise or dismay us. The whole creation groans, waiting for you and me to come into our complete birthright, for that day we're sworn in as full-fledged citizens of the kingdom.

Between now and then, we need perspective. We need to view the broken earth from the glory not yet revealed. That glory at present is hidden in clay jars, in these thin brittle containers of ourselves and our relationships. But one day, in a blink, that will all change. For now, we rehearse the ethics of the coming kingdom, we enact the citizenship code of heaven, long before it arrives, years before we get there. We learn to act out of, not the lowliness that still plagues us, but the transformation that awaits us.

In hope of that transformation, in eager expectancy of the One who accomplishes it, we start living here as though we're already there.

Euodia, do you see this woman? Syntyche, do you? Do you see each other from the window of heaven, as the new creations you are in Christ? Stop beholding each other from a worldly point of view. By faith, not sight, take hold of the One who is coming, and of the work he will finish once he gets here.

Practice today what you'll inherit forever.

Not that any of this is easy. It's messy. It's hard. I find a twisted pleasure in gossiping, faultfinding, pigeonholing. I derive a bitter satisfaction in dredging up another's mistakes. It takes discipline and humility to do otherwise, to see others as new creations when there is scant evidence to support the claim, and when I'd rather muckrake. Many Christians look more fallen than redeemed. They look, not renewed, but shopworn, the same old same old.

And me too. I am a man of unclean lips, and I live among a people of unclean lips.

But what are our options? We can keep letting self sabotage intimacy. We can keep falling into the snare of blaming and hiding and withdrawing. We can keep joining Satan as accusers of the brethren.

Or we can practice seeing others as new creations. We can take up, here and now, the privileges and responsibilities of kingdom citizenship. We can adopt the perspective of heaven.

I'm learning this, slow, slow, but maybe the hardest lesson yet was with Betsy[1]. Betsy was in her late 40s and had been a Christian most her life. Only, that was hard to credit. She was a trial: barb-tongued and hot-tempered, with skin both prickly and thin. She was quick to blast another, and quicker to wilt when it got dished back.

And Betsy loathed me. She scorned virtually every aspect of my ministry—my preaching, my leadership, my pastoral care, the way I dressed—and this to my face. Who knows what she said when my back was turned?

The truth is, I loathed her too. I wanted her to leave, and told her so.

And then God got me. I was cutting the grass one sweltering summer day, meditating on the letter to the Philippians as I criss-crossed the lawn. I was thinking about what it meant to see myself and others from the perspective of heaven, as citizens of a place we hadn't arrived at yet.

And guess who God brought to mind?

Yes, yes: Betsy.

Was she a new creation? Was she a citizen of heaven? Was I enough of these things myself to see her, even her, not for who she was but for her she would be when Jesus was finished with her?

Then God reminded me of something else in Philippians. In chapter two, just before Paul calls us to have the same attitude of Jesus—humble, servant-like, selfless, obedient, sacrificing—he makes this little remark, subtle and subversive: "consider others better than yourselves."

I was stunned. I had to stop what I was doing.

"God," I said, "you don't mean, you couldn't mean, that I'm to think this way of… Betsy? Do you?"

He did.

And then God took me through a painful and wonderful discipline. He showed me His Spirit's work in Betsy's life, her Christ-like virtues, hidden and tiny as embryos, that one day he would perfect and reveal in glory. Her generosity. Her compassion. Her heart for the broken.

That day was an epiphany. It freed me to love Betsy, but not only her. Now, whenever I find myself struggling with anyone—my close friends, my wife or children, my enemy—and I find that I'm looking at them from a worldly point of view, I re-enact the discipline of that day.

I seek heaven's perspective. And it makes all the difference.

Betsy left the church anyhow. I don't know if she still loathes me, or even thinks about me. When I think about her, I don't always love her: there are times I'm so earthly minded I'm of no heavenly good.

But there are other times—times I'm heavenly minded enough to be of some earthly good—that I see her from eternity's window.

And then I'm crazy about her.

1. Names have been changed.
This selection was first published in *Discipleship Journal*, July/August 2005.

What Was God Thinking?

Non-fiction
Brad Burke, MD

I stood motionless by her graveside, asking the inescapable question, "Why?"

When life hurts, helplessness often takes over the helm and routine and pleasure jump ship. The loss of a beloved child, a soul mate, a sacrificing parent, or an endeared grandparent abruptly halts the mellow voyage of life, transforming the shimmering waves of happiness into towering waves of sorrow. Nothing we do, nothing we say, nothing we possess can bring our loved one back. Memories both comfort and pain us. Questions both flee and haunt us. Answers both calm and anger us.

Perhaps you've never experienced the loss of someone close to you. Your unutterable suffering may be a devastating divorce, a child with cerebral palsy, an unrelenting ache deep in your back, abandonment by your mother or father, the ruinous loss of your cherished possessions in a fire, or the painful memories of abuse suffered as a child.

Indeed, pain and adversity hold no prejudices. A good friend of mine, in his capacity with the Canadian government, had the rare opportunity to meet Diana, Princess of Wales, on one of her last visits to Canada. Shielded from the press, he met with the Princess. Later, he described her as personable, shy, soft-spoken, down-to-earth—yet restless. She asked my friend and his fiancée about their upcoming wedding plans, making the comment about how expensive weddings are these days (a bit funny considering the cost of her own wedding). And she laughingly joked about sneaking away from the press outside to get a few beers with him and his officers. My friend said she came across as a "very normal person," and he remarked, "In hindsight, I wonder if at some level, in her genuine desire to discuss our 'boring plain lives,' she wasn't longing for that."

Maybe Diana really was just like the average person in many ways. The world's favorite princess battled bulimia, wrestled with feelings of insecurity, experienced family feuds, and lived through a broken marriage. And at the age of 37, her seemingly "fairy-tale life" reached the final line in the final chapter in a tragic Paris car crash. Even the most popular of England's royal family—the most popular and well-loved person in the world at that time—could not escape the vise-grip of pain, suffering and death.

As I stood by my grandmother's graveside, staring blankly at her suspended coffin, tears sliding down my cheeks, the question *Why?* was grinding through my head. Toward the end of her life, my grandmother's final dream was to hold in her arms her first great-grandchild. When my sister became pregnant for the first time, you can imagine how excited my grandmother became. She knew that her dream would be realized in a matter of months. But less than two weeks before my sister gave birth to her first baby boy, Joshua, my grandmother, at the age of 72, died of cancer.

The minister at her funeral remarked that one life was ending and in a short time another would be beginning. The words left an indelible mark on my consciousness, and I wondered to myself, *Why, God? My grandmother faithfully served and worshipped you for decades, and you couldn't give her just two more weeks to see her first great-grandchild? You allowed Simeon, the righteous and devout saint, to live until he could hold the Messiah (Luke 2:25-35). Why, God, couldn't you have spared her life for just 14 more days? It would have meant so much to her. We weren't demanding a miracle—just two weeks. How hard would that have been?*

But as in the patriarch Job's situation, God never answered my questions. My grandmother courageously battled breast cancer, undergoing a mastectomy and the painful aftermath of radiation—only to find later that she was filled with more cancer from an unknown source. The explosively dividing cancer cells finally won out. The pain and abdominal bloating grew intense. And she spent her final days on morphine in the hospital where I had trained during medical school.

She was my last living grandparent, and there was nothing she wouldn't do for me. But in the end, I couldn't even be there for her. I was isolated 3,000 miles[1] away in Los Angeles, working day and night in my surgery residency.

My grandmother believed with all her heart that if she could just muster up enough faith, God would heal her of the cancer. One day she confided to my mom, "When I finally beat this cancer I'm going to write an article to *Reader's Digest* and tell everyone what my Jesus did for me!" She never got a chance to write that article. One summer evening, my uncle called to tell me she had passed away. The director of the Cedars-Sinai Medical Center surgery program kindly allowed me some time off, and I flew back to Canada for her funeral. My grandmother had more faith in God's power to heal than anyone I know, yet she still succumbed to the cancer—like millions of Christians and atheists every year.

I had spent many years, both as a young boy and as an MD, memorizing and meditating on Scripture. As a perceptive Christian medical specialist, I thought I held the key to the mystifying black box labelled, "Why do we suffer?" But now the questions surrounding suffering became much more personal. Heart-rending. Invasive. Almost haunting.

Suddenly, it was easier for me to explain why nearly 3,000 people died in the 9/11 tragedy than why my grandmother had been buried just days before my first nephew was born. Suffering had moved from the theoretical to the touchable; from something other people go through to tears falling on fresh dirt beside a raised coffin.

But if I thought the death of my grandmother was the pinnacle of my emotional suffering, I was in for a rude shock. After finishing my residency training at UCLA, I was forced to move back to Canada because my training visa in the U.S. had expired. I had just completed 11 arduous years of university training to become a medical specialist, only to discover that when I stepped off the plane at Pearson International Airport in Toronto, I couldn't practise medicine anywhere in the country.

I had completed a science degree at the University of Western Ontario in London, Ontario, and graduated from medical school at Queen's University in Kingston, Ontario. The predicament was that my specialty of Physical Medicine & Rehabilitation was a four-year post-graduate program in the U.S., but a five-year program in Canada. And to get that extra year of training that would allow me to work in the Great White North was nearly impossible. Nor would my degrees allow me to work as a general practitioner, because my residency had not been in family medicine. (I discovered five years later that I could have worked in Manitoba, but by then it was too late.)

So at the age of 30, with no car, no job, virtually no assets, and tens of thousands of dollars of debt, I moved back in with my parents in the small town of Bancroft, Ontario. I was living off my credit cards, paying the minimum balance of one card with another card. I traded my stethoscope for a paintbrush, painting my parents' jewellery store in the evenings and my bedroom during the day (Martha Stewart would have been impressed). Instead of caring for the medical needs of children, I was babysitting kids for free. Instead of serving up cortisone injections to my desperate pain patients, I was serving up juice and cookies to hungry pre-schoolers. Instead of decorating a fancy medical office with all the prestigious degrees and awards I had earned, I was decorating the town bridges for Christmas with twisted chicken wire spray-painted gold and strung up between sawed-off birch trees. I came very close to doing what every other foreign-trained, unemployed medical doctor does in Canada—driving a taxi cab.

I was sure God had forgotten about me. Why else would He put me through all that rigorous, sleep-depriving medical training, only to haul me back to where I had started 11 years earlier, thousands of dollars in debt, living in an isolated town with two stoplights, one hockey rink, and no movie theatre? My doctor friends were getting married and buying their own homes and purchasing cars, but I couldn't even afford to sign a cell phone contract. I was bitter—and I made sure that God knew about it.

The questions surrounding God and our suffering represent some of the most personal, heart-rending and difficult questions asked in all of history. Much to my dismay, I was now the one asking them.

I had observed my own patients struggling with their pain and their often debilitating diseases. When I was working as a surgery resident in the prestigious Cedars-Sinai medical center, and then at the Veterans Affairs Medical Center in Los Angeles, I noticed that I couldn't stereotype my model patients and my most obnoxious patients into any particular "faith category." Some of my best patients were Christians, while some of my worst patients (and their families) who consumed my time—and my patience—were also Christians. It was as if they wanted to shout out, "I hate you God for making me sick!" but instead, they hurled their anger, bitterness and frustration at the nurses, doctors, therapists, janitors, and whoever else set foot in their room. The day came when the leather-bound Bible lying on the patient's night side increased my apprehension, when it should have done just the opposite.

Admittedly, there were some faithful Christians suffering horrible adversity who acted much differently. I remember one middle-aged firefighter in particular. He was married with a young family. While responding to a fire one day in California, he severely damaged his cervical spine, leaving him a complete quadriplegic. Despite his inability to move his arms or legs, he always seemed to have a smile on his face. And even though he required an extraordinary level of care, the nurses enjoyed responding to his requests for help.

But the first time I saw him, I was afraid. I'd been ambushed by others who supposedly bowed the knee to the same God I did. When some of these rude and demanding patients who considered themselves born-again Christians found out I was a Christian, they automatically assumed that I would cave in to all their incessant demands. They'd say to the nurses, "Did you know that Dr. Burke is also a Christian?" And

I'd want to say to the nurses, "But I'm not like these patients. Please, you have to believe me!"

By the end of my rotation, when it was time to say goodbye to this courageous and kind-hearted firefighter, I realized that he wasn't like my rude Christian patients. And I felt guilty that I hadn't taken more time to talk with him. To pray with him. To encourage him. He must have been hurting so much on the inside, and while I treated him with kindness and respect, I could have done much more as a brother in Christ.

In wracking my brain for an answer as to how Christians could be both my best *and* worse patients, I came to this conclusion: *it all depended on their understanding of God.* Some Christians had built their theological tower on the shaky foundation that God promises us only health, good times and unlimited shopping sprees; while others did not.

After a year of painting, decorating, dish-washing, and cleaning kids' Kraft dinner off the floor as an unemployed medical doctor in Canada, I realized I wanted to write a book that dealt with some of the tough questions about God—the questions I myself had been asking. I wanted to reach as many hurting people as possible, people who were wondering, "God, have you forgotten about me?"

One book eventually turned into three books, and three books turned into 12 as I kept researching, thinking and writing.

Ironically, all the time I was writing this book series, I continued to wonder if God had forgotten about me and all that medical training I'd done. For 17 years, I'd hand-picked every high school class, every university course, every medical elective; I'd worked 36-40 hour shifts without sleep, and sacrificed most of my weekends and evenings to attain the position of a medical specialist. Yet, here I was, sitting around in a T-shirt and sweat pants, typing away on a desktop computer, writing a book series about God—never knowing if anyone would ever read it. And the strangest thing of all was that I'd hated English classes and done everything possible in my school years to avoid anything that had the scent of an essay.

Despite my sporadic outbursts of venting to God, my heavenly Father remained gracious and his wisdom and power outshone my weaknesses. I received so many rejection letters and e-mails in response to my book proposals, I thought I was crazy to even consider going to a Christian writers' conference. But I did—and at The Word Guild's Write! Canada conference in Guelph, Ontario, God introduced me to my agent, editors and publisher.

On almost the same day Cook Communications sent me a four-book contract for my series, *An MD Examines*, I began my extra residency training. I had contacted every physical medicine and rehabilitation residency program director across Canada, begging each of them to give me the opportunity to train in his or her program so that I could practise medicine in Canada. After months of e-mails, phone calls and governmental red tape, Dr. John Flannery at the University of Toronto created an opening in his program and gave me the break I needed. And I will be forever grateful to him.

However, jumping back into the rigorous grind of medicine was no easy task after being kidnapped for more than five years by my new writing career. There were peculiar challenges that had never crossed my mind. For example, I had spent so many years typing my book series on my computer that when I went to hand-write clinical notes, my right hand literally froze up. It felt like someone else's limb. Here I was, expected to see patients and write orders and notes quickly, and yet I had trouble completing even the simplest of tasks, such as writing a paragraph.

Added to that was the déjà vu feeling of working long and sleepless shifts in the hospital again. Only this time I had a second job, editing all four books at once on a tight deadline.

But as always, God was faithful. He had *not* forgotten me. He had carefully planned my five-year sabbatical from medicine to allow me the freedom to study his Person, to grow closer to Him, and to write the book series that would later help many people better understand the complex, yet beautiful, character of their Creator and Lord. Every time I get an e-mail from a reader sharing how much my books have helped in some facet of his or her life, I look back on that difficult time in my own life and see God's guiding hand every inch of the way.

God never told me why He allowed my grandmother to die a couple weeks earlier than we would have liked. And He didn't tell me why I couldn't practise medicine for more than five years. But He did tell me in His Word that He is in complete control of absolutely everything! (Isaiah 46:9-10). When this broken world seems to throw us more adversity, suffering and trials than we can handle, God seems to catch our problems in mid-air and use them for His highest glory. This may be the worst world possible from our perspective, but from God's perspective it is the best world possible.

This made no sense to me whatsoever 10 years ago. Like the patriarch Jacob, I had to wrestle with these truths for several years before God finally humbled me to the point where I could see life more through His eyes and less through mine. God's truth surrounding suffering is certainly not easy to comprehend. The truth about suffering can be difficult to accept… but it is ultimately freeing. For the truth will set us free from the guilt, discouragement, anxiety, bitterness, anger and confusion we experience in our suffering.

I've learned this important truth during my medical career: every single breath we're allowed is possible only by the universal grace and mercy of Almighty God. Every oxygen molecule we breathe into our lungs has been leased from God with no money down, no security deposit, and with no payments for life.

But oxygen isn't the only gift we take for granted. Probably the most overlooked and undervalued attribute of God in the last century has been his incomparable mercy—what God doesn't give us that we deserve. Never before in the history of the world have we had the medical technology and expertise we do today to prevent sickness, decrease pain and effectively treat our diseases.

Did you know that the average life expectancy in America in the early 1900s was only 47? In the United States and Canada, life expectancy has soared to more than 77 years today. Did you know that before penicillin became available in the late 1930s, half of the deaths over the age of 50 were caused by pneumonia?

We take so much for granted, yet only a very small percentage of the entire world's population since the beginning of time has been the recipient of such extravagant kindness and mercy from the Almighty. We expect so much from our hospitals and doctors, yet we fail to realize that it is only because of God's mercy that most of us endure so little physical suffering in our lifetimes, and enjoy life to the extent that we do.

The thought crept into my mind, *If my grandmother had been born just 50 years earlier, would she have survived to even her fiftieth birthday? Would she have died earlier from appendicitis or pneumonia? Was the fact that she lived long enough to develop cancer not evidence by itself of God's great mercy and grace? Would I have shared the memories I did with my grandmother if we both had been born a generation before? With such a high mortality rate at the beginning of the twentieth century, would we have even lived long enough to meet each other?*

I was asking God why He allowed my grandmother to die two weeks before the birth of her first great grandson, when I should have been thanking God for His amazing mercy in allowing her to live as long as she did.

When we pray for healing, God may not grant us an instant miracle on the spot. But that doesn't mean our heavenly Father isn't right beside us in our earthly work camps. He is there, all right, *and he is not still!* He is beside us, holding our hands, hugging us close to his chest, crying with us, grieving with us, every step of the way. During the darkest moments of our hurt we can't see God, but we can feel our Father's presence. He holds his dear children close to his chest, whispering, "Be still, and know that I am God...." (Psalm 46:10a). *I am here for you, my precious child. And I will never, ever leave you. My grace is sufficient, for it is all you will need to get through this hurt.*

When we are suffering the devastating loneliness of a divorce, enduring the heart-rending grief and confusion of losing a loved one, or suffering the bitter pain of widespread metastatic cancer, we whisper out from the depths of our hearts, "Father, it really, really hurts." Hugging us even closer, God, with tears in His own eyes, replies, "I know my precious child. I know...."

Even though we may experience long periods of silence, we can know beyond a shadow of a doubt that God has His arms wrapped snug around us. God carried me and my family through the grief to a sunset of hope and renewed devotion. Will He not also be faithful in carrying you through whatever adversity you may be suffering?

It has been said, "The key to joy is not God's *presents*, but His *presence*." And we know, by faith, that with our heavenly Father's ever abiding presence and help, we will get through these tough times.

Our Father's love and guidance are the only assurance we need.

1. 1 mile = 1.6 kilometres.

Hurtled into the Valley

Angelina Fast-Vlaar

After a week of tests
and tubes and toilets,
my doctor stands at the foot
of my hospital bed
and says in an everyday voice,
"The tumour is malignant."
He pats my covered leg and says,
"You'll be all right."
His words are lost in the reeling room
that screams at me from all sick sides—
"It's cancer! It's cancer!"
My limbs freeze but
I make them move
and drag them down the hall,
repeating to make the truth sink in,
"I have cancer—I now have cancer."
I grope for the telephone.
Shaking fingers fumble to find
the buttons to press.
The ringing starts and stops
and his soft voice says, "Hello."
I'm dumbstruck, realizing that one
word will shatter his joy,
his recent-found joy.
Finally, while choking,
"Hon, it's malignant."
A muffled groan wells up

from the depths of his loving heart.
"Oh no, my love—I'll be right there."
He comes and we collapse
in each other's arms and cling
as we're hurtled,
        crying,
into the valley of the shadow of cancer.

Later,
when our tears are dried,
we see the Shepherd
with outstretched Hands
ready to comfort and to guide.

He knew we were coming.

People Matter Most

Non-fiction
Grace Fox

*T*he scene will forever be etched in my heart. While the outside world raced from one activity to another, my mother-in-law Betty lay motionless in her bed. Nearly 14 years of battling Parkinson's disease had reduced her body to a mere shadow of its former self and robbed her of her ability to communicate.

Four days prior, hospice workers had evaluated Betty's physical condition and said she had less than a week to live. Her five children were taking turns sitting at her bedside, holding her hands, stroking her forehead, and speaking words of encouragement.

One morning I watched as my husband Gene shared fond memories with his mom. The family had enjoyed a waterfront home, so most stories revolved around boating and beach-related activities. One experience in particular stood out.

When Gene was in ninth grade, he'd decided to build a 16-foot sailboat. He began work in the carport and laboured diligently for months. When winter rolled in and outdoor temperatures dropped, however, progress ground to a halt.

Betty rushed to the rescue. "Don't quit," she said. "Bring your boat into the living room. It's warm in the house. You can finish your project there."

And so, with his mother's blessing, Gene hauled the sailboat, plywood, nails, varnish, and sawhorse into the house and plunked everything in the middle of the carpet-covered floor. Several weeks later, the finished boat was carried through the sliding glass doors and launched on its maiden voyage on the nearby saltwater bay.

Tears filled Gene's eyes as he recalled that experience. Leaning close to Betty's face, he said, "Not many women would let their kids build a boat in their living room. Thanks, Mom, for being the exception. You taught me to believe that people are more important than things."

The scene challenged me to think about the messages we communicate to our kids. What's our initial response when they return home from a sports activity and throw their duffel bags and dirty socks in the entryway? How do we react when they spill juice on the couch, or on the kitchen floor moments after we washed it? What are the first words we speak upon hearing that they've had a fender-bender with the family car?

I remember the day my youngest daughter, Kim, accidentally broke a wee cup belonging to a glass tea set I'd received as a little girl. "I'm so sorry, Mommy," she cried. "I'm really, really sorry!"

I tried to comfort her but she refused to be consoled. Puzzled by her over-reaction, I asked why an obvious accident upset her so much. Her answer filled me with remorse, "Because you said you could never replace these teacups if they broke."

I hugged Kim and reassured her that I valued her far more than my teacups. And I purposed in my heart to teach my kids that, while things are nice, people matter more.

This selection was first published in Women Alive's online magazine, March 2007.

Broken Bodies, Shattered Lives

Non-fiction
Paul M. Beckingham

I don't remember the split seconds before the impact. Not the angry skid of tires, nor the fearful shrieks from my wife Mary, our son Aaron, and his young Kenyan friend Daniel. Not even the smashing of glass and the ripping of metal as the car crumpled on top of me.

But Mary remembers it all. Clearly. It is burned into her consciousness. The memory of our spinning car, smashing against the side of the military semi-trailer that struck us, spins in her mind like a nightmare smashing against the pattern of our lives. And Aaron, too—even more than one year after the accident.

Our car came to an abrupt halt at the edge of a sudden drop. And so did normal family life. The predictable rhythms of our lives were put on hold.

Mary's feelings stopped at the same moment. She froze them out, in a deliberate and conscious act of her will. She knew in that instant that she could either attend to the mammoth needs of her family or she could start to process her own deep grief—but not both at the same time. She didn't have the energy for two huge tasks. So, just like a million other mothers, she chose to put the demands of her family above her own needs. She went into automatic pilot—into rescue mode—busying herself with arranging for family life to continue as best it might without a husband and a father.

In those earliest hours, she thought I must be dead—if not at the roadside, surely before emergency medical help could save me. She arrived at the hospital numbed, cut, and in deep shock, guarding her badly broken collar bone. With her good arm, she coaxed Aaron along, whispering gentle, comfort-words of love. He was traumatized to the point of collapse. He screamed and wept, "I just want to go home, Mommy!"

But home as we knew it would never be the same. The accident had changed all our lives. Irreversibly. We had looked into the face of death. In one afternoon four of our children had come horribly close to losing both parents and their youngest sibling. Old securities disappeared. New anxieties emerged.

For five days, my family waited for me to die in the Aga Khan hospital in Nairobi, Kenya. I had broken or displaced 14 bones, fractured my skull, suffered a brain injury, and had to have my foot saved by the skill of microsurgeons. I frequently mistook Mary for my daughter Hannah. I kept telling her, "You know, I have been in a very serious car accident."

Each time she would reply softly, "So have I."

Just as frequently, I would look around my mosquito-filled private room and say with great satisfaction, "Isn't this a beautiful hotel room?"

Mary would hold my hand and try to speak above the roar of construction outside the window.

Then Mary told me she had made an important decision. We would go back to Canada for the advanced medical care critical to my survival.

I had experienced lucid moments in those first few days, but as I listened to her, I came back into reality for the first time since the accident. I realized how badly I was injured. My heart broke. I cried. I groaned. I felt an utter failure as a missionary. I hated myself for abandoning the people I had come to serve and had grown to love.

Mary assumed control. Completely. Magnificently. And, like so many wives and mothers in similar emergency situations, she paid the heavy price in stress, depression, and anxiety. The nurturing and protecting impulses kick into action—but at the expense of self-care and self-nurture. And so it is. When one family member suffers a trauma, all do.

So what does the road to recovery look like? Totally impossible. But just when we think the God whom we worship had better show up or all is lost, He does show up. Never in the ways we might predict or arrange if we were God for a day. Always too late by our busy schedule—but exactly on time by the schedule of His deep love for us.

"You see, at just the right time, when we were still powerless," God invaded our reality (see Romans 5:6). Just the way He does. Without pain? No. Without room for doubt and questions? Not usually. Then how? Mainly through His people. They furnished our house, provided winter clothing, met our financial needs. Strangers who had prayed for us brought hot meals to our door.

These ways of God gently but firmly remind my children that all things will work for good even when they scream that they cannot see it. They profoundly convince me that whether I live or die, God loves me.

They open Mary's tight grasp of control on our family security and slowly teach her to laugh again, to relax in God's love, and to rest in His care. Because He can, after all, be trusted in all things.

Fresh Perspectives on God's Will for Our Lives

Tragedy, loss and sudden change are unexpected, uninvited—and they really hurt! But they can offer fresh perspectives on God's personal love for us. God uses our pain to amplify His love. How will you receive those fresh faith perspectives? Here are seven ways that help:

1. Become an attentive listener—God sometimes whispers. Silence is His quiet invitation to be present to Him, even when you can't see Him.

2. Let God's people wrap you in prayer—especially when praying for yourself becomes hard.

3. Rest in God's love. Remember, He loves you. Not for who you are or what you do, but simply because He loves you!

4. Relax in God's care. When you reach the end of your own resources, allow God to do all that you cannot do for yourself.

5. When you're angry at God, read Psalm 77 (*The Message*) and invite Him to turn your anger to praise.

6. Sometimes, all you have to give to God are your tears. Trust Him with them—in His hands they become a healing balm.

7. When you lose your hope, let God gently give you His own.

Use these helpful hints as walking companions on your journey of faith. Invite God—the God above (Father), the God beside (Son) and the God within (Spirit)—to be your personal daily companion, friend and Saviour. He loves you and He will never let you go.

This selection is adapted by permission of the publisher from *Walking Toward Hope: Experiencing Grace in a Time of Brokenness*, copyright © 2005 by Paul Beckingham (Castle Quay Books Canada/*www.castlequaybooks.com*).

Be the CEO of Your Emotions

Non-fiction
Donna Carter

Whoever said that women marry men like their fathers has never met me and mine. My dad is a gentle, dignified, scholarly sort of man. He can do yard work all day in white clothes and not get dirty, a fact that astounds my husband, who can't stay clean for five minutes... in church. Randy is more the macho, action-oriented type. I'm sure he's never met an extreme sport he didn't like.

Although the two men in my life get along famously, my dad can't believe how hard Randy is on his own body. Randy is just so competitive and so completely involved in the game or task at hand that he is temporarily immune to pain. *Temporarily.* One day he was playing hockey when his face had an unfortunate and unscheduled meeting with another player's shoulder pad, opening a significant gash under his left eye. Presumably, the combination of the cold air temperature at the rink and Randy's refusal to acknowledge his injury kept it from bleeding all over the ice. When the game was over, he showered and dressed and started driving to an appointment. Suddenly, a trickle of blood started coursing down his cheek. He dabbed at it with a tissue, but the trickle became a gush and the gush, a torrent.

In the middle of rush hour traffic, there was Randy, frantically groping through the car for anything remotely absorbent with which to stem the tide. In sheer desperation, he settled for a sweaty sock from his hockey bag. It was now clear that he wasn't going anywhere until he stopped at a nearby hospital to have the gash stitched shut.

Ignoring or being numb to pain, physical or emotional, isn't healthy. It prevents us from responding appropriately to the people and the situations in our lives that can cause us harm. We have to learn to read our emotions for the warning system indicators they are, and determine what our emotional reactions are telling us. We can evaluate whether our hearts truly are in danger in the present moment or if there is something more complicated happening. Only then, can we respond appropriately to what is going on around and inside us, and keep an isolated over-reaction from becoming a predictable pattern.

I grew up in a relatively frugal home. My dad was a successful professional and money was not in short supply, but we definitely lived by the adage of "waste not, want not." I'll never forget something that happened once when Dad came into the house after cutting the lawn. Because he was trying to avoid spreading grass clippings in the house, he carried his shoes in his hands as he tiptoed past the kitchen table, which was set for supper. At precisely the wrong moment, the shoes slipped out of his hands and one of them headed, with the precision of a guided missile, toward a full pitcher of milk on the table. The projectile landed gloriously inside the pitcher with a dramatic splash.

My sister and I saw the whole episode unfolding in slow motion. We were faced with an enormous challenge: controlling our laughter without turning ourselves inside out. Holding our mirth in was necessary because we knew, even before seeing the angry expression evolve on our gentle dad's face, that he would fail to see the humour of the situation. We knew, in fact, that what to us was first-class slapstick comedy would be to him—someone who grew up during the Great Depression—a grievous waste of food.

Why such a mountainous reaction to such a molehill of a problem? Good question, because it happens to all of us, doesn't it? Your child does some typical kid thing and you unleash an angry response completely out of proportion to the crime committed. Your boss overlooks you for a great assignment and the rejection you feel penetrates right down to the bone. You see someone who reminds you of a dark figure in your past and the fear stops you in your tracks. The emotional reaction brought on by events like these is seldom a result of the event or trigger alone. There is something going on beneath the surface.

Our emotions are like warning indicator lights on the dashboard of a car. When the oil light goes on, it isn't telling us there is something wrong with the light. The light is telling us there is trouble under the hood. If all you do when the light goes on is yank out cables under the dash until it goes out, you have only dealt with the indicator that something is wrong. A short distance down the road, you will have more significant trouble to deal with than if you had dealt with the real problem when you were first alerted to it.

Our emotions are not the problem; they are the indication of a deeper problem. Several years ago my husband and I traveled to Haiti to meet two of the children we sponsor. Part of the trip involved a boat ride to an island called La Gonave off the west coast of Haiti. The trip to the island was uneventful. The trip back was anything but. Our first clue that things were not going according to plan came when the boats that had been hired for the return trip didn't show up. We waited two hours before two other boats arrived. One looked quite acceptable. The other looked highly questionable.

Knowing we couldn't stay on the island indefinitely, we got into the boats. By the way all 10 of us wanted to pile into the good boat, you'd have thought it was a lifeboat on the Titanic. But my husband and I, trying to be considerate, ended up in the other boat. It was old and filthy and had too few life jackets to go around. It sported two outboard motors, one of which was tied—yes, tied—onto the back.

"If one of those motors dies, we're toast," my husband Randy muttered.

He shouldn't have said it. Not 10 minutes later, one of the motors died and none of the efforts of our three-man Haitian crew could revive it. Our boat, no longer able to hydroplane, sank sluggishly into the water. This meant that with every wave the Caribbean sent our way, water sloshed over the side of the boat, soaking us and slowly filling our woeful conveyance.

At this point, I was being a good sport and kind of enjoying the adventure. Randy, on the other hand, who is by nature far more skilled at adventure than I am, recognized the trouble we were in. He began to bail water. While he bailed, he noticed that salt water was pouring into our gas supply. However, because of the noise of the boat and spray (not to mention his inability to speak Creole), he couldn't communicate the problem to our crew. So for the duration of our little Caribbean cruise, while my friend Karen and I prayed, Randy held the ill-fitting lid of the gas container down with one hand, furiously bailing with the other.

To this day I feel certain that if Randy hadn't been with us, we never would have made it to shore. Eventually our Haitian crew members seemed to recognize we had a significant problem. They changed course and headed for the closest point of terra firma, which was far from the place where our vehicle and the rest of our team were waiting. We didn't care. We were just so glad to be on land. Any land. As we tried to wring the seawater from our hair and clothes, our guide, a Haitian pastor, patiently debriefed us, saying, "De ocean is not de problem. De boat is de problem."

In the same way, when it comes to our emotions, what at first glance appears to be the problem is seldom the real problem. When we experience strong emotions like frustration, anger and fear, there is something going on under the surface. Something we need to investigate. Echoing the counsel of the Haitian pastor, the emotion is not the problem... Something else is the problem.

But like the Haitian boat crew, we often try to deal with the symptoms of the problem (bailing the ocean) without searching for the underlying cause (the boat). The underlying problem is our emotional conditioning. By the time we reach maturity, we have had all kinds of experiences that have become integrated into our perspective and affect the way we perceive life. We have feelings about every topic, every place, every event because they have been coloured and informed by our experiences.

Many years ago, while watching the evening news, I was reduced to tears in a matter of seconds by the image of an ultrasound scan on the television. Had I been in the company of anyone who didn't know me well, I would have had some explaining to do.

I don't recall what the featured news story was about. All I remember is the powerful effect that image had on me. Of course, my sensitivity had nothing at all to do with the news story being presented. It had everything to do with the fact that the one and only time an ultrasound was prescribed for me, personally, it revealed what the doctor already suspected. The child I carried in my womb was dead. The grief of that moment, when the devastating truth became obvious to everyone focused on that monitor, came rushing back to me. Powerful emotions flowed like turbulent water rushing through a narrow canyon, as I sat unsuspectingly watching the evening news.

When we feel intense emotion that seems out of proportion to the present catalyst, we need to "look under the hood" to discern what past event or experience is colouring the present. Once we know the cause of our exaggerated emotion, we can learn to manage it.

When I was a teenager, I took singing lessons from a woman who grew up in England during the Second World War. She had been severely scarred emotionally by the terror of the bombings she had survived as a little girl. One horrible night will live forever in her memory. She was awakened during an electrical storm by the awful percussion of an explosion and the frantic shouts of adults and cries of children. The German Luftwaffe had dropped a bomb near her home and flames surrounded her and her family.

They all escaped the fire by running through the storm to the home of some friends. The traumatized family hunkered down to wait out the bombing, the storm, and the night. But before the thunder stopped rumbling or dawn could come, another bomb exploded nearby, once again starting a fire and stealing their shelter.

I didn't know any of this when, in the middle of a music lesson, my 55-year-old teacher landed in my lap at the first crack of thunder announcing the arrival of a storm. Why the strong reaction? Because to her, every storm signified danger and every boom was a bomb and every flash of light was an explosion. Didn't she know the threat was not the same in the present as it had been in the past? Her head knew it, but somehow her head had failed to inform her heart.

We are completely incapable of controlling our instantaneous emotional reaction to an event. But we can manage those emotions by teaching our heads to talk to our hearts. When our heads tell our hearts the truth, we can bring an emotional volcano under control so that the response is a squirt of steam and not an eruption of lava.

But how does the head inform the heart? Consider this example. You've just left a job after 12 years of bashing your head against a glass ceiling that is dripping with testosterone. You have been disrespected, disregarded and passed over in every possible way because you are female. You have brought all 12 years' worth of frustration and anger into a new job that you took great pains to be sure was estrogen friendly.

You and your mostly male team have just finished a really great presentation and you are feeling very pleased with yourself. That is, until your boss individually thanks all the members of the team except you. He meant to thank everyone equally. He genuinely appreciates you. Excluding you was a simple oversight. But your previous work experience has set the lava to boiling. If you were able to think coherently at all you would yell out, "Get out of the way, boys... she's about to blow!"

This is what we'll call your gut reaction. It's that immediate, visceral, unmeasured emotional response. The next thing that must take place, if the eruption is to be avoided, is a sensible conversation between your head and your heart. You see, your head knows that based on everything you painstakingly researched about this man and your own brief experience with him, he is not sexist. You know that he values your contribution to the organization equally to those of the men on your team. You know that the only explanation for what happened is a brain hiccup.

While your lungs suck air in and blow it out, your head tells your heart the truth. Gradually your adrenal glands back off and the hammering of your heart begins to calm down. The decrease in volatility that you are now feeling enables you to refrain from lambasting your boss, who is blissfully unaware that he has even offended you. He doesn't get accosted, you don't get fired or go to jail. Everyone wins.

This story could have a very different ending. You might have let your careening emotions do your thinking for you. You could have told yourself:

- "I knew this would happen."
- "He's just like all the other men I've worked with."
- "It's impossible for a woman to get ahead in the workplace."
- "All men are jerks."

This would have added more baggage to the convoy you already drag along behind you, making you even more firmly entrenched in your belief that all men are chauvinists. Then you may have blown up at your boss, ending a career with an employer who really valued you.

The way the story ends depends not on what pushes your buttons to evoke an emotional response but on what you tell yourself in that moment. Telling yourself the truth will enable you to manage your emotions. The truth in this situation?

- "My boss is not sexist."
- "Excluding me was nothing more than an oversight."
- "He values me as much as his male employees."
- "This is a good job."
- "I have the power to control myself and keep my job or blow up and throw it all away."

In his letter to the Philippians in the New Testament, the apostle Paul writes, "Fix your thoughts on what is true and honorable and right. Think about things that are pure and lovely and admirable. Think about things that are excellent and worthy of praise" (4:8). He wrote that nearly 2,000 years ago.

Today, psychologist Dr. William Backus, among others, calls the apostle's advice "Misbelief Therapy: learning to replace our wrong or exaggerated impressions with the truth." When we employ this biblical strategy for managing our emotions, we first have to identify the lies that build the seismic pressure inside of us. Then we can defuse those emotional bombs by identifying, personalizing and expressing the truth as it applies to each situation we encounter. For example:

- "I'm such a loser" becomes "Okay, that was a stupid mistake but I am smart enough to learn from my mistakes and I am still a person of worth."
- "I'm so ugly" turns into "I'm not the most beautiful woman in the room but I have beautiful qualities most of these people know nothing about. Those who know me appreciate the beauty in me."
- "I can't do anything right" may be replaced by "This is clearly not my area of strength, but I'm proud of myself for trying and there are things I do very well."

- "I'm powerless" becomes "I am not a child anymore. The perspective and skills I've gained over the years have empowered me to deal with this situation decisively and effectively."

Our emotions are products of our thought life. In reality, we have very little direct control over our emotions, but we can control our thoughts. Replacing the confidence-killing, joy-sucking, rage-detonating lies in our minds with the truth is the way to calm our hearts. We can learn to manage our emotions not only by telling ourselves the truth but also by telling God the truth.

There are basically only three possible options for processing our strong emotions. First, we can suppress them by turning them inside, pushing them down where they will eat away at us and make us miserable. That is self-destructive. Second, we can explode all over everyone around us, wounding them and making the people we love miserable. That is also destructive. Third, we can vent our emotions to God. He has broad shoulders. He can absorb our outburst without our relationship sustaining any damage. In fact, the opposite is true. He *wants* us to come to him with our fragile hearts exposed. And it's not as if we can hide the truth from God anyway. By choosing to come to him with our hearts vulnerable, by telling him how we are feeling, we invite him into our experience much as we would unload after a bad day by talking to our moms, husbands or girlfriends.

Listen to this very "unholy" prayer from Psalm 109[1], in which Israel's King David dumps on God:

O God, whom I praise,
　　　　don't stand silent and aloof
while the wicked slander me...
Arrange for an evil person to turn on him.
　　　　Send an accuser to bring him to trial.
When his case is called for judgment,
　　　　let him be pronounced guilty.
　　　　Count his prayers as sins.
Let his years be few;
　　　　let his position be given to someone else.

May his children become fatherless,
and may his wife become a widow.
May his children wander as beggars;
may they be evicted from their ruined homes.
May creditors seize his entire estate,
and strangers take all he has earned.
Let no one be kind to him;
let no one pity his fatherless children.
May all his offspring die.
May his family name be blotted out in a
single generation.
May the Lord never forget the sins of his ancestors;
may his mother's sins never be erased from the record...

David's not finished yet, but I think you get the point. There's nothing noble or holy about his prayer. It's just real. And I think that's why God made sure it ended up in the Bible. David went on many of these little tirades before God. Yet He still called David a man after His own heart. God wants us to be real with Him, and He wants to make Himself real to us. He does that when we take our angry, frustrated or broken hearts to Him. As Psalm 34:18 says, "The Lord is close to the brokenhearted; he rescues those who are crushed in spirit."

When we know we can go to God with our strong emotions and be heard, understood, accepted and comforted, we just don't have the same need to dump on everyone else. And when we tell ourselves the truth, we manage our emotions by responding to reality, instead of reacting to our own subjective version of it.

Trying to function while at the mercy of our mood swings day after day is no way for us to live. Learning to manage our emotions will help us build a better life.

1. All scriptures are *New Living Translation*, copyright 1996. Used by permission of Tyndale House Publishers Inc., Wheaton, IL 60189.

This selection is taken from *10 Smart Things Women Can Do to Build a Better Life*, copyright © 2007 by Donna Carter (Published by Harvest House Publishers, Eugene, OR. Used by Permission. *www.harvesthousepublishers.com*).

Living Outside Our Comfort Zones

Non-fiction
Eleanor Shepherd

That unforgettable February weekend, I found myself repeatedly praying for my then-29-year-old son, John. I knew he would be driving back to Cambridge, Massachusetts, where he was studying for his MBA at Harvard Business School. John had rented an SUV for the six-hour drive to Montreal, Quebec, where he had spent the weekend visiting with his sister Elizabeth, who was studying music at McGill University.

I was in France, but I knew that the roads in New England could be slippery at this time of year. Finally, in desperation, I said, *Lord, send Your angels to watch over John on this trip.* How I wished I could take my children and hold them close to me and keep them safe from all harm!

Early Monday morning, as I was having my prayer time at our home in Paris, my daughter Elizabeth phoned from Montreal.

"Mom," she cried when I picked up the receiver, "There's been an accident. It's John."

"Is he alive?" I asked as an icy chill swept over me.

"Yes," she said. "But he broke his neck. He's paralyzed."

Once more, God had allowed our family to be thrown into a situation none of us wanted to be in.

We all have comfort zones; the non-threatening environments, either places or situations, where we feel adequate and at ease psychologically and emotionally. We want to stay in our safe havens. When people or circumstances challenge us to do things we don't think we're capable of doing, it's stressful and sometimes terrifying.

And yet, I've found that it's exactly those demanding situations that force us to grow in our faith and in our reliance on God. Looking back, I can see that my life has been a series of steps where I have been pushed, prodded and prompted to venture beyond what I thought was possible.

Early in our marriage, my husband Glen became extremely ill. I know now that if he had not gone into hospital that day, he would have died. We recently had become parents and now we learned that Glen had an incurable disease: diabetes. We had no idea how this would impact our lives.

In church that Sunday morning, I asked God, *Why Glen? You know that He loves You. He wants to serve You to the best of his ability. Why him?*

In the silence, I received my answer. God did not tell me why; but He enfolded me in His love and whispered in my heart, *My child, I know that you cannot understand, but I assure you I know what I have allowed to happen to you. Don't be afraid. I am here. I will always be with you.* I felt such a sense of His peace that I no longer needed to ask why or complain of the injustice of our situation.

I again had to leave my comfort zone when we sensed God's calling to leave the security of our life in a middle-class suburb in Winnipeg, Manitoba, to go into full-time ministry. At the time, Glen was working for the Manitoba Telephone System and I had chosen to stay at home and raise our children: John, who was seven, and Elizabeth, two. I was heavily involved in school and community activities.

For ten years, we had been wrestling with a calling to serve God in The Salvation Army. A crisis moment came in 1979 when we could no longer ignore the issue. Glen and I asked the Lord to show us His will clearly in the Scriptures.

The next morning, Glen picked up his Bible and read from where he had left off the day before. He recognized God's answer as he read I Corinthians 9:16: "Yet, when I preach the gospel, I cannot boast for I am compelled to preach. Woe to me if I do not preach the gospel."

We knew this decision would change everything. It would mean selling our home and furniture and moving across the country to Toronto, where we would be housed in a tiny apartment on the campus of the College for Officer Training while we studied for two years. We then would be ordained and commissioned as Salvation Army officers, to be sent wherever the Army posted us, to move whenever the Army changed our posting, and to inhabit homes owned and furnished by the Army.

As a homemaker, my time had been my own to manage as I chose. Because at that time The Salvation Army required both spouses to be ordained, we entered officer training as a family. During our two years of study, I seldom found occasions when I could quietly slip back into the security of a daily routine. I had to balance my roles as wife and mother, while meeting the challenges of completing assignments on time and learning to apply ministry skills.

Appointed as a student-leader during the second year, I was forced to make decisions and give direction to others, learning how to encourage them to develop as leaders at the same time as I was developing my own leadership capacity.

After ordination and commissioning, we served a congregation in southern Alberta for two years of pastoral ministry. I had hoped I could drift back into my role as a wife and mother. I figured Glen could handle whatever came along, and I could be nearby to quietly offer my support.

However, Glen unexpectedly was hospitalized for throat surgery, to remove polyps from his vocal cords. Forbidden to speak for three weeks while his vocal cords healed, he spent his days at a Catholic retreat centre where he could live as if he had taken a vow of silence. I had to lead worship services, conduct a wedding, participate in a funeral, and prepare and preach two sermons every Sunday, as well as visit the sick and counsel those in need.

As soon as Glen recovered, and before I had time to think about retreating into my comfort zone away from all of this public activity, we confronted a complicated marriage breakup involving elders in our small town church—a situation I felt totally unprepared to handle. The whole congregation was shaken by the event, which included the shattering of two leading families. Glen and I individually spent hours counselling each of the participants. Amazingly, the Holy Spirit equipped us with the necessary guidance and wisdom.

As that daunting experience wound down, I wanted so much to return to my cocoon where I could shut out the demands of a hurting congregation, but such a space continued to elude me.

I hoped that our appointment to Montreal, the city that we considered home, might permit me to retreat into a less stressful life. We were assigned to be Divisional Youth Directors, which meant that we were responsible for the youth work of The Salvation Army for Quebec and Eastern Ontario.

Our summers at The Salvation Army camp in Quebec's beautiful Laurentian Mountains were far from idyllic. We devoted large chunks of time during the year to organizing the weekly summer camp programs and finding leaders to facilitate them. Once on site, we discovered that supervising staff and facilities was a 24/7 task. Since most of the staff members were in their late teens, we needed to help them deal with their raging hormones, including making sure that the boys and girls went to their respective cabins at night and stayed there. This meant rounding up those who constantly found new places to hide, hoping we would not notice their absence.

The same staff who were so reluctant to go to bed were equally slow at rousing themselves to get up to prepare for breakfast and early morning activities for the campers. We often had spent part of the night sitting in the local hospital emergency room 20 miles[1] away with a camper who (inevitably right before bedtime) had injured him or herself by doing something like falling off the top bunk bed. Many mornings, it seemed we had just gotten to bed ourselves when the alarm would remind us we had to be out making sure that everyone else was at work.

On top of all this, we were responsible for overseeing the youth ministries of each local congregation in our area. We tackled the job of encouraging Corps Officers, or pastors, by sending letters and visiting with them, as we tried to fire their enthusiasm for youth programs.

In the really difficult times, I would dream of the day when the national Salvation Army leaders would send us to a situation where I would not have to live so far outside of what I believed were my competencies. But that dream was not to be realized.

From Montreal, we were asked to take an appointment in France, where I faced the tests of learning a new language and a new culture. As soon as I could communicate in French, my assignment was to develop the Corps Cadets program, which was a Bible study and leadership development program for teens. I also was responsible for Junior Soldiers, a catechism program for children. Activities such as writing curriculum in a second language, visiting groups of young Salvationists and their leaders all over France, and organizing national camps barely permitted time to catch my breath, let alone retreat back into my comfort zone.

After four years in France, in 1991 we returned to Canada. Surely the security of being back in my own country would offer some occasions to quietly slip into my comfort zone. However, I had forgotten what I had learned in France about cultural adaptation. Everyday habits like the time you eat, how you greet people, the colours you wear so you don't feel conspicuous, the amount of personal space you need around you to feel comfortable, and a myriad of other daily routines are part of our culture. To us they are perfectly normal—until we live in another culture where we have to abandon them and take on others, in order to accommodate to that culture.

I found out that I could not quietly slip back into my rut. While the English-Canadian culture was familiar to me, I had adopted practices that were characteristic of European culture. They were so second-nature to me that I did not shuck them off when I returned to Canada. For example, if someone spoke to me in English with an accent, whatever that accent was, I immediately switched and began to speak to him or her in French. It was a reflex. As soon as I encountered someone whom I had not seen for a while, my immediate response was to lean forward and kiss him or her on each cheek. It was instinctive. I received a lot of puzzled looks! I realized that back home in Canada, my comfort zone eluded me because I could not find where I fit any more.

In addition to the conundrum of cultural adaptation, I found myself in a taxing vocational situation. While we were still in France, we had exchanged correspondence with our Human Resources personnel in Canada. At their request, I gave suggestions about areas where I felt my skills and abilities could contribute to the ministry of The Salvation Army. I listed three different fields where I believed I had strengths and simultaneously could find some comfort and security. However, when I received my assignment, to my shock, it was in none of the areas I had mentioned!

I was named the national director for Corps Cadets, and my task was to travel all over the country meeting with young people and their leaders to explain the excellence of the program and to teach the leaders how they could be more effective. The problem was, I was trying to promote a curriculum I believed was outdated. I felt frustrated that I was not permitted to change the curriculum in the ways that the teens and their leaders suggested. And I still struggled with shyness, despite the frequent need to speak in public.

For several months, I tried to work through what was going on. Was there really a purpose in my being given an appointment where I felt so unqualified and uncomfortable? After a lot of soul-searching, I was driven to the conclusion that I needed to learn to find my resources in God and not in myself. This challenging assignment provided the opportunity for me to do that. And I discovered what I needed to share with the leaders: the most important gifts they could give the young people they were teaching were their time and their respect (shown by listening to what the young people wanted to say).

Secretly, Glen and I had always longed to return to Montreal, the place where we had met and married. We were ecstatic that day in 1998 when we received the news that we were being posted to Montreal, with responsibility for the work of The Salvation Army in Quebec. Now that I knew I would be able to return to the comfort of home, I could hardly wait.

But, after only eight months in Montreal, we were reassigned to France once again. This time, we were responsible for all of the work of The Salvation Army in France. To return to Europe and to a place we already had lived offered some possibility of going back into the groove of the familiar. Little did I know the challenges that we would face.

French legislation had changed the way that The Salvation Army financed itself. Funds donated by the public to The Salvation Army could no longer be used for general administration; the money only could be used for specific social programs. Our task was to find ways to reinvent ourselves in the light of the new reality. Economic challenges foster fear rather than creativity. Such an environment is not conducive to comfort-zone living, though the temptation is strong to retreat to one.

Strangely enough, I found a way to create a sanctuary for us—not where we could retreat, but where we were fortified to go out to face our challenges. In desperation, at Glen's request, I created a prayer-support team of people from around the world. Each month, I sent them prayer requests about our ministry. Their prayers fashioned a safe haven for us, one that held us during the difficulties we were facing and sustained us in the dark days that we were unaware lay just around the corner.

Mid-January of 2003, we received a call from the Army's International Headquarters in London, England, informing us that we had accomplished the task required in France and that in June we would be returning to Canada. I was thrilled—we would be going home again. I would be closer to my children, who were now young adults. I would be in my comfort zone at last.

But that Sunday night two weeks later, as we traveled back to Paris on the TGV, the high-speed train, from a ministry trip in Valence two hours to the south, I could not stop thinking about our son John.

Early the next morning, we got the call from our daughter Elizabeth, informing us that John had been in a car accident and was paralyzed.

By mid-morning, Glen and I were at Charles de Gaulle airport, booked on an Air Canada flight to Montreal. The overseas flight seemed interminable. I could not focus on reading or watching the movie. The young men on the screen seemed to mock me as I saw them walking about freely. In my head, I cried out, *It's not fair. You can walk and my son can't!* Before we left Paris, we had been able to contact the hospital in Vermont where John had been taken. We found out more about his condition, but we did not yet know that John instantly had become a quadriplegic.

Our friends met us at the airport in Montreal, ready to drive us to the hospital in Burlington, Vermont. They held out their arms to us and we dissolved into sobs as we gave vent to the bottled-up fears of what we would face. While we were en route, Elizabeth called us from the hospital. She warned us to be prepared to see John hooked up to a lot of machines—but she didn't say that his whole body was swollen up like the bulky "Michelin Man," and that a metal halo brace was bolted to his skull.

Over the next few days, we pieced together the accident story. John's rented SUV had spun out of control on black ice, rolled over, and come to rest in a snow bank in the wide median between the lanes of the divided highway. The vehicle was white and the road was deserted. In the winter night, it would have been hard to distinguish the car buried in the snow. John was alone and could have perished in cold and shock.

The accident site was about 10 miles[2] south of the Canada-U.S. border. Some U.S. Customs Border Patrol officers spotted the vehicle and contacted the Vermont State Police. The emergency workers had to cut the roof off in order to extract John. I am sure that the Border Patrol officers were the earthly angels whom I had begged God to send to watch over John.

John initially was taken to the local hospital, but when they ascertained that his neck was broken, they sent him to the Fletcher-Allen Medical Centre in Burlington, Vermont. Since it was in the middle of downhill ski country, the hospital was well equipped to deal with spinal cord injuries. In spite of such a terrible tragedy, the Lord provided a comfort zone for John.

By the time we arrived, John was in the intensive care surgical unit. It seemed incongruous that he could be hurt so badly—the only mark on him was a small scratch on his forehead.

John showed great courage in facing this tragedy. He assured us that he was determined to use this experience redemptively—to make the most out of the challenges that were presented to him by his situation. None of us knew at the time just how difficult that would be.

My admiration and appreciation for John grew as I watched him struggle with learning to live life a new way. Before the accident, he was a six-foot, two-inch, fun-loving young man who had the world by the tail. He'd worked in London, England and New York City. He'd spent three months in Barcelona, Spain to add Spanish to his fluency in several other languages before returning to Harvard Business School. He was in his last semester and had been hired by an investment bank to work in London.

Now, with no control of his hands or fingers, he had to learn how to hold a fork to eat; to use his computer; to put in his contact lenses; to cook and dress and wash his clothes; and even to look after his kitten. John has shown me, in a way I could never imagine, what perseverance means.

I continue to watch John, wanting so much to encourage him in his pilgrimage; yet often finding myself silent in the presence of the courage and tenacity that he has demonstrated. When he was a child, I tried to teach him how to cope with life. Now, he shows me how to overcome. John has learned to live outside the comfort zone of a strong body that you can depend on. He had to leave that option behind forever.

My life experiences—and especially John's accident—have taught me a lot about living outside my comfort zone. Something strange has happened to me through it all. I am no longer sure that I would want the security of what I thought were my safe havens, even if I could have it.

I have discovered that I do not need to be within my comfort zone to experience a sense of protection and well-being; rather, God provides the refuge of His comfort wherever we are. I now know that when I venture outside of where I feel safe—however timidly or unwillingly— the Lord can use me for His purposes.

Within my comfort zone, I can operate solely out of my own strength. I rely on my own resources, confident that I can handle whatever comes. Outside of my safety net, I am less confident, and I fear that my own resources will fail me. I am forced to rely upon the Lord for strength and to draw on His resources.

He has never yet failed to provide me with all I need. Because I acknowledge—to myself and to others—that He is the source for all that I am able to do in these situations, what I do brings glory to Him.

I want more than anything else to live to honour Him, even it if means spending a whole lifetime outside my comfort zone.

1. and 2. 1 mile = 1.6 kilometres

Dylan

Brian Austin

They sneak up without warning,
these hot and painful tears.
They squeeze the chest and crush the will;
they aggravate the fears…

Pure torture—though the worst
has already taken place.
A little one so longed for
has hid from us his face.

So great was our rejoicing!
Was it only days ago
when the coming of this little one
set all our hearts aglow?

Parents, loved ones, grandparents,
we thrilled to speak his name,
treasured the glimpses of each day,
and spread abroad his fame;

Longed for the chance to hold him,
spoke his name with deep delight;
were sure the world shone brighter 'neath
the glow of his small light.

He's gone now and we're aching
with the great unanswered *Why?*
God loans a child for so few days
then lets that child die.

Not first to feel such sorrow;
and we will not be the last.
Still, this boundless pain has seized us
And keeps us all downcast.

Yet God shares in our sorrows,
knows how deep his children grieve;
saw His loved and cherished Son die,
hung high between two thieves.

He does not let a tear fall
where He does not share the pain.
And He sees beyond our grief
to when we'll meet again.

'Tis a promise that we treasure
though the tears still fall today.
God keeps our precious little one
To rejoin us one day.

The tears, so deep and painful,
cannot out-reach His love.
We'll trust our precious Dylan
in the hands of God above.

This selection is adapted from *Laughter & Tears*, book and audio CD, copyright © 2005 Brian Austin (LittleBoxStudios/Word Alive).

How Big Is Your Umbrella?

Non-fiction
Sheila Wray Gregoire

Sometimes life is lousy. And when storms come, frequently our first reaction is to lash out at God. Why me? Why don't You do something? Why are You letting this happen?

I've done my own share of wailing at God. The worst occurred when I was 26 and pregnant with my second child. The day after my ultrasound, everything seemed to go into slow motion when the phone rang and the doctor said, "You'd better come in, because there's something wrong with his heart."

Over the next few weeks, as I had every test imaginable, my husband and I learned that our son had Down Syndrome and a serious heart defect that would require a series of surgeries. These operations, however, would only postpone his death, not save his life. The doctors couldn't be certain when he would leave us, but they believed he would deteriorate, grow very short of breath, and suffer until he finally died, whether it be as a baby, as a toddler, or as a 20-year-old.

I walked through the rest of my pregnancy in trepidation and, frequently, cold brutal terror. Yet when my son Christopher arrived on August 6, 1996, he was healthier than we expected him to be. We were praying that he could avoid surgery, and that he might even improve on his own, but God did not answer that prayer as we would have liked. As his heart began to fail, Christopher grew increasingly tired and lost weight instead of gaining it. The surgery was his only hope, even though the doctors gave that only a 25 percent chance of success. By that time my son was down to four pounds[1], far too small for the ordeal that lay ahead of him.

On the morning of his operation, when I handed him over to the anaesthetist, I was terrified I would never hold him again. But the surgery went well, and the doctors grew optimistic about his chances. Five days later, however, Christopher's breathing again grew rapid. That evening, my mother watched our daughter Rebecca so my husband Keith and I could visit our son together.

"Mommy loves you, sweetheart," I whispered as we left his room.

He was only 29 days old when he died later that night.

I had never known what it was for a heart to truly break until that moment.

C. S. Lewis, after the death of his wife, remarked that grief feels a lot like fear. It's like the sickening ache in the pit in your stomach that precedes something truly awful. That's what I felt, too. But what is it, exactly, that we're afraid of? Waking up tomorrow morning and dealing with the loss again? Facing the future alone? Forgetting? Going crazy? That God really is malicious? Or that this feeling will never end?

Perhaps it's a combination of all of them. After Christopher's death, I was simultaneously afraid of forgetting and of never being able to cope well again. During his illness and after his death I wailed many questions at God to try to make sense out of what was happening to me. In many ways, though, this quest was self-serving. I reasoned that if I could just find the reason for this storm, then it would stop. I could move on. This pain would end, or at least my ability to cope could begin. So I searched my repertoire of explanations for suffering in order to make sense of it. As I did so, these are the questions that vexed me.

What is God Trying to Teach Me?

About a decade before my son's illness, my mother was diagnosed with breast cancer, and the surgeon believed, based on the size and type of tumour, that it had already spread. As my mother lay in the hospital, I remember sitting on the subway returning from visiting her, thinking that this must be happening because I hadn't been reading my Bible enough lately. God was using her illness to try to get my attention.

It's easy to dismiss such adolescent musings now, but many adults entertain similar thoughts. The reason the storm is raging is that God will use anything at His disposal to make His point. When Christopher died, my husband Keith and I received some condolence cards from very well-meaning people who wrote things like, "Smile through this! God is teaching you something!"

Besides being a ridiculous thing to say to a grieving parent, I am not sure that this presents a proper picture of the cause of our storms. The insinuation is that the reason that this hurricane is blowing is that God wants to get my attention. It's for my own good, you see, because God loves me. And if it's for my own good, then I had better smile, as if it really isn't so bad. After all, shouldn't I be grateful that God is reaching out to teach me, a person who is obviously so unteachable that God had to send this catastrophe to get my attention?

But is there any evidence that this was Jesus' attitude to storms on this earth? After all, when Jesus' friends died, Jesus wept. When Herod had John the Baptist murdered, Jesus went away by Himself. He wrestled in prayer for His disciples. He even wept over Jerusalem! Jesus felt the pain that we all experience as part of life, and didn't try to deny the reality of that pain by saying, "It's all for your good." Even when it was for our good—when Lazarus was raised so that we could see Jesus' power—He still wept! Feeling grief is not denying God's goodness in our lives; it's being true to our humanity.

But even if storms are legitimate occasions for grief, does God really send horrible things to lead us to Him? True, throughout the Old Testament, the nation of Israel was consistently punished because its people didn't listen to God. However, this only happened after Israel had been told repeatedly what to do, and had ignored it. It wasn't God's first choice for making His point.

More than this, when Jesus wanted to teach people something, what did He do? Instead of inflicting suffering, He often retreated with them for some one-on-one time. He laughed with them, spent time with them, entered into their lives. He showed them love. He even performed miracles! While He did rebuke the Pharisees on a number of occasions, His *modus operandi* was to woo with love, not to zap with lightning. There are times when God does send hardships to call people back to Him, but this seems to be the exception, not the rule.

Of course, storms are excellent growth opportunities, as Jesus' brother James told us, "The testing of your faith develops perseverance" (James 1:3). You will mature through this storm. It does not necessarily follow, though, that a spiritual deficiency in you caused the storm in the first place—so learning a lesson may not necessarily end it, either, as much as we would like it to. There's probably more going on here than a simple spiritual lesson.

Whom Is the Storm Really About?

Trying to figure out what God is teaching us or how we're to blame are common reactions to storms, even though these reactions often block us from the comfort He longs to give. But there's another fundamental problem. Think about all of these questions: *What do I need to learn? What did I do wrong? How could I have caused this?* Do you notice how all of them centre around "I"?

When my son was ill, I remember talking to our minister about why God might be doing this. Trying to appear very mature, I said, "I just want to learn whatever God is trying to show me." And then my pastor said something that absolutely floored me. "Why do you assume any of this has anything to do with you?"

What did he mean? Of course it had to do with me! Christopher was my son! Nothing had ever affected me this much! And yet, the beginning of a nagging doubt was born: perhaps I was asking the wrong questions.

In 1964, Helen Roseveare was a missionary doctor in the Congo. When that nation erupted in a coup, rebels took her, along with some of her fellow female missionaries, captive. Over the next few months, she endured many beatings, rapes and other horrors. In the middle of one of the most degrading experiences, she remembers a question that was whispered into her mind. "God asked me, 'Can you thank me for trusting you with this, even if I never tell you why?'" And Helen realized that God did trust her, that He was using her, even if she never saw the fruit. She was part of a plan that went far beyond her. And God was in control.

History is filled with examples of people who have endured horrendous storms because God was accomplishing something bigger through them. Martin Luther King, Jr., the biblical Joseph, and the martyrs of the Christian church all suffered, and their families shared in their agonies. Maybe you can't see God's purposes now. Joseph certainly didn't when he spent years in prison. Maybe you never will see what God is doing on this side of heaven. But you are part of the story that God is writing.

When my pastor challenged my assumptions, it was as though God was finally pulling me back from the cliff towards shelter. I'd had everything backwards. I hadn't realized that in trying to find answers I was actually walking further into the storm, rather than towards God. I thought God wanted me to seek out *reasons*, when really God wanted me to seek out *Himself*. He was the One who was going to provide the shelter, the way of escape, the hope and will and power to keep clinging to the offered branch. I may never know the reasons, but I can know God, and rest in Him. This storm, you see, is bigger than me, but it's not bigger than Him. And if I followed Him, He would lead me through.

Did this mean that trying to find spiritual lessons in what had happened was wrong? Not at all! But painting God as the will behind the storm paints a picture of God that's both smaller and more mean-spirited than the one we find in Scripture.

The reasons why something terrible happens may or may not be revealed, as Helen Roseveare found, but God is still there. As we seek Him, we will learn, we will grow more holy, and we will develop perseverance. These come best, though, not when we condemn ourselves, but when we trust God, no matter what comes.

Looking for reasons for those storms is only natural. But as we voice those questions, yelling into the wind, God is simultaneously calling us towards shelter. Even if He never tells us why, He is the one in control, He trusts us, and He will carry us through.

1. Four pounds = 1.8 kilograms (1 pound = .454 kilograms).

This selection is adapted by permission of the publisher from *How Big Is Your Umbrella: Weathering the Storms of Life*, copyright © 2006 by Sheila Wray Gregoire (Kregel Publications).

Jesus' Disciple Wears a Stethoscope

Non-fiction
W. Harold Fuller

Whatever you did for one of the least of these…
you did for me (Matthew 25:40).

"Harold, you've just got to meet Dr. Bell," I was told several times. "She's from your country, and she's doing amazing work in the middle of the monsoon rains in Northern India."

I found Dr. Bell, a farmer's daughter from Bruce County, Ontario, sitting at the wheel of a four-wheel-drive Jeep.

"Hop in!" Aletta (pronounced Ah-LEE–tah) called, giving me the impression she was anxious to get going on her rounds of the village health centres she'd set up in the area. Fifty, I guessed her to be at the time—although guessing a woman's age can be reckless! Fresh-faced and dressed in an Indian-style long tunic over slacks, she acted more like a 30-year-old. The only indication of her profession was a stethoscope dangling from her neck.

As the Jeep bumped along unpaved trails, I learned more about this Canadian medic whom local people looked upon as their own "Mother Teresa." Of course, most of the world knows about the Albanian nun who spent her life caring for the dispossessed in the slums of Calcutta. But who has heard about this ordinary Canadian doctor who has invested her life caring for remote, poverty-stricken villagers on India's border with Nepal?

Aletta frequently changed gears to negotiate muddy potholes, while I, the eternal journalist, plied her with pesky questions about her upbringing. The youngest of a family of nine, Aletta recalled that Canadian rural society in the 1950s didn't expect farm girls to go into professions such as medicine. In fact, all of her older siblings left school after Grade 8 to enter the workforce and help support the family.

But perceptive teachers and principals noticed the intelligent girl who was at the head of her class, and urged her on. One even arranged bursaries to help pay for university. With those memories, Aletta grew up to become a constant advocate for improving women's lives.

"Okay," I persisted, "but how did a farmer's daughter from Kincardine, Ontario end up as a medical doctor here on Nepal's border?"

She told me that after graduating from medical school at the University of Western Ontario and completing a year's internship at Victoria Hospital in London, Ontario, she moved to Chicago to specialize in family medicine. But missions were already beckoning her, and she went to Saudi Arabia on a short-term assignment during her schooling.

After graduating, Aletta moved to India in 1964 to serve with the Ceylon and India General Mission, where she started Prem Sewa Hospital in Utraula in the northern state of Uttar Pradesh. The hospital served women and children in an area where 50 percent of the population was Muslim, and Muslim women were not allowed to go to a male doctor.

Due to changes in government requirements, Christian nationals and expatriate missions in India formed the Emmanuel Hospitals Association (EHA), under which Aletta's mission placed its medical work. In 1975, EHA asked Aletta to move to Duncan Memorial Hospital on India's border with Nepal. Aletta had already heard that "Duncan" had major tensions. But she couldn't have anticipated the difficulties she was about to go through.

Her problems started when one of the hospital's department managers, who had been raised by a missionary benefactor and was an active church member, tried to cover up his role in a fatal car accident. EHA attempted to transfer him. He refused to move, and with the help of a non-Christian politician, he arranged for the police to charge Aletta and her staff with making and selling drugs illegally!

That started a dragged-out court case. If Aletta had returned to Canada on furlough without court permission, she would have been refused re-entry into India. So she stayed in India for 17 years.

Not only was she separated from family and friends, at a time when long distance phone calls were rare and e-mail was unknown, but she lost her position.

"I had been invited to run Duncan Hospital as its Medical Superintendent. Instead, because of the internal conflict, EHA designated me as Director of Community Health—a position that I knew nothing about. It was a blow! At Utraula, I'd been in charge, full of self-confidence. Now I was exhausted, out of control," she explained.

"I told the Lord I couldn't handle it," she added. "He told me His grace would be sufficient for me and for the job. I had to die to my own ambitions and let God live through me in whatever circumstances He chose. That's how I found peace!"

As we followed the rural trail in the increasing heat, the doctor gave me a juicy "lychee"—a refreshing grape-like fruit she had brought to slake our thirst. But now a crowd of waving villagers told us we'd arrived at Champak Community Health Centre. "Champak," Aletta explained, was the name of a fragrant flower, but it also formed the acronym of three villages the Centre served.

How had this Canadian medic approached the complex cultural problems of undeveloped rural areas? For instance, how did she convince adults that spirits didn't cause fevers, and idols didn't need placating to prevent disease? I was about to witness the revolutionary power of the gospel.

Aletta parked the Jeep beside a mud-and-wattle hut. As cheering children rushed to grasp her hands, we wended our way along muddy footpaths between the huts. I almost felt as if I was walking alongside Jesus. Except that Jesus, when He walked in Judea and Samaria, didn't wear a stethoscope. And in this Indian village, no disciple tried to keep the laughing children from crowding around their favourite visitor!

Anxious mothers brought feverish infants. Squatting down to balance a child on one knee, Aletta checked a baby's glands and listened to its breathing. Then she stooped to enter a shack where a woman had dysentery.

"How many times have you had a bowel movement today?" Aletta asked, in perfect Hindi.

"Fifty times!" the woman answered weakly. Aletta patiently asked her to count to 50.

"One, two, three, one, two, three…" the woman counted over and over. Obviously, "50" was an impressive figure she'd heard. But because dysentery is the most common ailment (and causes death from dehydration), Aletta gave her an oral re-hydration packet.

At the Health Centre, we watched children making those rehydration packets. Sitting on mats, the children filled small plastic bags with a mixture of sugar and salt. One child carefully spooned out the right quantities while other children filled the bags and sealed them with heat from a candle.

"We pay these children for their work, and we use the packets in the villages and back at the hospital, which buys them," Aletta explained. "That's one of several ways we make Champak self-supporting. The children use their money for school books and pencils."

The work was also an educational experience. The children learned that evil spirits don't cause dysentery, and illness can be overcome with the right treatment, not with sacrifices at the local shrine. Moreover, they learned to follow directions and measure accurately while they earned money for schooling and helped their communities. The World Health Organization talks about promoting holistic, sustainable development. This was it!

But sadly, such an opportunity is not given to most of India's 70 million children under the age of 18 who labour "without benefit of education," according to World Health Organization reports.[1] The statistics are staggering. It is estimated that 10 million children are bonded or enslaved, paying off inherited family "debts." Two million "children at risk" are living on the streets, including hundreds of thousands of child prostitutes. Thirteen million of India's children are considered homeless, and more than one million are orphans.

Child labour was another concern. "It's illegal" she said, "but it still exists because of poverty. No one is convicted of it, because parents don't admit it, and employers never will. Besides, a bribe can quickly divert justice. We oppose exploiting children, of course, but we also realize it's more complicated than people overseas realize."

"If children don't work, there will be less food for the family, and in most cases the children would be sitting idle. Working children is a family tradition," she went on to explain. "The only way we'll get rid of child labour is by improving opportunities for the poor and making school attendance compulsory."

Aletta discovered that some areas might have a government school, but no pupils because teachers, equipment and books were missing. Winning the confidence of authorities, she encouraged communities to build their own one-room schools. The villages provided labour and half the cost; the Centre donated cement and basic equipment, and paid a responsible teacher for the first three years.

Champak improved farming yields, developed fish "farms" (villagers dug the pond; the Centre stocked it), and introduced rabbit breeding. Aletta developed a tree nursery and encouraged men to plant bamboo for building projects. For villagers, she opened up new vistas through adult literacy and small business seminars, so peasants could start cottage industries (one of Mahatma Gandhi's goals), such as candle-making, sewing, and other handicrafts.

"We don't press projects on villages—they'd only collapse after a while," Aletta explained, as she felt for a child's pulse. "We wait until the people see the benefits a neighbouring village receives. When they ask for the same, we're ready to help. Our formula for leader-ship? Teach as many people as possible, give responsibility, and require accountability."

That makes management sense in any language!

Aletta's rural background had taught her the value of self-reliance. She was determined to alleviate grinding poverty, ignorance and abuse in villages. Through the Champak Health Centre, she sought to meet the most basic preventive health needs: sanitation and clean water.

Aletta clearly had the gift of organizing. She started by numbering the houses, an unknown practice at the time. From there, it became possible to list every household, every child, access to water and sanitation, immunization, illness (especially TB and leprosy), and habits hazardous to health, such as smoking and drinking. These statistics, which graded households on an economic scale of 1 to 5, enabled the clinic to identify health needs quickly, and to charge patients according to their ability to pay. (The lower the income, the less the charge—right down to zero.)

The contrast between villages was dramatic. One village had refused medical treatment for its children and wouldn't provide a plot for a school. I noticed men lounging in the shade of a dilapidated hut, smoking while they gambled. A wizened grandmother, who looked to be 80 (but was likely under 50) held a coughing baby, obviously malnourished. Her 30-year-old daughter, wearing soiled clothing covered with flies, looked listless—likely suffering from parasites and dysentery. Instead of attending school, girls carried far-too-heavy water pots on their heads from a distant muddy hole. Refuse littered lanes; the smell of decay hung over the village.

In the next village, which had accepted the doctor's help, people looked healthier and were better clothed. We could hear children reciting lessons in a classroom. We saw men tilling gardens, and women adding peelings to compost heaps. In one villager's hut, a sow was tethered to the centre pole; six piglets slept on a raised platform. Beside the village market, I noticed a community water pump surrounded with guava trees. Even though India does not lack basic food, Aletta told me that when Champak started its project in that village 70% of the children under five had been malnourished. Now, five years later, only 10% were malnourished.

Aletta also was determined to help the plight of local women. First, she faced male village leaders who opposed educating women. They claimed that a Grade 10 education—which no village woman had ever reached—was required to enroll in the government's free small business course. Aletta found out that wasn't true, but she still had to fight for places in the courses because the male leaders claimed all places were taken.

Aletta then organized a Champak program to provide piglets for anyone who'd look after them. The Centre chose pigs because the only ones who'd keep pigs were low-caste, the people the Centre most wanted to help. Village men weren't interested, but women were—again, the most needy sector. So Aletta organized community committees that placed pigs and arranged breeding. When a sow gave birth, the owner had to give away two piglets to two neighbours—and so the benefits spread.

"I've noticed the men around here respect you," I commented after we'd dropped in at an administrator's office in another town. "How come—when you're not only 'a woman' but also not married!" I added, tongue in cheek.

"Ah-ha!" Aletta chuckled. "Partly because of my professional training. Indians respect that. But another reason is my willingness to work in the villages. That administrator you met once told me, 'Most of our own people aren't willing to do this, but you—a foreign doctor—you come and live among the poor!' So he's very cooperative."

In the next village, I noticed that Aletta was not only respected by the officials. A hubbub drew us to its little market, where drunken men from another village were trying to drag away a health worker. The worker was the brother of the chief, who wouldn't allow the intruders to sell or drink beer in the market. The drunken brewers wanted to beat up the young man in revenge. Disregarding the cursing and shouting, the stocky doctor waded into the melee, which suddenly became hushed.

"Now, tell me what this nonsense is about!" she demanded in perfect Hindi. After listening to the complaints, she told the intruders to leave—and it was over!

"Okay—you're certainly respected here!" I said. "But is it true that a traditional male thanks his god he wasn't born as a woman or dog?"

"Sadly, that's true," Aletta confirmed. "The treatment of women is really dreadful. At a Hindu girl's wedding, the customary greeting of guests is, 'May you be the mother of a hundred sons.' That's also the name of a book exposing the treatment of many Hindu women. The author cites bride killing, female infanticide, forced abortions, and widow burning—all are outlawed but secretly perpetrated in some places. Bribery and status make prosecution difficult."

In fact, India accounts for an estimated 10 million abortions annually. Some 20,000 ultrasound clinics identify the sex of fetuses, leading to female fetuses being terminated before they are born.[2] The reasons are traditional, cultural and economic. Parents pray for sons, and daughters are seen as burdens. Sons are more prestigious: they carry on the family name, provide labour for the family business and support their parents in their old age. Girls are viewed as an expensive liability, because they're destined to leave the family to live with their in-laws, and cost a huge dowry to get a marriage proposal. This is causing skewed birth statistics in favour of males, and a growing gender imbalance in India's 1.1 billion population.

Aletta said that in some cases if a husband or his family is not satisfied with the dowry payments, or the wife's servitude, or her inability to provide a male heir, they simply douse her with kerosene and set her alight. One newspaper reported that police recorded 4,000 bride burnings in one state ("And if those are the recorded ones, the total is likely double," commented Aletta). Few of these murders come to trial because of corruption. In a nearby village, Aletta knew a beautiful bride whose bruised and strangled corpse was dumped in a pond. No inquest was held.

"Even for women who survive, life is often miserable," Aletta stated. She recounted that some Muslim and Hindu men restrict the movement of their wives, keeping them virtual prisoners and slaves. Their women have no say in life—in fact, most men do not want an educated wife because she would speak up against injustice.

"Although most women are malnourished because the family males eat first, they are baby factories," Aletta added. She ought to know—having personally delivered some 20,000 babies and supervised more than 45,000 births. One mother was only 14.

"If a woman doesn't produce a baby, or if she only has girls, she's to blame," the doctor explained. "If she's sick, she's sent back to her parents for them to look after her. Since many husbands are away working, a relative may not bother taking a woman to hospital—and she's not allowed to go by herself. If she needs blood, most male relatives are reluctant to give it."

"If that's how many men here look upon women, how do you account for the great women who have risen to leadership in Asia?"

"Interesting paradox!" Aletta responded. "Women are becoming educated, especially in the higher caste, and family dynasties account for several women leaders. Education hasn't filtered down to the illiterate masses yet, but literates are becoming more aware of human rights and are entering public life. There are a lot of women's movements. However, we don't get involved in politics—only in doing what the government agrees with us needs to be done, which is helping the common people."

"So what's the best way of doing that?" I asked, remembering that ailing mother who couldn't count past three.

"Of course, the gospel is the answer," Aletta said. "But as William Carey showed, communicating the gospel means a number of practical things. We must educate women, which we're doing through village health workers. They become 'human beings' in their own eyes then. And their husbands respect them more once they begin to earn money."

Aletta added, "The villagers know that we are followers of Jesus. When they come to know Jesus Christ themselves—that's when they find true liberation!"

Some members of higher castes oppose uplifting the poor in lower castes, and insinuate that missionaries bribe people to "convert." The Champak staff members are careful not to attach any strings to their work. For those who ask for spiritual help, an evangelist is always available. Other staffers at the Centre include a teacher, agriculturalist, nurse, and crafts instructor.

When we returned to the Duncan Hospital, patients were lined up to see Aletta. Others on staff had their own line of patients waiting.

Later, Aletta told me about another concern. India has the world's second highest number of people infected with AIDS, second only to

South Africa. Much of the infection is spread by truck drivers who visit prostitutes on India's busy trucking routes.

I heard about Sarabjeet, whose husband had contracted HIV from a prostitute but didn't tell his wife. Their baby daughter was born infected and died before her third birthday. When Sarabjeet's husband also died of AIDS, her in-laws blamed her for both deaths. The distraught widow wanted to kill herself, but a worker with AIDS Care Training Services (ACTS) took her to Shalom, a Christian clinic. Today Sarabjeet has hope—and a job that provides her support.

"We help with projects such as ACTS in Delhi," Aletta explained. "Our mission, SIM, also sponsors Hope for AIDS projects here and worldwide. A recent India-wide survey showed that 36% of respondents thought all infected people deserved their fate and should kill themselves! We empower churches by educating volunteers in a Christian approach to sexual health education and teaching them how to help those who are suffering."

"I can still see the face of Shanti, a beautiful child," Aletta says. "The Hindu temple had thrown her out when her mother, a 23-year-old temple prostitute, died from AIDS. A pastor found Shanti sitting in the rain holding her baby brother, and brought her to our Home of Hope. Shanti found more than food and shelter—she found Jesus. Now her eyes sparkle."

Although presently AIDS affects only a small percentage of India's burgeoning population, the World Health Organization predicts it will explode unless the government takes urgent measures. After denying the problem in the past, the federal and several state governments now are developing programs of treatment and education with the assistance of missions and other aid organizations.

That Jeep ride with Aletta Bell gave me insight into many of the issues affecting the people of India and other developing countries. Now, when I read about seemingly insurmountable global problems, I remember the unpretentious Canadian doctor who quietly brought about spiritual and physical changes in the lives of thousands of men, women and children.

Aletta Bell recently retired and returned to London, Ontario. She makes periodic visits to India and other Asian countries as an adviser to medical services. Between overseas trips, she keeps busy speaking in churches as an advocate on behalf of the people of Asia. Many will "rise up to call her blessed."

1. Figures from TRACI (New Delhi), World Bank (Geneva, 2002), *Operation World* (Paternoster, 2001).

2. 113 million to 200 million females are estimated to be demographically "missing" worldwide, due to such causes as sex-selective abortion, infanticide, child abandonment, abuse and violence, according to a report titled "Women in an Insecure World" that labels it "hidden gendercide." *The Economist*, November 24, 2005.

This selection is adapted from *Sun Like Thunder: Following Jesus on Asia's Old Silk Road Today*, copyright © 2008 by Harold Fuller (Serving in Mission/SIM).

Shards of Silence / Seasons of Hope

Non-fiction
M. D. Meyer

A little girl lies still in the night. The darkness is complete. There are no street lights outside her window; only silent trees and rocks. Even the stars are too far away to have an effect, and the moon hides its face behind the clouds.

A shard of light abruptly pierces the darkness and startles the child. The form appearing in the doorway is only a silhouette, all human features hidden in shadow.

The little girl is frozen with fear. This nightmare has come before. She knows it is useless to cry out. Her Mommy does not hear. Her Mommy does not come to rescue her.

She weeps silently as the pain and the terror overwhelm her.

The years pass slowly and the silence grows, carefully guarded and kept hidden. The untold secret...

The little girl creates a fictional world. In her stories, there is always a hero; someone who rescues the one who is being hurt.

He will come to rescue her someday.

She insulates her heart in daydreams. She insulates her body with thick layers of fat, like a sumo wrestler. No one can hurt her now.

She is a good girl, ever anxious to please. But she trusts no one.

In her religion, she strives hard to please God, who calls himself "Father," but she does not trust this love He offers her, He who calls himself "Father."

Mary's first encounter with "counselling" comes during her college years.

She gets very good grades, but her professors note her detachment from the other students. They tell her that she has "low self-esteem," and advise her to seek counselling at a nearby mental health facility.

She goes.

The woman is very adept at diagnosing. Perhaps her job is "intake" or "assessment." Her questions probe deep, slicing down through the years of protective layering. Mary answers truthfully. No one has ever asked her these questions before. But she is very nervous; the "counsellor" is dispassionate and seems almost hostile.

The session is over.

Mary is left open and bleeding as if a giant meat cleaver has torn through her.

No attempt is made to staunch the wound. That is not this woman's "job."

Another appointment is set up for Mary.

But it is the end.

Mary determines never again to open herself to another person in that way. She buries it all, puts a cement seal over the deep well of pain, and vows that it will remain shut up tight forever.

It is also at college, though, that Mary meets people whose love is so undeniably genuine that she cannot help but feel it. She goes with a college friend to her home for the weekend and is met at the door with hugs from the girl's parents. Not knowing what to do at first, Mary eventually learns to release her frozen arms and hug back.

The mirrors in her friend's house are different, too. Perhaps it is the lighting… Mary looks in their bathroom mirror and feels she is not unattractive, perhaps even pretty. Back in the home of her childhood for Christmas vacation, Mary looks in the mirror and is once again repelled by what she sees. Perhaps it is the lighting…

Mary spends all her spare time working in a rescue mission. The director is a zealous, outspoken man who has totally dedicated his life to God and to those people living on the edge of despair whom he encounters every day. Amos becomes a mentor to Mary, a kindly grandfather figure who is bold enough to tell her that she should stop attending the church that "needs her" and attend one where there might be suitable young men to date. Mary is told that she should be thinking about marriage in her future.

God uses this man and his wife, and other couples as well, to show Mary that there can be true love between a husband and a wife.

It prepares her for the man she will meet. A man who tells her, "I can't prove my love for you. You'll just have to trust me."

The decision she makes to trust him feels like a bungee jump off a cliff, but as the months and years pass, she learns to rest in his love. And she finally understands that she must take the bungee jump of faith, and trust in her Father God as well.

This could be the end of the story. It is a happy ending, complete with a loving husband and three happy and healthy little boys. It could be the end, but it isn't...

For the silence still remains unbroken and the carefully shut up room in the little girl's heart prevents her from knowing... joy. She smiles, but cannot laugh. She sings, but cannot dance. There is no carefree abandon. The dark secret only she knows still isolates and insulates her from those she loves.

One night, she goes to bed before her husband. The light is off. The darkness is complete. There are no streetlights outside her window; only silent trees and rocks. Even the stars are too far away to have an effect and the moon hides its face behind the clouds.

A shard of light abruptly pierces the darkness and startles the woman. The form appearing in the doorway is only a silhouette, all human features hidden in shadow.

She is frozen with fear. This nightmare has come before. The little girl knows it is useless to cry out. No one will hear. No one will come to rescue her.

She weeps silently as pain and terror overwhelm her.

Her husband speaks her name and puts his arms around her. Mary sobs with all the repressed pain of her childhood. Her husband comforts her.

She tells him, "Something bad happened to me when I was a little girl."

It is the beginning of her healing.

The silence has been broken.

As the years pass slowly by, there are other flashbacks and times when the subject is brought to her attention. Mary feels she is in a giant "counselling session" with her Heavenly Father. Unlike the counsellor of her college years, this Counsellor breaks through one small chink in the stone wall of her heart and then rebuilds that part into a soft but strong heart of compassion for others. This kind of healing takes time—a lot of time.

In these intervening years, Mary's life is good for the most part. Bouts of mild depression occur but don't last for long. There are some things that Mary's husband comes to accept. She insists, for example, that the bedroom door be locked at night, and even on the hottest night, Mary needs to have some covers on or she cannot get to sleep. Battles with insomnia are frequent, and finally accepted as routine. Mary sleeps best after the sun has risen. She enjoys working nightshift and can sleep well during the day, spending time with her family after they arrive home from school and work.

A child's cries upset her to an abnormal degree. She tends to be overprotective of her children, but her husband's carefree joy is infectious and their children grow up healthy and whole.

An early menopause breaks wide open the remainder of the cement wall of protection she had built over her childhood pain. At the same time, people are entering her life who are talking about child sexual abuse. They are talking out loud in meetings and in books displayed prominently on shelves. It is now permissible to mention such things.

Secretly at first, and then in company with others, Mary reads and studies and finally talks.

Prying the cement pad off the deep well of emotions is painful beyond words, but with the pain also comes joy. Mary is shocked to realize that by sealing up the feelings of sadness, she also had sealed up the emotions of joy and hope. Not allowing herself to cry all these years had also made it impossible for her to laugh.

The dam of emotions breaks. But things seem to get worse before they get better. Flashbacks, hidden memories and feelings flood over her. She awakens to the realization of how these events have affected her life. Her husband, graciously, kindly, is on the journey with her. It takes time.

People who have not seen her in a while tell Mary that she is looking younger. There is a new strength. Mary becomes more decisive, surprising her family at times with her new confidence. She had been afraid to disagree with her husband before. Now she becomes more vocal and angry words are sometimes exchanged, but the freedom of speech only deepens and strengthens their love.

The unleashing of joy comes just in time for Mary to greet her new grandchild. Mary holds the baby girl, aptly named Hope, in her arms.

And they dance and they laugh together, their joy complete.

Crisis and Character

Non-fiction

Paul M. Beckingham

"If suffering builds character, your life must have been in pretty bad shape! God gave you a dose of radical suffering to build some character in you!" says Mary, my wife. She refers to an automobile accident we had a few years ago that required more than two-and-a-half years of rehabilitation. There is a smile and some laughter in her voice, but her point is serious; character and crisis are firmly linked. Their tight connection is central to our biblical perspectives on God's transforming activity in our lives.

The apostle Paul was no stranger to suffering. He maps the crisis-and-character landscape in his lived experience. He suffered the 40 lashes minus one no less than five times; was beaten with rods three times; stoned once; shipwrecked three times; spent one night and a day treading water in the open sea; was constantly on the move; experienced danger from bandits, his own countrymen, and Gentiles; was in danger in the city, in the country, at sea, and from false brothers (2 Corinthians 11:24-26).

When such a man recounts suffering's connection to character, he has my respect—and my full attention. I hang on his every word. I'm at the stage in life where I need to see a preacher's scars; they lend authenticity to his sermon outline. Has the preacher paid her prerequisite dues, or is her ministry cheap? God calls us to the cross, not to cottage country.

The apostle shows scars aplenty. His qualifications speak of crisis and of character as he walks their steep trajectory. I long to hear faith's lessons for life, and to hear them from someone like him.

Paul draws a straight line of connectivity, a direct causality, between suffering, perseverance, character, and—oddly, at first blush—hope. God's indelible love connects those realities that operate higgledy-piggledy in a believer's experience. When I hear the apostle declare that hope lies here, it sounds like no dry Sunday School material I may have heard before. Instead, its truth rings out; it is life as I know it, in the way I need to hear it.

Writing to Christians in Rome, Paul insists: "…we also rejoice in our sufferings, because we know that suffering produces perseverance; perseverance, character; and character, hope. And hope does not disappoint us, because God has poured out his love into our hearts by the Holy Spirit, whom he has given us" (Romans 5:3-5). Hope may not disappoint us, but life often does.

In *Overcoming Life's Disappointments*, Rabbi Harold Kushner writes, "Many of us look at the world and see two sets of people, winners and losers: those who get what they want from life and those who don't. But in reality life is more complicated than that. Nobody gets everything he or she yearns for."

The rabbi is right, of course. Yet disappointment can work in our favour as we allow God to build our character. He strengthens us through our disappointments. Some, by their denial and avoidance, become bitter and twisted. Either hardship helps us grow, or we simply grow hard of heart. The Spirit of God leads us gently forward, if we will let Him. Like the blind, we must stay close behind Him, tightly holding the hand of God.

Kushner continues, "I look at the world and see three sorts of people: those who dream boldly even as they realize that a lot of their dreams will not come true; those who dream more modestly and fear that even their modest dreams will not be realized; and those who fear to dream at all, lest they be disappointed."

God gives us hope through suffering, renewing our sense of a future through crisis and pain. Through the crisis-character continuum of spiritual formation we learn to dream again, for it is the dream that takes us forward.

Some imagine that the crisis-character connection does not require their active participation, but Paul's timely corrective is "Do not be misled: 'Bad company corrupts good character'" (1 Corinthians 15:33). Keeping company with God is the key.

How does the believer handle crisis? Is it a matter of steeling oneself against the threat? Can one escape to a far country? Will friends provide the shelter from the storm? Can stout denial and stubborn refusal to admit one's problems immunize a person from pain? The answer, clearly, lies in none of the above.

Resting in Jesus, trusting God alone, and listening for the promptings of the Spirit for each step, for each new day, is the ultimate way forward. The hymn-writer Annie Johnson Flint understood this intuitively. She puts it this way in her hymn "He Giveth More Grace":[1]

> He giveth more grace when the burden grows greater;
> He sendeth more strength when the labors increase.
> To added affliction he addeth His mercy;
> To multiplied trials, His multiplied peace.

God's grace alone turns crisis into character, and His grace says, "Welcome home!"

1. Hubert Mitchell and Annie Johnson Flint, "He Giveth More Grace" © copyright 1941, renewed 1969 by Lillenas Publishing Company. Used by Permission. *Hymns of Faith and Life* (Winona Lake, Indiana: Light and Life Press and the Wesley Press, 1976).

Searching For Something That Fits

Non-fiction
Marcia Lee Laycock

There's a beach on the north shore of Lake Superior that fascinated me as a child. It was a bit hard to get to, unless you had a boat, because the only land access was up over the back of a high cliff. My brother and I made that high trek often, spending hours rock climbing and walking on the beach. For me, it was always a time of searching.

It was a pebble beach, its entire length strewn with rounded stones of all sizes and colours. My favourites were the black ones. They absorbed the heat from the sun and felt warm and comforting when I held them in the palm of my hand. I spent many days searching for the perfect stone, the stone that fit my hand as though it had been cut from it. Sometimes I was successful, but more often than not I walked away from that beach dissatisfied. I would carry a stone around for a while, but usually drop it in favour of another that looked more promising. Sometimes I'd take one home to add to my collection.

As I think back on my life since those days of childhood and adolescence, I realize much of it was spent searching in the same way. Just as I hunted for that perfect stone, so I searched for something in life that fit, something I could hold on to that would bring me satisfaction and fulfillment. I picked up a lot of stones that didn't fit: jobs, hobbies, diversions, even friends and closer relationships. All were efforts to fill the void in my life. All were attempts to find something that fit my needs. But like my search for the perfect stone on the shore, I was never totally satisfied.

It was not until many years later that I discovered I was going about it all wrong. I was trying to fit something external to my shape, my way of thinking, my way of dealing with life. It wasn't until I turned to spiritual things that I realized I was the small round stone that had fallen away and had to find its place again, in God's hand.

In John 15, Jesus tells us how to do that. He says, "As the Father has loved me, so have I loved you. Now remain in my love." He also says, "Abide in me."

Abiding is effortless. It's a simple act of rest. Jesus is saying, "Live in me. Live as though you were being held in the palm of God's hand. There is no safer place, no place that offers more comfort and peace, no place that gives more satisfaction or more sense of fulfillment."

You are the stone. Jesus is holding out His hand, waiting for you to curl up in it. It's the place where you will always fit.

Friday, 8:50 a.m., April 7, AD 30

Biblical fiction
David Kitz

*I*n *The Soldier, the Terrorist & the Donkey King*, the events of Passion Week are shown entirely from the perspective of the Roman centurion who, at the foot of the cross, bore witness to the deity of Christ. In this excerpt, Marcus Longinus finds himself in charge of the military detail leading Jesus to Golgotha, the Place of the Skull.

See to it yourselves.
Pilate's words still reverberated in my ears, setting them on fire.
See to it yourselves.
They were fine words for him to say.
Take him yourselves and crucify him.
I heard him say that earlier to the high priest, Caiaphas. Fine words indeed!

Pontius Pilate wasn't the executioner. He could wash his hands and walk off into the palace. The provincial ledger books awaited his attention.

Joseph Caiaphas wasn't the executioner. He could crow over his victory, and crow he did, as he returned triumphant to preside over his resplendent temple domain.

Herod? Herod Antipas could get back to what Herod did best, chasing and bedding women.

No, the mighty could blithely pronounce judgment and then walk off. But it fell to me and my men to execute this, their rendering of profane justice.

Justice? What justice was this?

I walked over to where Claudius stood with the beaming, exultant Barabbas. "You're a free man, Barabbas," I announced, stating the obvious.

"God be praised!" he shouted with hands uplifted. "God be praised!"

Why a just God would want this leprous dog out roaming freely defied all earthly logic. This filthy dog's joy made my blood boil!

But then the completely unexpected happened. Barabbas turned to his two comrades and suddenly his head dropped. He had led them to this fate. Now he would walk away while they bore the burden of the cross. I saw the weight of it all suddenly come crashing down on him. In an instant he caught the despair etched on Thaddaeus's face.

It staggered him.

Barabbas, the free man, pinched his eyes shut and then began to tremble uncontrollably. He sank to his knees and turned away from his brothers, his two fellow terrorists.

The weight of his responsibility was too much for him. He was free. But now it was guilt that seized him—unbearable guilt.

"Get out of here," I yelled to the kneeling figure. "Get out before I run you through."

He was a sack of wheat rooted to the stone pavement.

I let fly with a kick to his fat rump to add force to my words. My hand rested on the pommel of my sword. It took real effort to keep it there. If he hadn't moved, I would have made good my threat.

"Move!"

Slowly he picked himself up and lumbered off—a sobbing, blubbering idiot, suddenly seized with remorse.

Surely I thought, for such a man, an accident could be arranged in the dark of the night. The common Roman soldier knows a few things about justice, even if the Roman governor doesn't. At a later date we could see to him—to this bit of unfinished business. Right now, we had another bloody job to do.

Flavio, the tribune, caught my eye, then beckoned me over. "I'm heading back to the fortress now," he announced. "I'll have a dozen cavalrymen meet you at the Fish Gate. There may be a big crowd out for this one," he commented, referring to the public crucifixion. "If you need help, send a dispatch."

Without waiting for a reply he walked off.

In the meantime Claudius had three crossbeams brought out of the fortress, one for each man. The condemned would carry these to their death. In length, the *patibulum*, or horizontal crossbeams, were the span of a man's arms fully extended. I inspected these rough-hewn, squared timbers. They were notched in the center so as to fit into the similarly notched uprights now standing at the ready on Golgotha. Since crucifixions were quite common, why go to the trouble of removing the upright poles from their secure position on the hill? Besides, their public display, even in the singular empty state, served our purpose well. They acted as a deterrent for the hostile, the tempted, and the wayward. On more than one occasion, I have heard Jewish mothers warn their young sons, "Bad men end up there."

The crossbeams were reused time after time, until rot set in or the wood became hopelessly splintered due to repeated nailing, hence the need for this inspection. The first two cedar beams were showing signs of long service.

"I think these will do for today," Claudius commented. "But we should get these two replaced for the next trip to the Skull."

I nodded absent-mindedly in response, and then motioned for Thaddaeus to pick up his beam. The man we called Animal spewed curses as he shouldered his cross. The third beam was heavier and more recently put into service. It went to Jesus, the messiah king.

As Jesus stepped over to receive it, a messenger arrived. He was clutching a crumpled purple robe in his left hand. He addressed me, "Sir, the governor sent this garment. He said it belongs to the prisoner."

I took the filthy thing from him, and then flung it over to Claudius. "Tie it on him," I said in disgust.

The Christ seemed to receive it willingly. But it came on him like a weight—the weight of the world. It was his now, and every stain on it. And now royally dressed, the *patibulum* was placed upon him. The notch in the beam fit neatly over his bloodied shoulder. He staggered and swayed under it.

The condemned were ready to set off.

Setting this death procession in motion took only a few brief moments. With the final sentencing of the Christ, a more relaxed atmosphere prevailed. Part of the angry crowd began to disperse. I was now free to call on my men who had been used for crowd control. I reassigned the same pike men who had served us earlier. They would advance in wedge formation before us. Then 20 foot-soldiers were arrayed on either flank of the procession, and finally an additional half dozen pike men brought up the rear.

I specifically assigned two soldiers to guard each criminal. At the back, Claudius oversaw two soldiers with his prisoner, Thaddaeus. Then came the two guards with the Animal. Jesus led the way with two more guards escorting him on either side. I walked directly behind him. If there would be any trouble from the public, I knew it would erupt around him.

"Forward!" I shouted.

The column lurched into motion.

Jesus moved on unsteady feet. Each step seemed to be summoned with effort.

We were heading north, out through the Fish Gate. We were retracing the same route that Herod had followed on his gloriously ignoble entry on Tuesday. The very thought of him made me grimace and reflexively clench my fist in rage.

Bloody Fox! He had brought this on. In my mind he was the reason I was leading the Healer out to the Skull.

I reached down for my nail pouch. The worn leather held its grim treasure. They were there. Five inch spikes. Hard iron. Ready for use. Ready to pierce bone and flesh.

And before me the victim struggled beneath his burden. Wrong victim. Dead wrong victim. Hell's choice for a victim.

But then, where is heaven's justice in this world?

I caught sight of Renaldo as we marched past the Antonia Fortress. Strangely, it was seeing him that served to remind me that the notices had not been picked up. The notices were to be posted over the head of each crucified man. Each flat wooden board announced to the world what crime had been committed—what brought the malefactor to this wretched state.

I hastily beckoned for Renaldo to approach.

"I forgot the notices!" I cursed while gesturing my frustration with the upraised palm of my hand. "They're with the jailer in the southeast turret. You'll need to get Pilate to rewrite the notice that was meant for Barabbas."

Then, with a shake of my head and a huff, I added, "I don't know what he'll write for this man." I motioned in the direction of the stumbling messiah. With a shrug, I said, "I guess it's Pilate's problem."

"Don't worry, Marcus. I'll look after it," Renaldo confirmed. "I'll have one of my men deliver the two notices that are ready. And when the other one is ready, I'll bring it out myself." He shot a glance at my thorn-crowned prisoner. Then he pressed his lips tightly together, shook his head, and turned from me. It was his way of signalling his displeasure with this turn of events. He too would have preferred seeing the backside of Barabbas heading off to the Skull.

Barabbas! He was the reason I was on this assignment. I detest crucifixions, but for him I had made an exception. I had needed to be here to oversee his bloody ending. I owed it to the dead, to Andreas and Hermes, the men from my company that he had butchered. And I owed it to the living, the men alongside me now.

But the murdering dog walked free! Free!

I was left fuming—in a killing mood.

The wrong man trudged slowly, each step conceived and born in pain. He was mocked continually by the angry mob surging along both sides of the street.

But why had the free man buckled? Why had Barabbas folded?

His fall before Thaddaeus, just minutes earlier, reminded me of the siege of a wood pole stockade back in Germania. My twenty men and

I pushed forward, straining every muscle. Suddenly the wall gave way, and we all pitched forward and collapsed right along with it. Then the arrows showered down.

That's how he fell, how Barabbas came down. He resisted Rome, pushed against Rome, until Rome backed off. Then he fell flat on his face. Only the arrows were missing.

Or were they?

The response that a pardon can bring is well beyond understanding. But then bloodguilt has a way of fashioning its own sharp arrows.

We were advancing slowly, far too slowly. The guard to the left of Jesus barked at him, "Move your feet, Jewish dog!" He followed this up with a slap to the shoulder. It was a light enough slap, but it caught the king off balance, sending him sprawling in the dirt.

Chest heaving, Jesus struggled to get to his feet, but the crossbeam was clearly too heavy for him. After an initial attempt to rise, he sank down again.

"Halt!" I shouted up the column to the advancing pike men. Then with a backhanded jab to the guard's shoulder, I demanded, "Pick up the beam."

He obeyed with a reluctant scowl aimed at the Christ.

Jesus rose.

I silently motioned with a jerk of my head for the beam to be passed back to the king. He shouldered it once more, and advanced again on struggling feet. I could tell the effort was valiant, but from the laboured breathing I knew he had very little left to give. I was beginning to wonder if he would make it to the hill.

"Forward!"

We were soon in the market section where the evicted temple merchants had set up shop. Many of them were still there. It seemed that none missed this opportunity to jeer and heap abuse upon the man they viewed as their nemesis. I half-expected Timaeus to appear among them and lead the verbal assault. But he was nowhere to be seen.

Timaeus, the leader of the temple merchants, had disappeared. Disappeared like Barabbas.

Timaeus too had fallen. His vitriol had been silenced by Jesus. Silenced by a pardon…. A healing pardon.

The Christ stumbled again. He spilled forward like the tipping of a stone water jar.

"Halt!" I shouted once more.

Both guards shouted obscenities at him. But then they glanced my way, and moved to lift the crushing beam off his bleeding back.

He rose slowly. Street dust stuck to his sweat-drenched face and beard. A bit of yellow straw had been speared by one of the thorns in his crown. He sucked in each breath as though he was drowning. With effort, he straightened and then slumped forward again, unable to hold himself erect or assume his burden.

He drew in three more gulps of air and straightened once more. Now he was ready and the beam was shifted back to him.

"Forward!"

The Fish Gate was now within sight. He pressed onward with whatever vigour he could summon.

The crowd changed now. Here for the first time we encountered his supporters. Women. Wailing women in full anguished lament over his fate. They fell to their knees on either side of the narrow street.

Pleading. Hands outstretched. Dishevelled. Begging for his release. A pathetic sight.

Not a few were kicked or pushed aside by the soldiers on either flank. And they were incessantly heckled by the high priest's mob.

Suddenly, Jesus fell again. He had reached his limit. His collapse was complete.

I stood over the fallen wreck. It was clear that further progress at a reasonable pace would require a change in tactics.

"Halt!" I bellowed above the wailing voices.

Off to the right, behind the weeping women, I spotted a tall young man. He appeared to be making his way into the city. Here he was, a fish swimming against the current. I stepped his way, aimed my index finger at his dark-skinned face and demanded, "You! Carry his cross." With my other hand I stabbed my thumb in the direction of the fallen king.

Startled by my approach, the man took a half-step back. His eyes darted to the two boys half-hidden behind him.

His sons.

I dropped my right hand. It came to rest on the pommel of my sword. A gesture well noted by the man.

His eyes took in the whole scene.

I pumped my thumb once more in the direction of the fallen cross-carrier.

The tall man stepped forward, but the boys desperately clung to the backside of his robe. Terror marked their faces. Surely, they dreaded the worst.

"Papa! Papa!"

He nodded his willingness to comply, but then stooped before his sons to whisper some words of assurance.

The youngest boy would have none of it. "Papa!" he bawled as tears streamed freely down his face.

A twitch of my eyebrow signalled the soldier next to me to intervene. He drew his sword, and then put a hand to my conscript's shoulder. Seeing the situation take on a deadly urgency, the conscript turned from his children to assume his service.

My soldiers became a wall between him and his sons.

He was a fine choice, tall, broad-shouldered, muscular. He shouldered the crossbeam with ease.

The boys were another matter. They reminded me of my sons. They trailed along the whole way to Golgotha, crying piteously, gnawing an ever-deepening hole in my conscience.

"I'll be fine, Alexander," he shouted across to them. "I'll be fine, Rufus! I'll be fine."

They clung to one another, but seemed little comforted by their father's words.

With his burden lifted, Jesus rose to his knees. Then with gasping breaths he addressed the kneeling women just beyond the military cordon, "Daughters of Jerusalem, do not weep for me; weep for yourselves and for your children."

In fact the two boys were weeping. The women sobbed as he spoke.

But his words grew dark. "The time will come when you will say, 'Blessed are the barren women, the wombs that never bore and the breasts that never nursed.'"

Slowly struggling to his feet, he continued in ominous tones, "Then they will say to the mountains, 'Fall on us!' and to the hills, 'Cover us!' For if men do these things when the tree is green, what will happen when it is dry?"

Having let him speak his piece, I motioned him on. "Forward!"

Soon we were through the Fish Gate, and we were joined by the promised escorts on horseback. It was a very mixed throng that surged around us in the more open space. Mostly it was made up of his enemies, the men who had endured his trial. Now they would gloat over his demise. They would see this through to the bitter end.

His disciples, the men I had seen around him earlier in the week, were strangely absent. All the better from my perspective. No hostile confrontation. No need for reinforcements. Perhaps they knew better than to mess with the Roman army.

Only the women were here vainly pleading his case.

Jesus slowly limped on. He was free of the burden of the crossbeam, but not the burden of the robe.

On his own power, he limped right on up the round stone hill.

This selection is adapted from *The Soldier, the Terrorist & the Donkey King*, copyright © 2003 by David Kitz, reprinted 2004 (Essence Publishing).

A Fertile Heart

Non-fiction
Keturah Leonforde

I proceeded down the corridor of the labour and delivery ward at the pace of a snail. Step after reluctant step simultaneously brought me forward, into a friend's uncertain future, and backward, into my own tragic past.

I recalled, with remarkable clarity, a very similar hospital ward where we had received news that forever shattered the dreams my husband and I had of growing our family biologically. Although that episode had taken place seven years earlier and several cities west of my current location, the emotions that overwhelmed me as I proceeded down the hospital hallway were as raw as if it had been that very day.

But Duty has a way of calling at the most inconvenient times. As a church leader and friend of the family, I'd been notified of the arrival of our newest member. It was expected that I not only show up at the hospital, but also display joy as I congratulated the excited, anxious and admittedly inexperienced Nigerian-born parents.

Despite my best intentions, my initial response was practiced indifference. To the others present in the nursery, I likely appeared cold and heartless, but the reminder of more than seven years silently spent waging war against the misfortune of my own infertility made me momentarily forget to be concerned about "appearances."

At less than 48 hours old, the new arrival was tiny, brown and wrinkled. She looked like she had struggled for far longer than the nine months of her incubation. They told me her name translated into English meant *The Lord is my support* and—knowing she had been born to newly-immigrated parents who were struggling to adjust to a strangely isolating culture, climate and community—I whispered under my breath, *He'd better be!*

For some strange reason, since their arrival in Canada nearly a year earlier, this young family had been drawn to my husband and me. Prior to and throughout the duration of their surprise pregnancy, they had maintained mid-weekly telephone contact with us— thrusting us into an unfamiliar but not entirely unwelcome extended family role. Nevertheless, I had subtly facilitated a separation in our relationship as they transitioned into the coveted status of parents and we remained shamefully childless. As a result, over the next few days I didn't give much thought to their altered family dynamics.

Through the years, I had mastered the technique of guarding my heart against attachment to any young child, babies in particular. This strategy was designed to protect me from losing my mind within an unproductive abyss of bitterness, anger and inconsolable grief. In fact, by the time this child was born, I had mastered the art of feeling absolutely nothing. Without realizing it, the barrenness of my womb had slowly made its way to the recesses of my heart.

Little wonder then that the news of the mother's hospitalization caught me completely off guard. I briefly recalled that, somewhere between the two- and three-week mark following the birth, an urgent message had been left on my answering machine. Fortunately for me, by the time I responded to it, the "situation" had been temporarily resolved by a neighbouring friend.

At the time, I had thought it strange that a distress call would come my way but, as was my practice, I simply dismissed this information and went on with my overly-full yet unfulfilled life. At least *that* was something I knew how to do well. Between launching my consulting practice, completing course assignments, and preparing and delivering programming for numerous high-profile community and church commitments, I certainly had no time or expertise to offer to these struggling young parents. I also reasoned that their more experienced and culturally matched African-born friends would be in a far better position to provide them with support and assistance.

However, another skill I proudly possessed was a reputation for crisis management. So, upon learning of the mother's diagnosis of profound post-partum depression, I swooped into immediate action. I rallied father and neighbouring friend into an emergency think-tank session to determine what action should be taken to address this cranky, restless and temporarily motherless three-week-old bundle. Always preferring to be part of the design rather than implementation side of a solution, I prepared to offer the best of my consultation skills. I then planned to do what I did best: delegate, sending everyone on his or her way to execute my plan promptly.

My husband cautiously observed this from the background, and wisely chose to remain silent. More than anyone in the room, he was acutely sensitive to the emotional toll this situation was having on me. While on the outside I appeared calm and collected, in my mind I was seething, asking God why *I* was taxed with the role of coordinating emergency provisions for a child that was not my own. As I silently muttered my complaints, little did I know that His requirement for me would far exceed "coordination."

As our discussions and strategizing continued far into the evening, we began to run low on options for childcare. Response after response came back from culturally-matched friends and spiritually-matched church members, all with legitimate reasons why they were not able to take in this child for an undetermined period of time. Finally, we proposed that the only viable solution would be to establish a rotating schedule, shifting the infant from house to house nightly as schedules permitted. Even in my inexperience, I realized that this type of solution hardly seemed acceptable. So our discussions continued.

The evening grew darker and our options fewer. Finally, my husband called me aside for a private word. With extreme caution and, reading my face closely for any sign of rejection, he quietly suggested that perhaps we could take the child for the time being. Sensing the alarm in my eyes, he hastened to add that having overheard the discussion, he was deeply worried about the impact that house-to-house, hand-to-hand disruption would have on this tiny child. I knew he had a point—not only as a concerned friend, but even more so as a professional educator who daily witnessed the results of disruption and lack of structure on children's development.

In that private moment, I knew what we would have to do…

If anyone had told me then that the child who arrived at my doorstep that cold February evening would end up remaining in our home for the next two months, I would have requested that he or she too be hospitalized! I never dreamed, even for a moment, that I would be called upon to actually step *into* this situation as a surrogate mother, caregiver and homemaker. My valiant attempts to identify and defer caretaking accountabilities to and through other agencies had failed. Instead, I was left with a disoriented infant, a case of formula, and a diaper bag filled with colourful sleepers.

Thankfully, I also had a willing and supportive partner. His readiness to take night shifts and to assist with caretaking duty provided much-needed relief throughout the eight-week period. I also had a nearby friend who was a home-care nurse. She patiently guided me through a crash course in Infant Care 101 that commenced on the very evening the baby arrived at our home. The child's father was another key team member—although he had the daunting task of juggling time spent with his wife in the institution with time spent in the classroom and library completing final-year course work. We all recognized that much was resting on his successful attainment of his nursing degree, as it was the family's sole ticket to financial independence and future stability within "the land of opportunity."

Over the next few days and then weeks, I marvelled at how the perfectly controlled and autonomous life my husband and I shared as a couple had been shattered into indistinguishable pieces. Schedules were tossed, rooms were overturned, and social plans were cancelled to allow a single-minded focus on this high-maintenance new roommate. The same determination that characterized my approach to professional matters was now channelled into nurturing the health, stability and well-being of this tiny charge.

As our former world disappeared, slowly, but wonderfully, an infinitely more fulfilling one began to emerge. Night after restless night, I rocked this tiny one in my arms and whispered her name in the Yoruba dialect, so very different from my own. But as my lips literally called out, *The Lord is my support*, a miracle occurred. What was spoken became real, and what was broken began to heal. A lasting bond of unconditional love began to form, and the transformation soon was evident for all to see.

If I claimed that my transition to parenthood was a smooth one, I would be lying. My transition was far more imperceptible and gradual, almost mirroring the winter melting into spring outside my windows. Likely due to her rocky start in life, this child came with many challenges. As a result, I was ushered into a whole new world that included unfamiliar pediatric challenges including chest infections, digestive complications and even disfiguring facial eczema that her tiny hands simply could not resist scratching. Yet through it all, God not only proved that He was her support—He became mine too.

By the time her mom returned to health and home, my heart had grown in ways I never thought possible. After all the years of disappointment and angst, God had used a tiny, comfort-seeking bundle to touch and transform a barren, indifferent heart into a heart now bursting with passion and life...

Many months have passed since that awesome encounter. Although my womb remains empty, my heart remains full. I am thankful that God allowed me to encounter this little one. Although she cannot yet speak, when I see her brilliant smile and feel her trusting hugs for my husband and me, I am constantly reminded that keeping my heart open and welcome to human souls in need is truly what makes life worth living.

And in those times of emotional pain, disappointment or longing, which accompany birth announcements as surely as night follows day, this little one continues to remind me that I do not need to be bitter, indifferent or fearful. I can face and embrace each tiny one I meet with passion, joy and unrestricted love. I now know beyond any doubt, that my heart can remain forever fertile because *The Lord is my support.*

The topic of dealing with life's disappointments is explored more fully in *Reflections from the Waiting Room: Insights for Thriving When Life Puts You on Hold*, copyright © 2006 by Keturah Leonforde (Essence Publishing).

The Joys and Surprises of Giving

Non-fiction
Diane Roblin-Lee

Hmm. I surveyed myself from head to toe in the full-length hall mirror. *Not bad.*

That Sunday morning, my hair had turned out perfectly. I loved the way the gold highlights accented the golden brown pelts of my new fur coat. It was 1979 and animal rights activists had not yet challenged the fur industry. Slinging my tan leather bag over my shoulder, I admired its perfect match with my knee-high leather boots. I lingered in front of the mirror, turning this way and that. They would think I looked great in church today.

At last, I pulled myself away from the mirror and rushed out to the car, where my husband and two young sons were waiting. As we drove to church, I thanked God for the coat.

Luxuriously insulated from the cold windiness of the day, I enjoyed the crisp fall air as we walked from the parking lot into the church.

"Hi, Di!" It was seventeen-year-old Jana London[1] waving cheerily to me. As I waited for her to catch up, I noticed that she wore only a thin cotton bolero over her summery dress.

"Jana, you're going to freeze. Why didn't you wear your coat this morning?"

"Oh, I'm okay. I haven't got one." Quickly she changed the subject and went on to tell me about the escapades of the youth group the previous night. As she chatted, I listened, but the fact that she didn't have a coat haunted me.

However, all thoughts of Jana soon left as she went her way to look after the children in the nursery and I went my way into the sanctuary. Hoping that people were noticing my glamorous entrance, I settled into my chosen spot. But it wasn't long until Jana's mom arrived and just "happened" to sit next to me.

As the service progressed that morning, I felt a growing burden for our community. There were so many people in our town aching in their lives apart from Christ. If only they could know that all of their needs— physical, emotional, intellectual and spiritual—could be met through accepting Him and living according to His principles. I was oblivious to the words of the minister as my heart overflowed with compassion. My old friends had mocked my sudden change in lifestyle when I became a Christian. Why couldn't they understand the beauty of Jesus and His great love for each of them?

Oh God, I cried in my heart, *pour Your Spirit out upon this community. Touch people's lives with Your love and make them see Your reality. They have so many hurts and longings in their lives.* I didn't care that my perfectly applied mascara was running down my cheeks.

Jana needs a coat.

The silent words intruded upon my thoughts. I resented the sudden shift in subject and tried to return to my prayer for the community.

Oh, God, just move upon these people.

Jana needs a coat.

Again the foreign thought imposed itself upon my mind. Again I tried to reject it. *Lord, You said that it was not Your will that any should perish, but people all around me are perishing. Please make them understand,* I wept.

Jana needs a coat.

This time I knew that I had to address the thought before I could get it out of the way. I thought about my three ski jackets. Which one could I give her? Maybe the red one. I didn't wear it much, anyway.

Give her your fur coat.

Astonished, I tried to shove the offensive thought out of my mind. Perhaps I should give her my good brown cloth coat.

Your fur coat.

This time I knew that it was to be the fur. But suppose that I had misunderstood and that she really did have a coat at home? I didn't want to be giving my cherished possession away needlessly. That would be silly. *Okay, Lord,* I bowed my head in submission. *I'll ask her mom at the end of the service whether or not Jana has a coat. If she doesn't, I'll know that you want me to give this one to her.*

The congregation rose for the closing hymn. I turned to Sandra. "Does Jana have a winter coat?"

Sandra smiled in embarrassment. "Well, no. We were hoping that we might be able to afford one for her by Christmas."

"This is for her." With tears streaming down my face and an incredibly deep peace in my heart, I handed the fur to Sandra.

"What are you talking about?" she exclaimed in astonishment, her eyes wide.

"The Lord told me that I was to give this to Jana. It's hers now."

We embraced each other with tears of joy in recognition of God's love.

As I walked out of church, my husband walked up beside me and asked, "Where is your coat?"

"I don't have one."

"Well, you had one when you came in," he said in confusion.

When I explained the situation to him, he removed his sports jacket and wrapped it around me. I felt far richer leaving the church without the fur than I did entering, wrapped within it.

The next morning, Jana got on the high school bus wearing the fur coat. The other kids were in awe. "Where did you get that?" Without hesitation Jana told them that the Lord had told someone to give it to her, and the reality of God was demonstrated to all who heard.

Once that coat left my back, its value increased a thousand-fold. As instruments of our pride, our material possessions can do nothing but depreciate in value. When we release them as tools for the kingdom, they become as heaven's gold. At the time, I had no idea what God was doing; I simply acted in obedience.

Later on, I realized that I had made a specific request. I had asked God to meet the needs of people in the area, to pour out His Spirit upon them and to demonstrate His reality. I wasn't expecting an instant answer. When it came, I didn't recognize it.

God is so practical. He is not just a mystical entity who deals only in vague hopes. He is real and will meet our specific needs as we ask Him to. He cares deeply about each of us individually. In having me give Jana the coat, it was as if He was saying, "Okay, this is where we are going to begin—with this one precious girl who needs warmth and something to make her feel special to Me."

"Well, what about you?" someone might ask. "Didn't God want you to be blessed and feel special in that fur?"

God blessed me far more by asking me to give it away than He possibly could have by allowing me to keep it. He could see that it was destructive to me. Rather than being filled with His love for others that Sunday morning, my heart had been full of pride. He must have felt tremendous concern. Rather than entering the sanctuary to praise and worship Him, my desire was to receive praise and worship for myself. It was that very sin that got beautiful Lucifer kicked out of heaven. God loved me so much that He didn't want me to be separated from Him by my pride.

Sometimes the things that we value the most in this world are the most destructive to us. In His gentle way, in His perfect time, God reveals those things to us and we are given the opportunity of choosing Him or them.

My specialness did not lie in a fur coat: it lay in the fact that I was a child of God and that Jesus loved me. I didn't have to impress anyone.

"Does that mean that we're not supposed to wear fur coats or expensive jewellery if we want to live the Christian life?" someone might ask.

Not at all. Some of the greatest examples of mature Christians in scripture were wealthy people; look at Solomon, Esther and Abraham, to name a few. God truly does want to prosper His people, but He has His perfect timing. If He didn't prepare us to be able to handle His blessings, they could destroy us.

Psalm 37:4 says, "Delight yourself in the Lord and He will give you the desires of your heart." When I think of that word delight, I think of an orange fizzy float on a hot day, of a child's first lollipop, of sparkling drops of water spraying up behind a water skier, of tender passionate moments with a mate, of dreaming about my very first pair of high heels.

That is exactly the way that God wants us to think of Him; with delight at the very thought of His presence. Sometimes at night, I wake up in the dark hours and feel a surge of joy and delight at the thought of Jesus. As we immerse ourselves in Him, His desires become the desires of our hearts. We won't ask for things that are not within His will.

When God created Adam, He delighted in giving him the very best of everything. However, on the horrible day that Adam chose to disobey God, he came under the dominion of Satan. He and Eve had to flee the luxurious abundance of the garden and were forced to toil and sweat amid thorns and thistles for their very survival. They were cut off from God spiritually. Sickness and disease replaced the radiant health that they had once accepted as a matter of course.

However, God so loved His creation that He provided a way through blood sacrifices and obedience for humankind to be reunited with Him. He made a covenant with Abraham and his heirs that He would make them exceedingly fruitful. Since the resurrection of Jesus—God's provision of the perfect blood sacrifice for all time—purification of the heart comes through belief in Christ. Now, all who walk in the faith of Abraham become heirs of the promise of the covenant.

Galatians 3:29 reads, "If you belong to Christ, then you are Abraham's seed, and heirs according to the promise." Thus, we as believers step into the shoes of the heirs of Abraham.

The will has been read. We have been granted our inheritance of fruitfulness. All we have to do is receive and use what is already there for us. God's will for Adam and Abraham and all of the heirs of the promise was abundance. Since His will doesn't change, we know that His will for us is abundance in every area of our lives—body, soul and spirit! The epitome of a doting father, God loves to give abundantly to His children.

Unfortunately, as with any attractive teaching, there has been a great deal of imbalance in the prosperity message. Second Corinthians 9:11 reads, "You will be made rich in every way so that you can be generous on every occasion, and your generosity will result in thanksgiving to God." Yes, God wants to prosper His people, but it is not so that we can wallow in spoiling ourselves; it is so that we will have the resources to reach out to others. Walking in divine prosperity means walking in abundance to share. It means having enough to enable God to minister to the needs of others through us.

Although God wants us to be open-handed in sharing our blessings, we can never outgive Him. In Mark 10:29-30, Jesus says, "I tell you the truth, no one who has left home or brothers or sisters or mother or father or children or fields for me and the gospel will fail to receive a hundred times as much in this present age (homes, brothers, sisters, mothers, children and fields—and with them persecutions) and in the age to come, eternal life." In Malachi 3:10, He tells us that if we are faithful in tithing, He will throw open the floodgates of heaven and pour out so much blessing that we will not have room for it.

Thus, if we are delighting ourselves in the Lord as we faithfully and cheerfully give our tithes and offerings, we know that He will give us the desires of our hearts.

When we moved from Quebec to Ontario, we invested the profit from our large Montreal home into an audio-visual production studio. The career opportunity was wonderful, but it meant sacrificing our large home for a much smaller one. I didn't mind at first because we thought that it was just a temporary measure until the business began to boom. However, as the expected two years stretched into eight, I became extremely frustrated with the crowded conditions. Our family was growing and there was no space to entertain large groups of people and host meetings.

I prayed fervently that God would supply the perfect home for us. My dream was a large rambling side-split home with a big fireplace and spacious lawns. I made a new prayer list. I wrote, "a large, five-bedroom home" because, having written my first book on the dining-room table, I wanted the fifth bedroom for an office. I added "well-appointed." After writing "well-appointed," I rubbed it out, thinking that perhaps I was getting too materialistic and shouldn't be asking God for luxuries!

When I found a great buy on a ping-pong table, I made the purchase in faith that we would soon have a home large enough for it, and we stored the table in the garage. However, months passed and we were still stuck in our little house. Finally, one day, in tears of frustration, I submitted to God's admonition to us to be content with such things as we have (Hebrews 13:5). With hands uplifted, I said, "Lord, if this is where You would have me serve You, then I am willing to stay in this little house for the rest of my life. All that I ask is that You take away this terrible feeling of being so closed in all of the time."

Just outside of town, there was a beautiful, nine-year-old home that I had admired every time that I passed it. It was about four times the size of our house. Owning it was just a dream, because it was far beyond our reach financially. Tragically, one day it burned.

For about a year it sat forlornly as the bank, insurance company and owners battled about the circumstances of the fire. Finally, one evening as my husband and I were driving by, we noticed a "For Sale" sign on the property and excitedly called the real estate agent to investigate. The house had been burned enough to make a massive clean-up job, but there was no structural damage beyond a missing floor in one of the bedrooms.

I fell in love with it. Beyond the charred ruins, I saw the wonderful potential in the ten-foot-wide hallways, the once-grand chandelier and the massive rooms. As we stood on the back deck with the real estate agent, I gazed at the fields and the apple trees and the woods and felt the gentle peace of God all about me. Fifty acres of land came with the house.

We offered the same amount as we put on the asking price of our little house. I enrolled the children in the new school in faith that our offer would be accepted. Every day I drove them to the new house to catch the bus—in spite of the fact that we wouldn't know for a month if we were the successful purchasers, and there were nine other sealed bids!

One month later I walked out of the lawyer's office with the key in my hand. We went directly to our burned home and walked through every room, asking God's blessing on each nook and cranny.

How could I begin to enumerate the gifts of God in this home? It was full of lovely furniture, dishes and all sorts of things that just needed to be cleaned up. The owners had removed many things but had left about as much as they had taken. I had asked the Lord for a new set of cooking pots because I didn't feel that we could afford them. I opened a cupboard door and there they were—a beautiful set of pots. All I had to do was wash off the smoke. Besides space for the ping-pong table, there was a pool table already in place!

God even supplied the workmen to do the renovations. A friend had just returned from a missionary stint in the Philippines and agreed to do the major part of the restoration. As we needed things, God supplied bargains and people step-by-step. Finally the time came when everything was all cleaned up. Every crystal of the chandelier glistened. There was no trace of any fire.

That gentle voice spoke again. *It's time to offer all of these goods back to the owner.*

What? I cried in my heart. *I've worked so hard, Lord. All of these things are mine now!*

What is of higher value, these earthly things or souls for My kingdom?

And so one day, I called the former owner and invited her over for coffee. After showing her all through the house, I told her how the Lord had instructed me to offer anything back to her that she would like to have. I explained how I knew that He loved her in a very special way and why we had committed our lives to Him. She listened politely and firmly refused to take anything back, saying that we deserved it after all of our hard work. I have no idea what happened as a result of that obedience except that my heart was at rest.

God used that house in a wonderful way. While He blessed us with the privilege of living in it for 28 years, His purposes in giving it to us were much wider than spoiling us with His love. It became a regular meeting place for Bible studies, Full Gospel Business Men's gatherings, women's groups, youth gatherings, children's parties, weddings, and retreats. We knew that if we were to begin hoarding our blessings for ourselves, they would eventually destroy us and we would lose them.

If we don't give, we will become useless. Even in the natural world, the principles of receiving and giving are clearly evident. For instance, in the Middle East, the water from the mountains in Lebanon flows into the Sea of Galilee and the Dead Sea. The Sea of Galilee is healthy and prosperous, full of life. The water flows from its source in the mountains, through the Sea of Galilee and on out to the Jordan River. Because it both receives and gives, it is a source of abundance for many.

The Dead Sea, on the other hand, is a stagnant body of water where very little life can survive. The water from the mountains is received, but not passed on. It simply evaporates slowly. Because there is no giving, the Dead Sea is truly a sea of death.

In the same way, what we receive from God must have an outlet so that we can pass on our blessings to others.

"Well, that's great for you," some may say, "but what about Christians in countries where there is famine or war? They would probably like to have nice big homes and chandeliers too. So, if the Bible is supposed to be true for all people, where's the equality?"

Abundance is relative. What may be abundance to me is not abundance to Bill Gates or Oprah Winfrey. What would be abundance to someone in a prison camp might mean very little to me in my circumstances.

Giving is grace that flows naturally out of a heart dedicated to the love of God. You can give without loving—but you can't love without giving. When you take the risk of giving what Christ asks you to give, God will honour you. He will give grace to enable you to give whatever He may ask.

God asked Abraham to give his precious son. In obedience, and carried along by the strength of God's grace, Abraham made preparations to do that very thing. When the condition of his heart became clear both to himself and to God, God made provision for a less costly gift.

With Himself, however, our Heavenly Father was not so tender-hearted. When the sacrifice of His own Son was required for our salvation, He gave without question the most precious gift He could give. "Thanks be unto God for His unspeakable gift" (II Corinthians 9:15).

1. Names have been changed.

Where Have All the Mothers Gone?

Non-fiction
Thomas Froese and Jean Chamberlain Froese, MD

> We are one, after all, you and I.
> Together we suffer.
> Together we exist.
> And forever will recreate each other.
> –Pierre Teilhard de Chardin, 20th-century French philosopher

For men, there really is no knowing what motherhood is all about.

Before I met my wife, an obstetrician who has delivered too many hundreds of babies to count, the above quote was about as close as I could get to that mystery of bringing new life into the world. My own mother died when I was a boy, and years later I found that de Chardin's verse held something of what I imagined was motherhood, at least on a certain esoteric level.

Since then, awed and a little fearful, I've twice watched Jean labour in childbirth. And, as a journalist who has lived in the developing world for seven years, I've had some experiences that only add to those feelings—especially the fear.

Once, while Jean and I lived in Yemen, an impoverished Arab nation where women have, incredibly, a one-in-eight chance of dying in childbirth, I talked with young Ramzy, a bright and caring enough newspaper office colleague whose wife was about to deliver.

"When are you leaving to be with your wife?" I asked.

"After the delivery," he said.

He was three hours away from his pregnant wife. She was a week overdue, and having complications. Concerned, Jean offered to help with an induction or C-section, if needed.

Ramzy assured us that his wife Wedad had a doctor. Besides, he said, "It's better if she delivers naturally, isn't it?"

No, it's better not to risk her life and the baby's. And it's better if you're with your wife, regardless of your culture's ways.

Thankfully, Yemeni medics induced Wedad, and all went fine in her delivery of a baby boy. But this, I've learned, is how women in the developing world die: at the quiet hands of ignorance.

More recently, here in Uganda where Jean and I and our two young children Elizabeth and Jonathan now live, I had a more personal scare. A friend of ours, Alice, was delivering. Jean was out of the country, ironically at an international conference on maternal mortality. Still, I felt good after ensuring Alice had arrived at a clinic safely, with the gloves, buckets and cotton-batting that Ugandan mothers are required to bring.

But later, Alice called me. "Mr. Thom," she screamed, in horrific pain, from her mobile phone into mine. "The baby's not coming out." In a surreal 911 moment where anyone can now relay his or her own death via mobile telephone, I knew Alice could be perishing in childbirth, just as 6,000 Ugandan women do every year.

She survived, as did Baby Divine. And we're thankful. But in the developing world, such is everyday experience—always somewhere on the fine line that separates life and death.

Here's another all-too typical story about another Ugandan woman, Charity, told by Jean.

Charity hoped for a quiet delivery, with just her mother and sister beside her in her small African hut. She would hear the roosters crowing and the dogs barking in the distance, just as she always had.

The 18-year-old tried to imagine what giving birth was like, but that was difficult. People told her different things. Some women said that the discomfort was mild and the sense of fulfillment was wonderful. Others told her hair-raising tales that sent cold shudders racing down her back. Who should she believe? There was not much time to decide. She would soon be in labour.

The sun was setting, the crickets were chirping, and the fires around the little hut were shimmering with heat as she began to feel the early pains. No rest tonight; it would be a "night of labour."

Charity called for her mother, who was overjoyed by the news. This would be her first grandchild. The generations were starting to multiply, thanks be to God!

Her mother quickly shooed away the men, and then waited patiently for labour to start in earnest. She knelt beside her daughter and laid her hand on her abdomen. "These are good tightenings, my dear child," she said. "You must be strong and deliver this baby with courage." She kissed the perspiring brow of her young daughter.

Midnight came and went, and the contractions intensified. But the baby was not coming out. "Mother, what is the matter? I am trying to be brave. What more can I do?" Charity cried.

"I fear your baby may be coming out buttocks first. Remember, the midwife warned about this at your last visit. She said we should go to the hospital for your delivery. I did not think that it was necessary then. The hospital will want money, and even the transportation is more money than we have."

Charity grimaced at the next contraction, then asked, "Mother, is it too late? Can we still go to the hospital?"

"Remember your sister. The doctor said that she needed a Caesarean birth. I will never forget my last sight of her, wheeled on the stretcher towards the operating theatre through the large white swinging doors.

"They told me later that she died from the needle in her back that was meant to give her pain relief. I never knew if I should believe their story. The one thing I know for sure is that I brought in a living daughter and carried out a dead one. I fear the hospital and all who work there."

Still, she reluctantly placed her labouring daughter on the back of a neighbour's motorbike. The ride to the hospital, three miles away, was rough, but she braced her daughter between the driver and herself. Three silhouettes without helmets sped through the night in the direction of the small government hospital.

The night watchman met them at the gate and said he would tell the midwife that they were there. The doctor's shift had ended at 5:00 p.m. The hospital was mostly dark, and silence hung like a sheet as they hobbled to the labour area. The midwife found Charity a bed and confirmed the earlier midwife's diagnosis and her mother's fear: the baby was indeed a breech.

However, it seemed to the midwife that Charity was doing okay so far. Her cervix was two centimetres dilated, with eight more to go. Her frail mother sank into the cold steel chair just outside the room. She would not be able to deliver her grandchild herself, but perhaps this hospital visit would not be tragic, like the last one.

Two more hours passed. Water from the birth sac continued to flood everywhere. Surely, Charity would deliver soon. The new day awoke. No baby, no new life, just ongoing pain. Worse, the contractions seemed to be lessening.

A new crew of midwives took charge of the labour and delivery ward. Charity was re-examined. Not much change was noted. She was only three centimetres dilated. This was not good.

The labour and delivery ward was busy. Women came and went, delivering their babies and then leaving. It was now three days since Charity had presented in early labour. She did not move much now. Her water had been broken during this entire time, which meant that she was dangerously exposed to bacterial infection, and a fever had started.

The midwife seemed relieved that Charity's labour picked up on the fourth day, and it was not long before she was nine centimetres dilated. Despite the many examinations, very little had been written on the chart that hung still at the end of her bed.

Another change of shift, and another examination. She was so close to delivery, why not get the process started? The midwife told her to start the pushing motion. She puffed up her face and gave the mightiest blow she could muster. "That's not hard enough," the midwife snapped. "Give it all you've got and then a little more."

After an hour and a half of the strongest effort Charity could muster, she delivered her newborn son's buttocks and legs. A look of panic appeared on the midwife's face. It reminded Charity of her mother's look a few days before. What was the matter? The baby was nearly out—she would give all she could to get his precious little head out.

Despite her valiant effort, the head wouldn't budge. For a long time, the dangling little body struggled, as if to wiggle out. But after four hours of partial delivery, no life was left in him. The midwife continued to pull and tug on the body. It was like a key stuck in the lock.

For Charity, it was a nightmare she could not awaken from: a lifeless body trapped between her legs.

Charity was exhausted. And her heart was broken. Was there no one who could help her? The midwife was paralyzed with fear. Why didn't the doctor come?

The midwife announced, "I have made arrangements for you to be transferred to another hospital. It is a mission hospital just ten miles away. There is a doctor there who specializes in maternity. He is called an 'obstetrician.' I will send for the ambulance."

The cloud of dust behind the old ambulance was the only thing Charity remembered from the glum ride. The twinkling stars seemed to taunt her. They drove through the whitewashed gate and entered the hospital compound. This time, things seemed a bit better. Lights flickered in the maternity ward. A midwife from the labour and delivery ward greeted them at the door, and assured them that the doctor would be coming soon.

By now, Charity's mind was wandering. The face of her mother was blurred and horribly distorted. She wondered where her sister was. Shouldn't she be here?

A plump *Mazungu* (meaning "white") doctor with glasses and white coat appeared. Charity could not understand his quiet words, but he seemed gentle and caring.

The baby's legs still lay motionless between the young mother's legs.

After giving her some medication to dull the pain, he delivered the baby's head with instruments that looked like large metal spoons. But by now, she hardly noticed what was happening.

Intravenous fluids and antibiotics were pumped through the young girl's veins. But delirium was overtaking her, and she attempted to pull out the lifeline. Apart from that, she was too weak to even lift her head. Her mother, who slept on the floor on a wool blanket, began to worry that she would slip into eternal rest. She knew by the frequent visits from the nurse that things were not looking good. She dared not ask what was happening. She could only sit and pray that the night would not steal yet another life from her family.

Once again, the doctor returned. Charity was strangely still. Beads of sweat lay on her brow. The intravenous fluid continued to flow from the suspended jar.

He approached the bedside and laid his hand upon Charity's chest. He waited and hoped. He reached into his pocket, and withdrew his stethoscope. He laid it over young Charity's heart. Then he gently placed his instrument back into his pocket, and his hand moved slowly towards Charity's mother. He rested it on her head-covering.

Words were not needed. His eyes told her. Her daughter's life was over.

Charity's mother had done all she could. She did not understand the medical term for the cause of her daughter's death: overwhelming sepsis, or infection.

Perhaps she did not clearly realize that the mismanaged care at the first hospital had contributed to her death. What she did know was that safe motherhood was not a priority in her country. She had two dead daughters to prove that.

She started for her village that night. There was no telephone, so she could not call to tell her husband and son-in-law the terrible news in advance. She wondered whether they would even believe her. Charity had been working in the field just a few days ago. Well, they would have to believe her, because they would have to go and collect her body.

Of one thing she was certain: intense wailing and tears would soon shatter the African night.

Of course, Charity's story is just one of many, and most are never told. Millions of mothers perish silently. In fact, from the time you have your morning coffee today until the same time tomorrow, some 1,450 women—most of them in sub-Saharan Africa and Asia—will die from totally preventable complications of childbirth. That's three jumbo jets filled with pregnant women quietly crashing to earth, every day—or 525,000 mothers every year.

This often surprises Westerners who have advantages of modern health care. In a typical Canadian city, one mother dies for every 4,000 births. In the developing world, the rate can be 150 times more. Often it's nearly impossible for women to reach a clinic. Sometimes families refuse medical care because of the cost, or cultural misconceptions. One in four of these mothers simply bleeds to death.

Those who do survive prolonged labour are at risk to develop a fistula, a hole between the rectum and vagina that causes chronic incontinence. The leaking urine and feces leave these women with such an unbearable smell that they become social lepers. Obstetric fistulas are almost entirely preventable, yet affect about two million women in the developing world. Incredibly, the surgical procedure to repair the fistula was developed in the 1850s. Yet it's simply out of reach for many.

Jean can tell you scores of other stories. There's Geraldine, whose "two year pregnancy" turned out to be an ovarian cyst; there's Faithful, who, with terrible results, bowed to social pressure to deliver naturally after two "unnatural" Caesareans; there's Juliette, the Ugandan dwarf whose first pregnancy presented extraordinary challenges.

Imagine a pregnant woman strapped onto a wobbly motorcycle, travelling a bumpy, dirt road for 30 kilometres, the only way to a clinic. Picture giving birth while guns of war rattle outside your hut. Or having, like Charity, the body of your half-born child dangling, lifeless, between your legs, in a breech delivery that could have been avoided with proper care.

Charity's story is among the true accounts in Jean's book, *Where Have All the Mothers Gone?*, a series of vignettes about mothers in developing countries. The title deliberately mirrors "Where Have All the Flowers Gone?," the anti-war song by the '70s folk group Peter, Paul and Mary. So, yes, where have all the mothers gone?

In the twentieth century, more women died in childbirth than soldiers died in either World War. Why, in the information-saturated West, haven't we heard more about this? Why haven't more Westerners been made aware that during the two decades between 1980 and 2000, more women—about 12 million—died from childbirth than from AIDS? Why haven't more of us been outraged that more than half of these "women" are between the ages of 13 and 24, many of them girls barely out of the playground?

One reason is, unlike other global tragedies such as AIDS or child hunger, this issue hasn't been given a much-needed personal face. No film icons or entertainers have campaigned to save the world's neediest mothers. No rock stars speak out on their behalf. Even Western feminists, who historically have fought so hard for other rights for women, have been silent. I wonder if this is partly because motherhood isn't the West's highest priority. Cheering "Rah, rah motherhood!" in fact, might be rather unpopular, cutting against post-modern Western values of independence and freedom.

Fortunately, there are good news stories, too. Consider Sylvia Ssinabulya, a Ugandan parliamentarian who knows first-hand the dangers of childbirth in Africa. Two of her four deliveries were breech, one with the baby's umbilical cord wrapped dangerously around its neck. "But I had a doctor for one, and a midwife for the other. If not," she told me, "I could have lost my life."

Sylvia knows that the largest single cause of mothers dying in childbirth is lack of a skilled attendant. But in places where life hangs by a thread, even that is no guarantee of a successful delivery. She tells of her own sister-in-law. "She said she was hungry, and then she complained of stomach pain. Thirty minutes later, the midwife checked in on her and she was dead."

Sylvia, an influential politician, is now a champion for maternal rights.

In Uganda, a mushrooming African nation with about the same current population as Canada, women have, on average, seven children—pushing the projected population to 180 million by 2050. Recently, Sylvia was able to get money allocated for maternal health in Uganda's budget for the first time. She's also mobilized three dozen other Members of Parliament to form the Ugandan Women Parliamentarian Association, which is focusing on finding solutions for the various needs of their country's mothers.

In the summer of 2007, Sylvia travelled to Canada to speak with Ottawa's parliamentarians and other advocates about these huge issues. Then she went to the U.K. to attend Women Deliver, the same international conference Jean was attending during that frightening delivery of our friend Alice.

How has this happened? Sylvia—and this is the good news story—has become one of the Uganda's emerging champions for maternal health because she enrolled in a new Master's degree program in Public Health Leadership sponsored by Save the Mothers (*www.savethemothers.org*). Launched in 2005 at Uganda Christian University, near Uganda's capital of Kampala, the program incorporates a groundbreaking multi-disciplinary approach, and is open to both medical and non-medical professionals. Students such as Sylvia represent the revolution that's possible.

Think of "training the trainer." Teach indigenous leaders—politicians, educators, lawyers, journalists and social services professionals—to understand why their women are dying; then send them back into their spheres of influence to initiate broader societal change. New attitudes. New infrastructures and networks. New futures.

Jean founded the Save the Mothers organization (which is part of a Canadian charity called Interserve) and created the Master's degree program because her experience had convinced her that an innovative strategy was needed to generate grassroots change. International debate, such as took place at the Women Deliver conference, tends to verify problems we already know exist, rather than explore and implement new solutions.

Of the 68 people now enrolled in the Save the Mothers program, four are Ugandan Members of Parliament. Another, a local politician who governs 40,000 people, is mobilizing women's groups in his villages. A teacher educates teens about the importance of avoiding pregnancy. A national newspaper journalist informs readers. Other participants are using their vocations in radio, a vital communications medium in a country with high illiteracy.

"We in the West don't have all the answers, but people in their own cultures can make it happen if they want to," notes Jean. "Even in the West, there's been change. Three generations ago, our rate of maternal death during childbirth was 10 times higher than now."

Save the Mothers is planning to duplicate this approach in neighbouring developing countries, while making the Ugandan location both a regional and international training centre.

Training hundreds of developing world professionals may seem like a drop in the ocean of battling maternal mortality, this under-reported global blight that's been called "the last unreached frontier of modern medicine." But on the long journey to create safety for the world's mothers, on-the-ground torch-bearers like Sylvia, and supporters who give them resources, do give some real hope.

I'll never forget, shortly after I got to know Jean, seeing her weep for women whom she'd never met. She knew that the poorest women in the world's forgotten villages have no voice in the global agenda. In fact, Jean's parents tell me she was just a little girl when she first announced her desire to "be a doctor for poor people far away." That would have been about the time my own mother died, the summer before I started Kindergarten.

Today, others are hearing the stories and shedding their own tears for the world's dying mothers. A couple of Canadian business leaders, men who are supporting this work, equate the human rights violations of these mothers to the slavery confronted by William Wilberforce, the

British Parliamentarian who, after decades of struggle, saw abolition become reality 200 years ago.

"I see this (Save the Mothers) as a 'Wilberforcian' moment in time, and I want to be part of it," one of these men told me.

"One reason that many African women are dying in agony on dirt floors in mud huts during childbirth, is because they're denied the right to seek basic medical help," said the other. "The question is, do we believe that allowing African women to die because they lack basic human rights is as outrageous as having African men chained to slave ships, moved across the ocean, and sold into slavery?"

Having observed men in developing nations, I don't think most of them intend to hurt or kill their wives, or sisters, or daughters. Like my Yemeni friend Ramzy, they simply don't realize how big a difference their attitudes can make.

Concurrently, too many Westerners assume little can be done because, "It's just the way things are."

So—like Charity—more mothers will die agonizingly and needlessly. But with these new voices, something is stirring. Maybe the tragic stories of the world's mothers are now growing so deep and so wide that, like rushing water, they're building into a great force.

If so, the reality of Pierre de Chardin's verse—that "we are one, living together, suffering together, and forever re-creating each other"—will become more meaningful to more people. We'll realize that even mothers on the other side of the ocean are our neighbours. And more modern-day disciples will truly practice The Way that Jesus showed so beautifully to the disadvantaged women of His own world.

Parts of this selection are adapted from *Where Have All the Mothers Gone?*, copyright © 2004 by Jean Chamberlain Froese (Epic Press/*www.savethemothers.com*).

Mama Nellie

Non-fiction
Paul M. Beckingham

*M*ama Nellie cleaned house for missionaries in Kenya. For a few months, while we were at language school, she cleaned our cottage. We lived in a tiny unit of accommodation. It was aptly called *Pango*—the cave.

Pango was tiny. And with seven of us (Mary and I have five offspring), we filled it to capacity. Our days—Mary's and mine—were taken up with language study and with ferrying children back and forth to Nairobi to their mission school. Mama Nellie's help was greatly appreciated.

Mama Nellie's real name was Phanice. Like all Kenyan mothers, she took her title by combining "Mama" with the name of her (usually first-born) child. Nellie was a lively three-year-old. She loved to play at our house with Tiger, the stray ginger cat that found its way to us on most days of the week.

Mama Nellie is a Christian believer—and a wise woman. She is full of information for greenhorn missionaries. In her opinion, none of them know how to carry on the simple business of life—at least not in an East African setting. She was able to put us all right. And she frequently did.

She taught us the rudiments of food hygiene—which food goes with which. It all depends, she said, on whether the food is "hot" or "cold." These are the two basic classifications into which all food (don't you *know* that?) may be categorized. East Africans believe that all foods have inherent characteristics that either will heat you up or cool you down, regardless of their temperature.

"Bwana," she said, "if a missionary doctor comes to a village, the elders will ask him many questions."

"What will they ask him?" I inquired.

"First, they will ask him, 'If a man is sick with a fever, is he allowed to eat eggs?' And if the doctor says 'Yes,' then they will know that he knows nothing. *Everybody* knows that you are not allowed to eat eggs if you have a fever. How can an *mzee*, an elder, trust a doctor who does not know the simplest of things?"

Mama Nellie knew that she had much to teach us about the ways of wisdom in Africa. Our open jaws and rapt interest betrayed our ignorance. Clearly, like the good doctor in her illustration, we knew precisely nothing. Nothing, that is, that was really worth knowing.

To give Mama Nellie her dues, she *did* know *a lot* about living. One day, however, it was Mama Nellie's turn to stand open-mouthed.

It happened, as all good conversations happened, in our little kitchen. Mama Nellie was at the stove showing Mary how to make *dengu*. *Dengu* is a delicious meal of lentils mixed into a tomato-and-onion sauce poured thickly over rice and served with Mama Nellie's magnificent home-made chapattis, a warm, round flatbread.

Their conversation turned to childbirth. A woman in the village had just delivered her baby.

"It was a difficult birth with much pain!" announced Mama Nellie. "It is different for you mzungu, white women."

"How do you mean, *different*?" asked Mary.

"Well, everybody knows," started Mama Nellie, with that note of authority in her voice, "everybody knows that *wazungu* women do not have pain in childbirth!"

Coughing over her mug of *chai*, a sweet milky tea made with cardamom, Mary spurted, "Pardon me?"

Mama Nellie pardoned her. Then she repeated her well-known fact.

Now, Mary freely admits that she knows very little about all kinds of things—like rocket science, nuclear physics or the Romantic Poets of the fourteenth century. But childbirth? Let's just say that Mary has given birth to five children—one at a time. That might qualify her to comment. She does, after all, have some unfair insider knowledge when it comes to trading in the marketplace of childbirth.

"Ooooh…" Mary said very slowly. "Tell me more about how white women give birth to children."

"Well," said Mama Nellie, "It's so easy for you. You're just able to squat. And out comes the baby, alive and well—and there is no pain for you. It's as easy as coughing."

"Really?" said Mary. "When I was a girl, growing up in England, we heard the same story."

Mama Nellie suddenly looked interested.

"Only," Mary continued, "we heard that it was African women who could just sit down beside a tree and give birth. They do not, we were told, need any help from other people. And they do not have any pain. None."

Now it was Mama Nellie's turn to be open-jawed and wide-eyed in wonderment.

"No, ma'am," she began, "you are telling me a joke."

"I am telling you the truth," said Mary.

As a strange new angle of vision opened up for Mama Nellie, she paused. She was deep in thought. Then, with her big warm smile beaming at Mary, she shared her wisdom.

"Maybe we should not believe the lies that people tell about each other. It makes it hard for us to understand other people."

"Mmm…" said Mary, "I think you may have a point."

You can learn a lot in Africa about the art of living well.

Will My Baby Die Without Me?

Non-fiction
Grace Fox

"Congratulations! You have a girl," announced our midwife, Margaret Brass, after my Caesarean section on Tuesday morning, March 19, 1985. But instead of allowing my husband Gene or me to see or hold the baby, she and a pediatrician whisked her to an examination table across the operating room.

From where I lay, I caught a glimpse of the baby's head. It looked like a swollen melon, much too large for her wee body. *Something's very wrong*, I thought. At that moment the surgeon began stitching my incision, tugging and jerking the thread. No one spoke.

I cast a glance toward Margaret and the pediatrician but saw only their backs as they huddled over our baby. *Why doesn't someone tell us what's going on?* I wondered. The jerking and tugging sensation escalated until I felt I'd lose my mind.

"I can't handle this!" I cried. "Put me out!" Within seconds, the anesthesia put me to sleep.

When I awoke an hour later, Gene was sitting beside me and stroking my cheek. "We're going back to the States," he said softly. "We're leaving Kathmandu as soon as possible."

"Why?" I asked. I tried to make sense of his words through my mental fog.

"The baby has massive hydrocephalus—excess water on the brain," he explained. "She needs a shunt in her head to drain the fluid and reduce the risk of brain damage. Doctors can't do that type of surgery here."

The situation was serious. Our location complicated matters. We lived in Nepal, one of the world's poorest countries. Neurosurgery was impossible without modern medical technology. Returning to the United States—my husband's homeland—was our only option. The trip would be anything but easy: we lived 12 hours from Kathmandu's international airport. The winding mountain roads made travel difficult at the best of times.

We'd worked for the United Mission to Nepal (UMN) since 1982. Gene, a civil engineer, was involved with a hydroelectric power project. I taught basic health care and literacy. Our blue-eyed, blond 20-month-old toddler Matthew entertained the Hindu villagers with his chatter and antics. We'd committed our lives to serving these people whom we'd grown to love. Now this.

Hours passed, and my mental fog slowly lifted. This wasn't just a bad dream. It was real, the climax to a nagging uneasiness I'd carried throughout the pregnancy. Each time I prayed for a healthy child, I felt as though someone put a finger across my lips and shushed my request. I'd experienced none of this during my first pregnancy. I expressed my concern to Margaret several times during the pregnancy, but without the necessary medical equipment, our unborn infant couldn't be checked. The intuitive sense that my baby had special needs grew stronger as the months passed, and several occurrences helped prepare me for the blow.

One afternoon four months prior, Gene and I met a woman plodding up a steep path, carrying her unconscious five-year-old son. His head seemed massive compared to his limp body.

"What's wrong with him?" I asked.

The woman's eyes filled with tears. "The doctors in America (referring to the UMN hospital about two hours away) can't help him. I'm taking him home to die," she said.

I described the child's appearance to Margaret at my next pre-natal appointment. "He probably had hydrocephalus," she said.

"Hydro *what?*" I asked.

"Hydrocephalus. The brain produces cerebral fluid that circulates down the spinal column. If the neural tube is blocked during the embryo's development, the fluid remains in the head and causes it to swell. The condition requires neurosurgery to insert a shunt into the head so the fluid can drain into the abdominal cavity. Can't be done here with our limited facilities."

As Jesus' mother pondered the angel's words in her heart when he told her that she would bear God's Son, so I pondered Margaret's words in my heart. I just *knew* they bore significance.

One month after meeting the mother and child, the UMN's economic development board asked Gene to consider directing the Tansen hospital reconstruction project. If he said yes, we would have to move from our village.

In our early months of village life, we gladly would have abandoned our mud-and-rock, grass-thatched house to live in a brick home with glass windows, electricity, and running water. But not now. Our hearts had bonded with our villagers.

"No, thanks," Gene said.

"Please reconsider," came the reply.

We did. "No thanks," Gene said.

An urgent message arrived a few days later: "We need you in Tansen. Please come." We reluctantly left our remote mountain village and moved to a house next door to the mission hospital. We now had access to phone lines and medical help.

Several days before the birth, Gene's mom, Betty Fox, had arrived from Washington State to lend a hand with the new grandchild. For two years, she'd tried to visit us. Each time she made plans, however, circumstances prevented her from coming. This time her arrangements were trouble-free.

I remembered a conversation while waiting for Grandma's arrival. "What will we do if this baby has special needs?" I'd asked Gene.

"Love him or her all the more," he replied with quiet confidence.

News spread quickly of Stephanie's birth and her health concerns. Coworkers scrambled to help. Another UMN engineer assumed Gene's responsibilities. Friends began placing phone calls to arrange our flight back to North America. That night, three UMN women took shifts at my bedside so Gene could care for Matthew and get a decent sleep. As the hours dragged by, those women prayed with me, spoke encouraging words, and cuddled Stephanie.

I was exhausted, but sleep was impossible. I shared a hospital room with three Nepali women, one of whom cried in pain from burns suffered when her sari caught fire as she cooked over an open flame. A bare light bulb shone overhead all night—the women and their family members at their bedsides were frightened by evil spirits they believed to be hiding in the dark.

Wednesday morning dawned and friends carried me on a stretcher to our house. I rested on our bed while Stephanie slept in a wicker bassinette nearby. Morphine lessened my physical pain from the Caesarean section but nothing numbed my thoughts. *What will happen to Stephanie? Where will we live? What about a job for Gene?*

Mid-afternoon, Gene entered the bedroom and sat down beside me. "I have some bad news," he said. "There are two flights leaving Kathmandu in the next week. The first flight has only two empty seats left. Obviously that won't work for us. But there's a bigger issue at stake: The airline won't allow you to travel because you've just had surgery and are considered a high medical risk. Besides, the airline doesn't want a baby less than a week old on board their planes."

His words nearly knocked the breath out of me. "You've got to be kidding!" I cried. "They can't do that! Stephanie needs help! How will we get her home?"

"I'll take her," he said. "You'll travel with Mom and Matthew six days from now."

"You can't take her without me," I gasped. "I'm nursing her!" Tears spilled down my cheeks. I wanted to yell, "Fix it!" but the strain on Gene's face made me hold back. In the midst of great difficulty, he was doing his best to get our family through this.

"It's the only way," he whispered, taking me in his arms. "God's in control. We can trust Him."

My head told me he was right. My heart disagreed.

Eight months earlier, Matthew had almost died from a mysterious virus. For a week we watched and prayed as his little body fought back. I'd hurled angry words at God then. "We've given up so much for You! Serving You isn't worth it!"

His response was gentle. "I gave up my Son because I love you. Please trust me in this."

I thought I'd learned the lesson well. I was wrong. My heart screamed while circumstances dragged me into the dark unknown. *Not again, Lord! This time You've gone too far!*

Thursday morning, amid tearful good-byes with coworkers, we climbed into a Land Rover headed for Kathmandu. Margaret cradled Stephanie while Gene and Betty took turns holding Matthew. I rested on a mattress on the floor. Oblivious to the seriousness of the situation, Matt squealed with delight when buses rumbled by. His innocent joy broke the silence and eased the tension. Twelve hours of twists, turns, and potholes later, we rolled to a stop in front of a UMN guesthouse. The hostess ran to our vehicle before we climbed out.

"You need a passport picture for the baby," she said. "A photo studio is staying open for you." Exhausted after the long day, Gene and Margaret climbed back into the Land Rover with Stephanie and disappeared into the night. The hostess turned to me. "We'll help you to your room," she said. Coworkers supported me as I climbed the stairs. I collapsed on the bed, my body aching from the day's travels.

Margaret slept in our room, rising periodically to help me nurse Stephanie and to check her condition. "I'm uneasy about her heart," she said. "Something doesn't sound right." With only a stethoscope in hand, it was impossible for her to say much more.

In the morning Gene raced to the embassy to process the passport. An American doctor whisked Stephanie to the city's UMN hospital. After inserting a needle through her fontanel (the hollow in a baby's skull where the bones aren't fully formed) into her brain, he withdrew 40 cc of cerebral fluid to reduce cranial pressure. The doctor brought Stephanie back to the guesthouse less than an hour before the flight's departure.

Only a few precious moments remained for me to hold my daughter. *I might never see her again. What if she dies before I get home?* I thought. *Memorize her face—her tiny mouth, her little nose!* I looked at her long, slender fingers. *I wonder if she'll play the piano someday.* I caught myself. *I wonder if she'll live long enough to play the piano someday.*

Gene stuffed an overnight bag with diapers and a change of clothes. He glanced at his watch.

"Let's pray," said Margaret. "Heavenly Father, You are trustworthy even when we don't understand what You're doing. We have nothing to fear. Protect Stephanie on the trip and reunite the family soon. In Jesus' name, Amen."

Gene kissed me and wrapped Stephanie in a blanket. "I'll call you from the States," he said. And then he was gone.

Three or four hours passed. I lay on the bed and held my toddler close. Feverish from a reaction to the measles vaccination he'd received a week and a half earlier, he wrapped his little arms around my neck and cried for his daddy. I cried to my heavenly Father.

What now? What will life be like for Stephanie if she lives? Oh, God, what are You doing?

As if in response to my questions, a melody came from nowhere and filled my mind with the familiar words of an old hymn: *Great is Thy faithfulness, O God my Father, there is no shadow of turning with thee; Thou changest not, thy compassions, they fail not; As Thou hast been Thou forever wilt be.*

The words replayed in my thoughts, and as they did, they washed my fear away. In a moment of surrender, I embraced the lyrics as truth and whispered the chorus through broken sobs: *Great is Thy faithfulness! Great is Thy faithfulness! Morning by morning new mercies I see; All*

I have needed Thy hand hath provided—Great is Thy faithfulness, Lord, unto me! (Thomas O. Chisholm, © Hope Publishing Co.)[1]

Would I see Stephanie alive again? I didn't know. But grim circumstances couldn't change the fact—God was faithful. I could trust Him no matter how the story ended.

Before Gene left Kathmandu, I'd given him a baby bottle filled with mother's milk for Stephanie. She'd finished the supply by the time he checked into a Hong Kong hotel room for the night. Gene knew she needed either formula or regular milk for the long flight home. He placed the baby on the bed and surrounded her with pillows, and then he dashed outside in search of a grocery store. To his amazement and relief, he found a convenience store still open a few blocks away, where he bought a small carton of cow's milk. He wasn't sure it was the best thing for the baby, but he didn't know what else to feed her.

That night, lying on the bed beside Stephanie, Gene fought to stay awake. He watched her chest rise and fall. *She's so quiet,* he thought. *What if she dies during the night?*

Choosing not to let fear overwhelm him, he focused on a different thought. *Not too many dads have the opportunity to do this with their newborns. This may be the only time we travel halfway around the world together!*

Saturday morning en route to Seattle, Stephanie no longer had enough strength to suck from the bottle. Gene fed her with a syringe, hiding her in her blanket to avoid questions. One passenger thought the syringe was a needle and alerted a flight attendant that a scruffy young man was "shooting up" illicit drugs. When she went to investigate, the flight attendant discovered an exhausted, unshaven young father feeding his four-day-old daughter. She asked a few questions, Gene answered, and she immediately found a doctor on board to check Stephanie's condition.

Before we left Tansen, Gene had phoned his father and dictated details about Stephanie's condition. His dad relayed the message to a cousin who was co-owner of a radiology company in the city. The cousin then arranged Stephanie's admission to the neonatal intensive care unit. So after Gene's family met him and Stephanie when their plane landed in Seattle, they drove 30 minutes to Tacoma to deliver Stephanie to the Tacoma General Hospital.

Neurosurgery the following day eased pressure on her brain, but doctors discovered a hole in her heart. When I returned to North America five days later, a pediatric cardiologist stood outside Stephanie's room and handed me a grim prognosis: "If your daughter lives to be two years old, we can try to repair the defect. That, however, is unlikely. She'll probably die of congestive heart failure within a month."

God had other plans. Two months later, Stephanie underwent medical tests for her heart. The same doctor looked at the results and x-rays. "I don't understand this," he said. He shook his head in disbelief. "Her heart is normal."

Gene and I looked at each other and smiled. We understood. Hundreds of people had been praying.

In 2007, Stephanie turned 22, graduated from a four-year Bible college program and got married. She still needs the shunt, but she's an overcomer. She knows God has a special plan for her life; so far, she has survived a heart defect, meningitis and 11 surgeries. Only two of the surgeries were related to the shunt; the others included two eye operations, a double hernia repair, and the removal of a cyst from her brain.

Despite the setbacks, Stephanie earned a position on the A honour roll in her junior year of high school. She plays piano, saxophone and flute. She has participated in short-term missions trips to Germany and Haiti. And now, as a young married woman, she enjoys cooking, spending time with her husband, and singing in the church choir.

More than two decades have passed since Stephanie's birth. I consider her early years rich with lessons that taught me what it means to trust God implicitly. It's easy to do when life rolls along smoothly; it's not so simple when the tough times hit. In the midst of difficulties, however, I've discovered that trusting God is a choice. I either can let

fear paralyze me, or I can believe God's promises and then live accordingly. Understanding that concept has enabled me to trust in the face of other difficulties.

For instance, when a kidney stone complicated my third pregnancy, I chose to trust God's ability to care for me and my family. He didn't remove the kidney stone, but He provided friends to help care for my two toddlers, prepare meals for us, and lend a hand with housework.

When my dad suffered two crippling strokes, I chose to trust God's ability to give the doctors wisdom and to bless my mother with patience and peace in the face of an unknown future.

Throughout the years, whenever our family's finances have stretched tighter than we liked, I've chosen to trust His ability to look after us as we've practiced wise stewardship. He has always provided for our necessities, often in ways beyond my imagination.

No matter how dismal our circumstances appear, God assures us that He is faithful. He will carry us through, not because of who we are or what we've done, but because of who He is—the faithful, unchanging One.

1. "Great is Thy Faithfulness," words by Thomas O. Chisholm. © 1923. Renewed 1951 by Hope Publishing Co., Carol Stream, IL 60188. All rights reserved. Used by permission.

This selection is adapted from an article that won first prize in the 2001 *Christian Reader* writing contest.

Jessie's Generation: Canada's Firebrands of Mercy And Justice

Non-fiction
Jane Harris

I can do all things through Christ which
strengtheneth me. (Philippians 4:13, KJV)

Jessie Robinson pulled up the fur around her collar and clasped her arms tight against her overcoat. She could not stop the autumn wind of 1909 slapping at her face and pulling hairs from pins tucked under her hat, but neither would the wind stop her. She had come to the edge of the town of Lethbridge, Alberta to see the "thing" that could not be built, the railway bridge that Canada's newspapers touted as a wonder of the modern age. The black steel lattices of the Lethbridge Viaduct[1] towered 314 feet[2] above the cottonwood-covered[3] valley, and stretched a mile[2] across Southern Alberta's coulees.[4]

The starched collar of her blouse pinched Jessie's neck as she gazed up at the massive railway bridge. Only completed a few weeks ago, the viaduct enabled coal to be taken from Jessie's hometown all through the Dominion of Canada and to the United States. It promised to make the city of Lethbridge richer and bigger: more jobs for men; better schools for children; many fine houses; even skyscrapers like the 10-storey, steel-framed towers soaring above Chicago and New York.

The Board of Trade said there was a prosperous future in Lethbridge for anyone willing to work. Any man could make money. Any family could live well.

So as she moved past the bridge, Jessie was puzzled by the sight of thin children playing along the coulees, and worn knees on pants hanging from lines beside tiny shanties on Brewery Row. What kind of people would live in these shanties? On a sudden impulse, Jessie walked over and knocked on an unpainted door.

"Come in," said a weak voice.

Jessie stepped inside, into a world where ladies' calling cards[5], finger sandwiches and teas were as exotic as the Taj Mahal.

Later, she would write to her friend, Mrs. Galbraith: *I found a young woman sitting in a rocking chair, looking very ill—and at her feet a little child playing on the floor. I spoke to the woman, and left wondering about it.*

Jessie was still thinking about the woman and her child the next day when the iceman made his weekly visit. As he filled the icebox in her kitchen, he recounted that his wife had seen a woman starving in a house by the viaduct. Jessie realized that this was the woman she had spoken with yesterday. Could she be starving? Jessie grabbed her coat and headed back to the shack on Brewery Row.

She was not starving, but far gone with T. B. and needing little comforts and kindnesses, Jessie wrote.

Jessie discovered that many residents of Lethbridge were poor and sick. They had come to Alberta looking for jobs in the brewery or mines. Some, like the woman Jessie had found, were dying. The squalid slum known as Brewery Row[6] was home to the unemployed, the addicted, recent immigrants, families who had been abandoned by their bread-winners... and one of the biggest red light districts in the prairies.

Jessie wanted to help, but what could one woman do? *I determined to try to interest others in doing something about it,* she wrote.

Jessie already spent many hours volunteering at St. Augustine's Anglican Church. Twenty of her friends from church met weekly at the home of Mrs. Chivers, the minister's wife, to sort used clothing for distribution to needy families. The next time they met, Jessie shared her story about the dying woman in the shack. The ladies agreed they could do more. They would bring food to the poor and visit the sick.

First, they formed a Relief Society and elected Jessie its President. Next, Jessie and her friends visited shanties along the coulees and in the river valley. Despite their own warm coats, they shivered when wind whistled through cracks in wooden walls. They put burn ointment on toddlers who had touched hot stoves while their mothers were busy washing clothes and cleaning houses for wealthy families across town. They discovered that the children were getting sick through drinking milk supplied by cows infected with bovine tuberculosis.

As they walked down crooked paths, they heard hacking coughs from men, women and children dying inside shanties. The Relief Society paid for hospital beds for the sickest people they found—but it was not enough.

There was more poverty and sickness in Lethbridge than we had imagined, Jessie wrote.

It was clear that Lethbridge needed a full-time nurse to care for the poor. Some members of the Relief Society wanted to ask the Victorian Order of Nurses[7] to take over the relief work. Others, including Jessie, wanted to continue their Christian ministry to the poor.

Jessie wrote, *The Margaret Scott[8] mission in Winnipeg, which was run independently, appealed to me more than the broader organization of The Victorians' Order. We discussed the pros and cons at several meetings. It looked almost impossible.*

The biggest hurdle was cost: a nurse's salary was $60 per month, plus additional expenses for medical supplies. That meant they'd have to raise more than $700 for one year. Where would women, without paid jobs, get more money than their husbands made in a year?

They decided to try. If they could collect enough money to pay expenses for one year, they would hire their nurse.

Jessie told Mayor Adams about her mission. She later wrote, *He listened to me and then said, "I will give you a cheque for one month's salary." I could scarcely believe my luck and I have never been sure whether I thanked him properly or not.*

Many citizens matched Mayor Adams's gift by pledging to send The Relief Society five dollars every month.

In a few weeks, Jessie and her friends were sure they would have enough money, so they sent for their nurse to come.

Our idea had been that the nurse would board... [but] she wanted a house where she could live and have people come to see her... That meant more begging, more talking, to convince people that we were on the right track.

It took two more months to raise the rent money and find furniture for the cottage, but soon, Lethbridge's poor had their own nurse.

Still, it was not enough. As new job-seekers arrived from across Canada and Europe, more shacks went up along the railway tracks. One nurse could not keep up with the work. So, Jessie and her friends raised enough money to hire more nurses and a settlement worker. They were moving toward Jessie's dream: a Christian nursing mission that could offer more services to Lethbridge's poor.

By 1913, that dream was reality. The Relief Society was renamed The Lethbridge Nursing Mission and moved into a new building. They hired Anna Tilley, a social worker from Ontario, as superintendent.

Tilley and her staff sent groceries, clothing and coal to impoverished families. They looked after sick mothers and babies, found jobs for unemployed men and girls, and handled adoptions.

The mission provided families with safe milk free of tuberculosis contamination. The nurses gave school children health checkups and toothbrushes. The settlement worker helped immigrants learn about Canadian society, and organized English classes, sewing classes and girls' clubs.

The poor paid when they could, but no one was turned away because he or she had no money. So there was always more money to raise.

The early years were anxious ones, wrote Jessie. *Many times near the end of the month, we wondered how we could meet our bills, but it was always done.*

Jessie and her friends held teas and rummage sales to keep the mission open. When those initiatives did not raise enough funds, they borrowed money from the bank—but that had mounted to a $100 overdraft by 1916.

Desperate to save the mission, Jessie and her friends visited the new mayor. But he refused to promise city funding. Undaunted, the women knocked on every door in the city. To their amazement, the rich and the poor alike emptied their wallets and wrote cheques to pay off the mission's debt. And Jessie and her friends discovered that door-to-door canvassing raised more money than their teas and rummage sales ever could.

However, there was no time to celebrate. Thousands of Canadian men were lying dead and wounded on battlefields in France and Belgium due to the horrors of the First World War.

Piles of wool and cotton sat on the polished wooden tables in Jessie's house. Every morning, dozens of war workers arrived to knit socks, mufflers, hats and mitts for soldiers. They made bandages for battlefield hospitals. And they went into all parts of the city to visit and comfort soldiers' families.

As busy as she was with war work, Jessie never forgot the day she had found the woman dying in a shack on Brewery Row. While president of the Lethbridge branch of the Council of Women, Jessie worked with fellow Albertans Henrietta Muir Edwards and Louise McInney. They fought to give women the right to custody of their own children and ownership of their farms—as well as the right to vote, so that women's votes could oust politicians who did nothing for the poor.

At first, politicians laughed at the thought of women voting. But by 1916, public opinion forced them to give Alberta women the right to vote for provincial Members of the Legislative Assembly; and on May 24, 1917, all Canadian women were given the right to elect federal Members of Parliament.

A few years later, McInney and Edwards were part of "The Famous Five" group of women suffragettes from Jessie's province who convinced the Privy Council in London, England in 1929 to acknowledge women as Persons throughout the British Empire. Women could finally run for Parliament and become judges in every nation over which King George ruled.

But Southern Alberta's poor had not disappeared, nor had its sick. So year after year, Lethbridge women canvassed the city to raise money for the nursing mission. With the help of city residents, their mission grew. By 1934, The Lethbridge Nursing Mission (9) was the largest independent nursing mission in Canada. King George V recognized its contribution to the health of his Canadian subjects by making Superintendent Anna Tilley a Member of the Order of the British Empire.[10]

Women such as these, driven by Jesus' command to "Love your neighbour as yourself" (Matthew 22:39), were instrumental in changing Canada forever. And those changes eventually rippled through the world's most powerful empire.

While times have changed, Jesus' words have not. The poor still line up at soup kitchens, and the sick still die alone in shacks and tenements. Will you help bind up the wounds of our century?

1. Construction on the Lethbridge Viaduct began in August of 1908. The bridge was completed June 22, 1909 and officially opened on November 1, 1909. It cost $1,334,525 to build. It is still the longest and highest bridge of its kind in the world.
2. 314 feet = 96 metres; 1 mile = 1.6 kilometres
3. Ravines that are very steep and craggy.
4. The cottonwood is a type of poplar tree.
5. Women left printed cards when they visited neighbours.
6. Brewery Row was finally condemned and torn down in the 1960s.
7. The Victorian Order of Nurses (VON Canada) was founded in 1897 to commemorate the Diamond Jubilee (60th anniversary) of the reign of Queen Victoria. It is a national, Canadian, non-sectarian, not-for-profit health care organization and registered charity that provides nursing services in the home and community.
8. A devout Christian, Scott gave up her job with the Canadian government in 1886 to care for Winnipeg's poor.
9. Alberta Social Services took over the Lethbridge Nursing Mission in 1954.
10. An award bestowed by a British monarch to honour achievement or service.

This article is based on original research done by Jane Harris, including her paper "Starting From Scratch: Social Reform By Pioneer Women of Southern Alberta 1900-1919", published in the newsletter of the Lethbridge Branch of the Alberta Historical Society (November 1990).

Jessie Robinson's quotations are taken from a 1934 letter to a friend, which is archived in The Galt Museum & Archives in Lethbridge, Alberta.

How I Found Jesus in a Drug Dealer's Apartment

Non-fiction
Deborah Gyapong

I grew up in a good, nominally Christian home in the Boston, Massachusetts area. Although I was baptized Russian Orthodox, my parents sent me to various Protestant Sunday Schools so I would learn Bible stories as part of my education. When I was eight or nine, my mother would give me an envelope containing her $2 weekly pledge to the Congregational Church, expecting me to drop it in the collection plate. Instead, I used the money to buy Superman comics, Wise Potato Chips and Almond Joy chocolate bars at the Parker Drug Store, conveniently on the route home from church. Somehow, the Jesus I met in Sunday school spoke to me less than the comic book hero did.

By the time I reached my early twenties, I had rejected the Christian faith altogether. However, "spiritual" things fascinated me, so I embraced Eastern religions, New Age teachings and the occult. I even dabbled in magic, because I thought it was harmless. I viewed spiritual forces as impersonal powers like electricity.

Out of college and unemployed, I smoked a lot of marijuana and embraced the remnants of the Sixties Cultural Revolution. Though my lifestyle left me depressed and without self-respect, I failed to see the connection. Instead, I took foolish chances, jeopardizing my emotional and physical safety. Had I continued on that path, I'm sure I would have died or lost my mind long ago.

One September night in 1973, I hitchhiked to a seedy bar in Cambridge, Massachusetts. The bartender, a large ex-con named Frank, invited me into a back room to snort cocaine. By closing time, high on the drug, I felt like Superwoman. No way did I want to go home to my lonely apartment on the other side of Harvard Square. So Frank invited me to accompany him on his drug-selling rounds. At each hippie-style apartment, we snorted lines of white powder through a rolled dollar bill.

"By the way, that was mescaline you just did," Frank told me.

That was fine with me. I'd had only one experience with that hallucinogenic drug and it had been deeply spiritual. I assumed that my second mescaline experience would be a good one too.

When Frank finished his rounds, we took a bus into Boston's South End. In those days, the South End was a slum near the elevated subway tracks, a dangerous area frequented by pimps, prostitutes and muggers.

Frank took me to his basement apartment in an old row house. Someone had gutted the walls in the hallway and kitchen, leaving piles of wooden laths, horse hair and plaster chunks. In the front room, a sleeping bag had been thrown on a bare mattress. Next to the bed was a pile of newspapers. On top of the pile sat a cardboard box of marijuana seeds and stems. Other cardboard boxes full of seeds and stems were strewn around the room.

Frank began to make physical advances, but I resisted. Thank God, he didn't force himself on me. Instead he said, "I want to be with a woman tonight. I'm going to leave now and I'll come back to get you at eight tomorrow morning. Here's a key."

Then he left.

I sat down on the bed in the damp basement room, expecting to be fine by myself. Soon, however, the noise in the room began to feel chaotic and invasive. Maybe the roar and buzzing sounds came from an elevated train or trucks passing by, but the noise created anxiety and seemed to be driving me crazy. What's more, I felt an evil presence in the room.

I studied dance in those days, as well as dabbling in magic, so I tried to create order by clapping and snapping my fingers. I started to "play" the room. The rhythm helped at first, but soon I was clapping fearfully and compulsively. Then I decided to do a dance to collect the growing evil presence and flush it down the toilet. With sweeping arm gestures, I gathered it up and pulled it through the plaster-strewn hallway, into a long narrow bathroom with a toilet at the back wall.

I flung the evil into the bowl and flushed. The toilet seemed to shudder as it roared and howled. Horrified, I ran out of the bathroom into the hallway. The evil and sense of impending doom mushroomed instead of disappearing into the sewer.

Terrified, I began to pace from the kitchen through the gutted hallway to the bedroom and back, saying aloud, "I want to live! I want to live!" over and over again, experiencing unbearable fear. Yet the wall clock seemed stuck on 3:00 a.m. I hallucinated wraithlike shapes in lurid colours rising up from the trash piles in the hall. I visualized myself running out into the night, screaming, gripped by madness. In that neighbourhood, being alone at night might have been a fatal mistake. But I was more fearful that the evil presence would get inside me and take me over.

Psalms from Sunday School came to mind. I tried reciting the 23rd Psalm out loud. "The Lord is my Shepherd…" I was surprised I remembered it. I recited the Lord's Prayer too. But my prayers seemed to bounce off the low ceiling. Meanwhile, the evil continued to grow in intensity, seething around me.

I sat on the mattress and flicked on the TV near the bed. On the black and white television set, a trio of musicians were playing guitars and singing folk songs. Tears rolled down my cheeks. *Humanity, precious humanity*, I thought. The comfort didn't last. The music stopped for a commercial break and a recruitment ad for the Marines came on, reminding me of the Vietnam War. A Marine in a dress uniform was performing various parade drills with his bayonet. To me, he looked cadaverous. My heart started doing a drum tattoo. The reality of war and bloodshed was more than I could handle.

I changed the channel to see a man dressed as the devil, introducing the nightly horror movie. Normally, I'd have thought this man looked silly, a parody of the devil, wearing greasy streaks of make-up. That night, however, his eyes burned with a hateful, malevolent intensity personally directed at me. It *was* the devil glaring at me through the television set. Then he seemed to leap out at me. Horrified, I jammed the off button.

I reached for a cigarette, my hands shaking. But instead of calming me, the red burning end of the cigarette seemed to have the same derisive, spiteful malevolence as the TV devil's eyes. I crushed it out and began to pace again, feeling utterly desperate.

Maybe if I clean up and restore order in the bedroom, I might feel better, I thought. So I lifted the box of marijuana seeds and stems off the pile of newspapers to carry it out of the room. The front page of the top newspaper showed a photo of three hooded Ku Klux Klansmen. I couldn't bear the horror.

As I grabbed the pile of newspapers to throw them away, I found a paperback book underneath. The title—*Hey God!*—made me stop and pick it up. What was this doing in a drug dealer's apartment?

The evil in the room swelled and buzzed as I picked up the book and opened it with trembling hands. I was afraid that it would decay into horror like everything else I'd turned to for comfort. Huddled on the edge of the bed, feeling surrounded by hundreds of evil spirits watching me and trying to get inside me, I sensed they hated my reading this book.

I read about author Frank Foglio's Mamma and her 10 kids and how she received the baptism of the Holy Spirit. I read about how she prayed, "Hey God!" and spoke to Him in simple straightforward prayers. I read about the miracles they experienced, like praying over the spaghetti and having it multiply to feed a crowd, or praying over an empty gas tank so the car would keep going.

Mamma was always telling people about Jesus. Whenever she asked someone in the book a question, I felt as if she was asking me.

Did I know I was a sinner? YES! Did I believe Jesus died for my sins? YES! Would I ask Jesus into my heart? YES! Would I turn my life over to Him? YES!

I was doing some heavy-duty bargaining. *Hey God! You save me from the hell in this room and I'll serve you the rest of my life. I promise.*

As I read, I understood how profoundly Jesus knew the depth of the evil in the world. I knew that was why He died on the cross. I also understood that without Him, I was powerless against it.

Despite my bargaining, despite my having said The Sinner's Prayer, the evil seemed to grow even stronger. Though terrified, I kept reading, eventually coming to a Bible verse where God seemed to be speaking directly to me. *Be still, and know that I Am God* (Psalm 46:10).

Everything in me was fighting for life, struggling to save myself. But God was telling me to let go, to stop struggling, to know that God is God, and Jesus is Saviour, and to be still despite what seemed like overwhelming evil. Could I trust Jesus? Could I stop trying to save myself?

Being still took such a tremendous effort of will that my sweat felt like blood. Being still was the hardest thing I'd ever done in my life.

But as I willed myself to release, to trust, to let go, a Bible verse that was quoted in the book came to me. *There is rejoicing in the presence of the angels of God over one sinner who repents* (Luke 15:10). I could feel heaven rejoicing. I felt as if God's invisible arm was reaching down and cupping me in His palm. His presence was stern, though, as if He was saying to me, "Look what kind of mess you got yourself in this time."

In His powerful presence, I felt safe. The evil vanished. So did any drug effects. The room became a normal, messy basement room. My tears of fear and angst turned to tears of joy and repentance as I experienced the peace that passes understanding.

When the drug dealer returned as he'd promised at 8:00 a.m., I was smiling, and so in love with Jesus that I could have gone down the street knocking on doors and witnessing about my new faith—just like the author Frank Foglio's Mamma.

I look back at that September night in 1973 and see how God carefully set the scene and used Frank Foglio's simple testimony about his mother's faith in God to bring me from darkness into light. Some Christian had stepped out in faith to witness to the drug dealer by giving him that book. God had made sure that book was there for me, hidden under the pile of newspapers, just when I needed it.

I wish I could say the rest of my life was perfect after my profound conversion. Unfortunately, because I found Jesus alone, I felt uncomfortable in churches full of "normal" people. Also, I continued to cherish the "truths" I had learned from various New Age and heretical sources. I had trouble with some doctrines. Despite a personal relationship with Jesus, I reserved the right to pick the parts of the Bible that "spoke to me" and to ignore the rest. My approach kept me a defeated Christian, easily confused and discouraged. It also made me vulnerable to impulsive and ultimately self-destructive relationships with men.

Two years after my conversion, I rushed into marriage with an alcoholic man and moved to Nova Scotia on Canada's Atlantic coast. This led to a period of unbearable suffering and insecurity. Eventually, I poured out my heart to Jesus, begging Him for release from my rage and hurt and self-righteousness. God didn't change my circumstances, but He gave me the grace to survive them with some evidence of the fruits of the Spirit.

After my second son was born, my husband tried to remain sober by substituting marijuana for the alcohol. But he couldn't stay away from alcohol for long. My husband disappeared when my second son was a little over one year old. He reappeared two weeks later, drunk and physically abusive. I left with the boys the next morning.

That winter found me alone in a drafty farmhouse, with no wood for the stoves or furnace, and no income. I sold real estate and tried other ways to make money, but nothing seemed to work for long. I prayed, not unlike Mamma in the Foglio book, begging God to do something.

Within days, God again altered the course of my life. I spotted an advertisement in the weekly *Digby Mirror* newspaper for a part-time reporter. I applied.

When I arrived for my job interview, the managing editor of the chain was distracted and agitated. "I really need someone for the big job," he said. "The editor quit this morning."

"I'll do it," I blurted out.

The managing editor thought for a minute and said, "How about if you try out the job for two weeks and we'll see how you do?"

I spent the weekend in almost-crippling anxiety. What had I done? I would not only be the editor, but the reporter and photographer as well. Would I be able to do it? Though I had loved to write as a child, and had even written "books" that I illustrated and stapled together, I knew nothing about writing for a readership of thousands of people. I knew, though, that I had to try for the sake of my children.

That Monday, I trotted off to cover the municipal council meeting, camera and notebook in hand. Later, as I typed the stories on an old electric typewriter, I thought to myself, *I love this!* In two weeks, the newspaper chain offered me the job, for the then-lucrative weekly pay of $150 a week.

With my demanding job and single motherhood, I had little time to go to church or to fellowship with other Christians. After a local pastor told me my heretical beliefs were partly responsible for my ex-husband's drinking, I felt so hurt that I started to avoid evangelical churches that might have helped me become solidly grounded in the Christian faith.

I continued to make mistakes in relationships. Though I had discovered Jesus was faithful, I had trouble being faithful to Him, even though I wanted to be.

I married for a second time on the rebound and began to work at the Canadian Broadcasting Corporation (CBC) in Halifax, Nova Scotia, in radio news and current affairs. Although I saw signs in our too-short engagement that my future husband had an anger problem, he had a good, professional job and seemed responsible. But after he slapped me on our honeymoon, I realized with horror that I had made my bed in hell for a second time. After two and a half years of verbal and sometimes physical abuse, I went to a psychologist.

"I don't want to be a two-time loser," I said.

"From what you are telling me, you already are," he stated bluntly. "I can help you become a better ballerina on eggshells but I can't help your marriage. Is that what you want?"

When my husband refused to go to counselling with me, I applied for a divorce. I had avoided Christian friends because I assumed they would lecture me on how I should be a more perfect homemaker and wife. Yet I was the one who put a terrible standard of perfection on myself, blaming myself for not being a strong enough Christian to bring my husband to repent of his anger and abusiveness towards me.

When I went to see my old Christian friends back in Bear River, Nova Scotia, they said, "You should never have married him in the first place." They invited me to a potluck supper where I felt the love of Christ that permeates Christian fellowship, a love from the Body of Christ that I had been so deprived of over those years.

My life slowly began to turn around. I started to consciously and strategically plan my social life, spending as much time I could with Christians, especially Christian couples, so I could have the influence of good, solid men in my own and my sons' lives.

I met my present husband, Tony, in 1998. Not only did he treat me with respect, he loved my boys and helped me raise them, hanging in throughout their sometimes difficult teenaged years. In our 20 years together, he has never called me a derogatory name or made me feel physically threatened. More than that, he is trustworthy, dependable, and emotionally stable.

We moved to Canada's capital, Ottawa, in 1989 and I took a job as a television producer with the CBC's cable news television network. My career and family life both were going well, but I felt something was missing. The suffering that used to force me to my knees was gone, and consequently so was that motivation to seek Jesus with all my heart. I missed the joy of being close to Him.

One day I told my new next-door neighbour that I needed to find a church, so she suggested I try hers. When I first met the pastor, I told him, "I'm a heretic and a maverick, and I've never been able to sign on the dotted line with any church."

"Maybe this church is big enough for you," he replied.

My Christian faith started to become more consistent through my fellowship at this Baptist church, though still I knew that I needed something more. Then one day, someone recommended I read Neil Anderson's *The Bondage Breaker*. I couldn't put the book down. What he wrote about demonic forces rang so true, I needed no convincing.

Nonetheless, I resisted taking Anderson's recommended "Steps to Freedom," a series of prayers to confess and renounce sin, including involvement in the occult and false religions. I rejected this as too narrow, too anti-intellectual, too unsophisticated.

Meanwhile, the CBC was going through massive changes and cutbacks. I felt so depressed I could hardly sit up straight. One day, I ducked into a vacant office to pray. I sat alone in the dark, my spine curved like "C," weighed down by an awful sense of doom. Suddenly, I found myself saying out loud, "Spirit of depression, I rebuke you in the name of Jesus Christ. I command you to leave my presence." I cringed once the words left my mouth, thinking, *What if someone heard me?*

However, what happened next amazed me. The depression lifted. My back straightened, my mind became quiet, joy filled my soul. I not only was able to pray, I communed with Christ, knowing that whatever happened, I wanted His will for my life.

Finally, in the mid-nineties, during a conference sponsored by Anderson's Freedom in Christ Ministries, I completed the "Steps to Freedom" prayers, telling myself I would not be renouncing anything that was true in non-Christian teachings, only the false. I confessed and renounced previous occult practices—such as getting my astrological chart done and reading tarot cards. I renounced the many false teachings that still influenced me. I confessed habitual sins, including my previous self-destructive relationships, as well as pride and bitterness. Afterwards, my mind became quiet, free of the almost constant mental chatter that had plagued my prayer life, just as the conference leader promised.

My focus had always been on how much of a sinner I was. I came to see that it is by believing the Truth that I am not only saved but also changed. Anderson made it clear that in Christ we have authority over demonic influences. He taught me the value of examining every thought and rejecting those that weren't of God.

I eventually resigned from my position with the CBC, trusting God to look after me. And He did, taking me through a challenging posting working for a federal politician and leading me to my present job as a freelance writer covering religion and politics.

During this period of my life, I poured out my heart in a novel, using long weekends and vacations to write my first draft. I wanted to put what I had learned into a gripping story that would reach other people, just as Frank Foglio's book *Hey God!* had once reached me. I wanted to show readers that through Jesus we not only can have salvation, but also victory over the very real forces of spiritual wickedness that operate in our midst.

In 2005, my manuscript for *The Defilers* won the Best New Canadian Christian Author Award, administered by The Word Guild. The prize included a dream come true: publication by Castle Quay Books, a Canadian publisher committed to promoting Canadian stories by Christian authors.

I look back now with awe, thankful God was looking after me all the way, helping me change from that girl in the drug dealer's apartment to the woman I am today, someone who can speak with confidence of God's love, patience and power.

Of Cobras, Culture and Change

Fiction

Don Ranney, MD, and Ray Wiseman

On an October day in 1970, water from a late shower covered the runway at Dum-Dum Airport in Calcutta. The plane skidded and bumped, but with engines in full reverse managed to stop just short of disaster. The pilot announced the temperature was 94 degrees Fahrenheit and humidity 85 per cent. "Enjoy your stay," he added.

Dr. Steve Manley smiled. His hand drummed impatiently on the arm-rests at his sides as he realized he would soon be where God wanted him to be. He would spend the rest of his life making crippled hands work again, helping the lame walk—and who knows what else God had in store for him. With this came the excitement of visiting a whole new world, one in which he might raise the standards of medical care.

Getting off was the usual airport hassle. He stood in line in a stuffy plane with sweat dripping from his forehead and clothes sticking to his body, waiting for the people ahead to start moving. Then there was the noise and bustle of an overcrowded airport. But he was pleasantly surprised to find none of his luggage missing.

Getting through customs was another matter. He found he had two problems. One, he was American. Nobody liked Americans. They loved American money, not the people who made it. He was also a missionary. He soon discovered that Indian officials treated all missionaries as suspected felons. His task was to prove he was not smuggling anything into the country. He began to sense this when he had to wait in a special line labelled "Immigrating Aliens," fill out similarly-named forms, and wait 20 minutes for an interview. He'd assumed that having a visa would be enough. But the customs officer's plan seemed to be to establish him as a smuggler and block his entry.

"Aha, vat is dis?" the man with the black cap asked him. "Film, film, film," he screamed, as he unwound reel after reel of audiotape on the floor. "You cannot bring movie film into this country. We have our own film. You buy here!"

"But it's not film!" Steve said. "That's audiotape, so I can learn Bengali."

"And why learn Bengali? So you can corrupt the minds of the people?"

Steve began to wish he were back in Toronto with Jennifer, talking about India, rather than in Calcutta experiencing it. Another American on Steve's flight, waiting in line behind him, began talking to the customs officer in some unknown language.

The passenger turned to Steve and said, "Give him a few American dollars and he'll let you through. You'll soon learn that in Bengali the word used for bribe is also translated to mean 'the usual thing.'"

Steve grudgingly handed over a five-dollar bill. Both the other men smiled. The bags were stamped and he was on his way.

What a joy to meet, at the end of the long hallway, a blonde curly-headed young woman carrying a sign with his name on it! She looked English. She was pretty too.

"Hello, I'm Bonnie Stubbings. I'll take you to the train. Quick. We must hurry! Your plane was an hour late and travel through town will be slow. There's a big crowd in Calcutta today, celebrating a festival. Taxis can't make it through crowds like this. We'll each have to go in separate rickshaws."

They managed to find two hand-drawn rickshaws, loaded half the luggage on each, and, with Bonnie in one and him in the other, they took off for the railway station. He soon lost sight of Bonnie. Steve found himself all alone in a sea of humanity with only half his luggage. He didn't really know where he was going and couldn't tell anyone if he did.

But the surgeon's keen eye took note of everything. Filth was everywhere. You could smell it. Cow dung and garbage mixed together by a recent downpour of rain flooded the streets. Yet people didn't seem to care. Their lithe semi-naked bodies pushed, pulled, twisted, and struggled in an endless battle to survive.

He passed close by a woman in a dirty, tattered sari, sitting in a pile of garbage. The stench of rotting cabbage filled Steve's nostrils as she hacked one of them to pieces with a large machete. After throwing away the most decayed parts, she put the remainder in a brown sack at her feet. Just beyond her, an old woman stuffed a banana into her mouth. It had just been run over by a bullock cart.

These two-wheeled bullock carts were grossly overloaded. Animals with little more than their bones to hold them together struggled to move them. One foamed at the mouth as it was fiercely whipped with a bamboo cane.

Clearly, the worship of cattle only applied to the female of the species. India was not for the sensitive heart. Jennifer, the one he had hoped to marry, was right to stay home.

At last he could say it. *Good-bye, Jennifer.*

They crossed a wide, turbulent, storm-swollen river on an iron bridge 300 feet long. It was built to take four lanes of traffic, but three were going one way and three the other. A truck abandoned near the center didn't help the situation. Somehow they got across and Steve found Bonnie waiting for him at the station.

"Hurry," she said. "The train is starting to move. We had to buy the tickets two weeks ago to make sure we got sleeping quarters. And there are no exchanges. You get in here. I have to get in the women's section. I'll see you in the morning."

"But—where are we getting off?"

"Assinsole," she replied.

The steam engine chugged slower and slower. Brakes screeched, metal on metal, as the train skidded toward a wooden platform crowded with people. The morning sun shone brightly into Dr. Steve Manley's eyes. It was 6 a.m., and for everyone but Steve the day was already well underway.

"*Chai, Chai,*" a boy shouted through the open window of Steve's railway carriage. A small brown hand reached between the bars that covered them.

"Chai? I'd hoped we were in Assinsole."

"We are." Bonnie's head appeared next to the boy's. "He's asking you to buy tea. *Chai* means tea. Get your things and we'll have some tea before leaving the station."

Steve opened the door, passed out his suitcases, and stepped onto the platform. Instinctively, he drew his broad shoulders together in the hope that by being thinner he would avoid bumping into anyone and being contaminated by typhoid bacteria or whatever other germs might be out there.

Bonnie handed him a cup of *chai.*

"Can we drink this? Is it clean?"

"Freshly boiled and served in cups that have never before touched human lips and never will again."

Steve stared in amazement at the terracotta cup in his hand as Bonnie explained.

"Hundreds of years ago the Brahmins invented disposable cups of unglazed pottery to avoid ritual defilement. These high caste Hindus must never drink from a vessel that has touched the lips of a lower caste person. So when you're finished, you throw it on the ground and the clay returns to the soil. Then a Brahmin won't face the risk of drinking from your cup."

Bonnie smiled. "Their idea of impurity is far removed from ours, but it serves us well."

"So does the tea. I'm so thirsty," Steve said, as the train chugged its way out of the station.

The boy came over and refilled his cup with the sweet, milky spiced liquid. *"Eck rupee,"* he said.

Steve wanted to show his appreciation and gave him a bill with number one on it.

"Did I tip him too much?"

"You gave him the exact price. That's about ten cents."

For the rest of the journey, Steve and Bonnie rode nearly six hours in a taxi. It was a black and cream-coloured, mid-sized car called an

Ambassador, with big round fenders front and back. A fifth hump, at the rear, formed the trunk lid, which was hinged at the top. It reminded Steve of the car his missionary friend Andrew had driven in Toronto, and made him wonder if Andrew had made it to South Africa.

They piled luggage in the back seat. Bonnie and Steve crowded into the front seat beside the driver.

"Why isn't the luggage in the trunk?" Steve asked.

"Some of these taxis are so old they won't start on their own," Bonnie said. "The boy who carries the luggage pushes the car. When it is rolling, he hops into the trunk and pulls the lid down. There's no room for luggage in the trunk."

The taxi rumbled along at 20 miles an hour[1] on an eight-foot[1]-wide ribbon of asphalt toward the village of Dhanbad. This "highway" was a public road, and the public made good use of it. People and cattle wandered aimlessly. Some women laid saris and blankets on the black asphalt to dry in the sun. The taxi was as much off the road as on. The driver blasted the horn repeatedly to declare his right to a part of the highway—any part.

The noise and confusion of the road stood in stark contrast to the tranquility of the lush green countryside on each side. A row of toddy palms bordered the road, some standing erect, most of them leaning to one side or the other. Between them Steve rested his eyes on lime-green rice fields interspersed with patches of taller mauve-topped sugar cane.

It was a long drive, but an interesting one, a picturesque introduction to the culture of India. Eventually the taxi entered the large village of Dhanbad, and minutes later, the hospital compound. It circled around to the right and stopped in front of a small sand-coloured stucco building. A wooden sign over the doorway declared it to be the Guest Quarters.

"Here's where you'll stay for now," Bonnie announced, "till the Hospital Superintendent, Reverend Archibald Smithers, decides what to do with you."

"What to do with me? I thought he'd been waiting for a surgeon for more than a year. Surely he must have everything planned."

"You're to meet him in his office at four this afternoon to talk about that. Meanwhile, get some rest. I'll send some food over."

While they were talking, the boy from the trunk of the car had carried Steve's suitcases into the room, two at a time on the top of his head. A few minutes later the taxi drove off under a dazzling noonday sun, leaving a swirling cloud of dust behind it.

Steve stood for a moment in the doorway, letting his eyes adjust to the relative darkness before entering. A small bed stood against the opposite wall. At one end of the room was a dresser and, at the other, a desk, chair and lamp. A two-inch-long cockroach scurried across the floor to find refuge under the bed.

Steve walked slowly across the room and sat down on the bed. It felt firm enough to support an elephant. But he was tired and it would do.

As his gaze drifted up toward the open doorway, movement attracted him—a green, sinuous, undulating movement. What he feared most about India, a large king cobra, had come out from under the dresser and slithered toward the sunlight.

It had almost reached its goal when it stopped, raised its head 18 inches[1] off the ground, and turned in Steve's direction. Its tongue darted from right to left and back again while its beady eyes studied him intently.

Steve sat motionless, paralyzed. Beads of perspiration formed on his forehead and dripped onto the bare floor between his feet. *What goes through the mind of a cobra—just before it strikes?*

Footsteps outside the door approached, and abruptly halted. Steve heard the sound of a stick tapping—followed by, *"Jao! Jao! Jao!"*

The snake turned toward the sound, and quickly slithered out the door.

"Food, sahr."

A bearded man wearing a dirty gray turban came in with a bowl of soup, a sandwich, and a large glass of lime juice. He calmly set them down on the desk and turned to leave.

"Thank you, thank you, thank you," Steve said hoarsely. "You saved my life!"

"*Bungla basha jano.* No English."

Steve smiled and placed one palm against the other in a gesture of thanks. The man did the same and left.

Steve thought, *If I believed in omens, that cobra might reflect badly on my future in India.* He had no appetite for food now. Neither could he rest.

Five thousand, two hundred, and eighty-one miles from Steve's room in India, his friends Andrew and Nancy Heath sped through a smoky haze into Soweto just south of Johannesburg, South Africa.

Nancy skillfully guided the Austin past bicycles, taxis, and huge green buses. "I love this car," she said, as she braked sharply to avoid a horse-drawn cart. "We're certainly well equipped for new missionaries. We've got a better house and car here than we had back home in Canada."

"We do." Andrew gripped the seat as Nancy accelerated past the cart. "I wonder if Steve is doing as well in India. That letter describing his scary standoff with a cobra worries me."

Nancy had her mind on her own fears. "I'm still not sure it's a wise thing to come to church in Soweto. I know it makes sense to identify with the local people and take our cues from our African friends—and Mumsa did invite us—but all of the other missionaries on the team attend church in the white community. They say it's safer." Nancy hesitated, "And yet—I don't know. That kind of talk sounds racist to me."

"You got it! We came here to work with black people, not to follow the ungodly laws of apartheid. We'll make up our own minds," Andrew replied. "Whoa, speed demon! Here's the church."

The pastor's wife, Mumsa, met them as they got out of the car. "Follow me."

Andrew kept her in view as he and Nancy weaved through the crowd toward the back of the cinder-block church building. Mumsa shooed away a group of teenage boys and girls sitting on a bench against a back wall.

"Sit here," she said, "One on each side of me. That way I can interpret so each of you can hear. Those kids should not sit here. I told them to go to their own sides."

Andrew watched the crowd as people continued filing into the building. The African men all sat to the left, the women on the right. Adults filled the rear third of the building, with teens ahead of them and children at the very front.

"We sit separately. It's the way we do it. But we save the back two rows for visitors and married couples who want to be together. So you aren't breaking any rules by sitting here," Mumsa explained.

People continued entering and squeezing onto the benches, always making room for one more.

"You put ten people where we would seat only five!" Andrew whispered to Mumsa.

She grinned back. "The service is about to begin."

The murmur of voices dropped, but Andrew couldn't see anyone preparing to lead the service. Pastor Thomas Makunyane, Mumsa's husband, sat on the men's side. Three latecomers slipped into an overcrowded row. The church became silent.

To Andrew and Nancy's complete surprise, Mumsa threw back her head and in a rich mezzo voice filled the building with the first line of a Zulu hymn:

"Hlengiwe-limnandi—"

Even before she finished the line, 300 voices began thundering out the words:

"Hlengiwe-limnandi lelizwi,
Hlengiwe ngegazi leMvana,
Hlengiwe ngomusa nothando:
Ngenziwe sengaba umntwana."

Bass, tenor, soprano, and alto meshed in superb accord. Andrew and Nancy had sung in church choirs, but had known nothing like this. Thundering, powerful voices beat together to fill the room with rich four-part harmony. Mumsa's voice soared above them all, leading, encouraging, worshipping in song.

By the third line of the hymn, Andrew had taken control of his emotions, recognized the tune, and joined in with the English words:

"Redeemed through His infinite mercy,

His child, and forever, I am."[2]

They sang three more choruses and hymns, passing the leadership around the room as though guided by some mysterious order known by all.

Pastor Thomas rose to his feet and moved to the front. He prayed, gave announcements, and invited the people to give. He returned to his seat, and the congregation, starting with the children, filed forward to drop money onto a plate as they sang, *"Bonga, Bonga, Bonga...."*

Mumsa, Andrew and Nancy went last, singing the words in English, "Thank you, thank you, thank you."

Following three more choruses, Pastor Makunyane returned to the front and stood behind a table. A middle-aged African man stepped up beside him.

Mumsa whispered, "Thomas will preach in Zulu, while Daniel interprets it into Sesotho. I'll try to keep up by giving you the English words."

Without warning, Pastor Makunyane fired out a line in Zulu, his powerful voice filling the room. Clicks, a characteristic of the Zulu language, shot from the roof and sides of his mouth like rifle reports. Before he finished the first sentence, Daniel began his interpretation in a softer tongue that, to Andrew, sounded much like French.

They continued with tremendous energy, overlapping each other, yelling, commanding, whispering, pleading. Daniel, standing slightly behind the pastor, mimicked every gesture. When the pastor imitated a woman walking seductively along a railway platform, Daniel copied every hip-swinging wiggle, looking like the second person in a chorus line. The congregation echoed its approval with bursts of laughter.

Toward the end of the sermon, Pastor Makunyane began to describe the crucifixion. He grabbed Daniel by the wrist, spun him around, and bent him backward over the table. His free hand imitated a hammer pounding nails into the hands of the prostrate Daniel enacting the role of Jesus. Even as they dramatized the scene, the pastor preached rapidly in Zulu while Daniel, lying on his back, fired Sesotho interpretation toward the ceiling.

As the awful scene grew in intensity, Daniel's voice became husky and the tears running from his eyes fell onto the table. Ultimately a great sob choked off his words.

Pastor Makunyane released Daniel and stepped back, freeing him to spring to his feet and wipe tears from his face. The staccato preaching with its echoing interpretation resumed as the two pleaded for everyone to come to the cross of Jesus.

Gripped by the drama of the event, Andrew heard very little of Mumsa's whispered English interpretation. He glanced sideways to see tears rolling down Nancy's cheek.

Andrew guided the Austin along the road homeward. Neither he nor Nancy spoke for the first few minutes. They barely noticed the Peugeot taxi lying on its roof in the ditch, the litter that had collected along the fence, or the naked teenagers swimming in a pond.

Andrew broke the silence as he slowed to steer around a big pothole. "I know you wanted to go to one of the white churches, Nancy, but I really think we've found the place God wants us. That was one of the most powerful services I've ever attended."

Nancy took a deep breath. "You're right, Andrew. Think what we'd miss otherwise. It's clear to me now that we have no reason to fear African people." She added after a moment's thought, "I just hope this doesn't build a wall between us and the other missionaries."

"We'll see," Andrew said. "We'll soon see."

1. 1 foot = .3 metres; 1 mile = 1.6 kilometres; 1 inch = 2.5 centimetres
2. Hymn, "Redeemed," Frances J. Crosby, 1820-1915. Public Domain.

This selection is adapted by permission of the publisher from *When Cobras Laugh*, copyright © 2007 by Don Ranney and Ray Wiseman (Waterford, VA: Capstone Fiction/ Capstone Publishing Group LLC, *www.capstonefiction.com*).

The Pink Blossom

Fiction

Eric E. Wright

*T*errance paused in his rocking to stare at the flowers in the ceramic pot in front of him. "Coral-pink," he muttered. "Just like… like…"

He reached over, picked one of the hibiscus blossoms, and tried to twirl it in his arthritic fingers. "Susan's dress… spread out around her… under the magnolia." A tear gathered at the corner of his eye.

A full-figured woman with coal-black hair, dressed in a blue uniform, marched down the veranda to his side. "You called, Mr. Webley? More coffee?"

He brushed away the tear. "No thanks, Rosa. Just an old man talking to himself."

Her eyebrows arched. "Seventy-two—old? You're not old. My grandpa's 85."

"You're kind, but not very honest, I'm afraid. Look at that." Terrance extended his left hand toward her. "See, I can't even keep it steady."

"Phah," she said.

"You can do something for me. Would you please bring the *Financial Post* as soon as it comes?"

Terrance turned to gaze toward the lake where Milford Manor's 45-foot power cruiser rocked in light swells. The lawn of the posh retirement residence swept down to the water in a flawless expanse of sculpted green. A meandering flagstone walk with formal borders of perennials on either side bisected the lawn. Here and there, clusters of evergreens and dogwood sheltered groups of Muskoka chairs, many occupied by residents soaking up the September sun.

Terrance glanced down at the blossom in his hand and sighed. *Susan...* Laughing eyes, slender fingers on his arm. So long ago. Secret meetings in the library. Breakfast at the Toddle House. Strolling through campus, hoping to catch a glimpse of her chestnut hair. Watching her residence window for a signal.

"That blasted missionary speaker!" Destroying all their plans.

He could still picture the bench where Susan had told him. Could feel the softness of her coral-pink sweater, and the gentle touch of her hands as she turned his face toward her so she could look at him. Her warm brown eyes, one minute full of dark intensity, the next swimming with tears, still haunted him, as did her gentle voice pleading with him to heed the call of God and go with her to India. His anger as he jumped up and stormed off.

"Here you are, Mr. Webley. Your paper."

Jerked from reverie, Terrance threw the blossom over the railing and reached for the paper. "Thanks, Rosa. Another coffee would be great with some of those imported biscotti. Better be decaf this time, though."

Terrance leafed through the paper. *Ah, a column about my coronary,* he mused. *Hah, got the pundits shaking in their boots. Gold up again. Oil down slightly. Sprint almost bottomed out. Should buy.* He leaned back and began to rock. *What's the point? Can't spend any more. Would only incite my ex-wives to ask for more alimony. And T. J., Jr., would pester me for a Lamborghini.*

Of course, maybe he could do some good with the money, even underwrite that mission Susan went overseas with. What was its name?

Susan... He sighed again. *Susan...* What was she doing? Where was she? Was she even alive? Maybe she had been right all along. What had he really gained?

He clenched his jaw. *Stop doubting yourself, old man! Gained a lot! A financial empire. Your name in* Business Today. *Houses on three continents...*

Of course, on the debit side, two bankrupt marriages and a coronary. Kids who can't hold down a job… and… and she would say, a tarnished soul. A tarnished soul.

Tarnished soul, huh? Wonder what Susan would think of him now. Would she be shocked? Of course, anyone who rescued prostitutes in Mumbai shouldn't be shocked at an old reprobate. She'd probably look into his eyes and tell him God loved him just as he was. Terrance laughed out loud at the thought. Would be nice if God did. No one else seemed to.

"Good to see you laugh, Sir." Rosa put a fresh cup of coffee and a plate of biscotti on the table beside him. "Sir, your lawyer phoned. He's got more papers for you to sign. Mentioned coming after lunch."

Terrance grimaced. "Always some lawyer disturbing the peace and quiet. Call him back will you. Tell him—tell him I'm not feeling well."

"Yes, Sir."

With a great sigh of satisfaction Terrance dipped his biscotti into his coffee and took a bite. *Now, there's a perk I can handle,* he thought. *Nothing like imported biscotti.*

Out of the corner of his eye, he caught sight of an ancient Honda with rusted fenders rattling to a stop under the canopied entrance. He was about to ring for Harry with instructions to give the driver a tongue-lashing for not going to the rear entrance when he stopped. Out of the passenger side stepped a stately woman in a black A-line skirt and coral pink blouse.

No, it can't be!

He turned away, shook his head and rubbed his eyes. *I'm losing it,* he thought.

The Ventilation Grate

Brian Austin

Ah, just a glimpse, the briefest glimpse
of a face that I once knew,
and the gentle touch of a loving hand—
yes, that would see me through…

This night as cold as the heart of Hell
and as lonely as the grave,
while I crouch here on this hard steel grate,
to its grudging warmth, a slave.

And mem'ries mock as the traffic roars
and the crowds walk blindly by;
so I curse the warmth that gives no life
but still won't let me die.

Ha!

Did you know I held a good job once?
And walked with head held high?
And dreamed my dreams and chased my goals
with sights set on the sky?

Did you know I wore a wedding ring
in some lifetime long ago?
And shared a bed with its wonders warm
and my spirit all aglow?

In those days I drove a Thunderbird
and I gazed with boastful scorn
on an old grey-beard—on this very grate
and I blasted with the horn.

And I rolled my window down once
and I shouted, "Get a job!"
And I felt disgust as he chewed a crust
from the gutter—like a dog.

But that old grey-beard is gone now.
Another fills his place.
And the grate gives stingy, meagre warmth
to another in disgrace.

And the mocking hasn't changed much
though I hear it with new ears.
And the joke's lost all its laughter—
I'm the target of the jeers.

And I haven't seen that smiling face
and I haven't felt the touch
of a loving hand with gentle warmth
though I long for it—oh so much.

And mem'ries mock as the traffic roars
and the crowds walk blindly by;
and I curse the warmth that gives no life,
but still won't let me die.

This selection is adapted from *Laughter & Tears*, book and audio CD, copyright © 2005 Brian Austin (LittleBoxStudios/Word Alive).

One True Friend

Fiction

Donna Dawson

*D*irt smudged across the tobacco stains that streaked the shaggy beard. Long grizzled grey hair had lost its tidy edge years ago and hung in chunks, like a wild pony's mane. How long the man had sat in his filthy heap upon the unforgiving sidewalk, Danny didn't know. Rheumy eyes nestled deep into the cragged and folded skin of his face and carried heartache so deep that Danny wondered if it could be erased. But he was determined to try. With a nod of his unruly red mop, he decided. *Yeah, this is the one.*

Matt, the new youth pastor at his church, had told them that Jesus befriended people before he tried to preach to them. So Danny settled his fleece and nylon-wrapped body onto the icy surface beside the old man and tried hard to ignore the pungent waft of body odour. The crisp, bright blue of his jacket contrasted with the worn denim that covered the scrawny arm next to his. He wondered if the man was even aware of his presence. Nothing moved; not a muscle twitched to show awareness. Eyes that watered because of the blast of the east wind continued their empty study of a spot of pavement somewhere between the second and third lane of traffic on the busy road.

A shiver wracked the elderly body. Danny noticed the old man's chapped and veined hands were tinged with the blue that comes from being too long in the cold. Pulling at the ends of his mitts, he removed them and then took one of the old man's limp hands. He worked a mitt onto it, careful to settle the fingers, stiff and gnarled with arthritis, into their proper places within the snug confines. The second mitt was more difficult. Danny was forced to lean across the old man, stirring up the pungent scents of an unwashed body. He turned his head and gagged once, disgusted by the smell. And then he settled his back against the scratchy brick wall behind him and stuffed his own hands deep into the pockets of his coat.

Silence wrapped around the two as car horns honked and music blared. The silence of the forgotten—the overlooked. Danny looked around, seeing with new eyes the street he'd walked on for 16 years. Litter skipped and tumbled down the gutter with each new blast of wind. Steam billowed, like the smoke of a passing train, from the mouths of the hurried and harried as they rushed to and fro, ignorant of his presence—of their presence. People he had smiled at, spoken to, just the day before, passed by without as much as a nod.

He frowned and turned his freckle-spattered face back to the old man. Legs covered with patched cotton pants were pulled up under the thin body in an effort to keep the cold away. He caught a glimpse of running shoes—broken-laced and worn through at the toes and soles. Why had he never seen this man before? The question tugged at him. Was this what Jesus meant when He said to love your neighbour as yourself? How long had this old man been an unloved neighbour?

Danny glanced at his watch. An hour had come and gone without a word spoken. *Well, this was a waste of time.* His stomach growled its empty state, and he pulled himself to his feet. The old man turned his eyes then and smiled—a faint lifting of the corners of his chapped and mustached lips. Danny nodded and turned to leave. He'd done what Matt had said. He'd been kind. Now he could have his supper and watch a DVD.

I was hungry and you fed me. I was thirsty and you gave me a drink. I was a stranger and you invited me in. The words dropped into his mind and he looked again at the old man. How long had it been since he'd eaten?

Danny shrugged away the thought. *I gave him my new mitts, for crying out loud.* Hunching against the wind, he headed for home.

A week passed. A week filled with video games, music, school, friends. Danny went through it all in a state of distraction. *I was hungry and you fed me.* He shrugged. *Yeah, like Mom and Dad would ever let me bring a homeless guy into the house for food.* Slamming his locker door shut, he flipped the dial on the lock, stuffed his hands into his pockets, and headed for the street. His left hand felt loose change and he pulled it out to count it.

There was enough for a burger at The Pit.

He didn't want to spend the money. He was saving for a really cool hat. One that would cover the thinning hair and baldness the cancer specialist had warned him would develop after he began chemotherapy.

Danny still hadn't worked through the whole cancer thing. *God seems to care more for the homeless than he does for the sick.* The angry thought brought a flush to his cheeks. Matt had said that Danny had to make a choice. He could let the cancer destroy him or let it define him. Danny didn't want to be a whiner about it, but it was scary.

Turning the corner, a huddled figure at the far end of the block came into sight, a rusted cookie tin pushed far enough forward to catch the wayward change that the odd passerby tossed to him. Danny sighed and felt the coins in his pocket. *I was hungry and you fed me.*

"OK, God. I get the point." He ducked into a greasy spoon and ordered a burger with the works and a styrofoam cup of water to go. Pocketing the few pennies left, Danny carried his small package to the old man and set the food on his lap.

The smell of grilled meat drew immediate attention and the old man looked at the bag with suspicion. "What do you want, kid?" His voice sounded like the offset gears of an old clock, scraping and grinding the words out.

"You looked like you could use some food. That's all," Danny said. He hesitated a minute, then added, "After you finish eating, I could walk you over to the men's shelter on Second Street, if you want. You shouldn't be out here in the cold all night."

He leaned a shoulder against the brick wall and waited as the old man unwrapped the burger and bit deep. Chewing gingerly, he tipped his head up and squinted a single eye, as though trying to see past the ski jacket. Danny offered a tight smile. The old man nodded once, his moth-eaten toque bobbling to the side with the weight of its shaggy pom-pom, and returned to his meal. When he was finished, Danny offered a hand, clasping hold of the familiar smoothness of his own mitts as the old man groaned and creaked to his hunched height.

Sandpaper tones assaulted the air again. "Your folks might not be happy seeing you with the likes of me."

Danny shrugged. "They'd say it's the right thing to do."

Scruffy eyebrows shot toward the toque's frayed rim as the two of them headed down the snow-blanketed street.

"So... How come you sit on the street like that and beg for money? Don't you have a home?" Danny couldn't help asking.

The old man grunted. "Nobody wants an old drunk, boy. And I can't seem to be nothing but an old drunk."

"Can't you just quit?"

Lifting his face to the sky, the old man swallowed hard.

Danny realized how callous his questions seemed. "Look, if you don't want to talk about it, no problem. I was just curious."

The old man shook his head then, and his eyes hardened. "The drink helps me forget. Helps me not think about the little girl I run down 14 years ago." Tears came suddenly, salty streaks of pain frosting pallid cheeks and crystallizing into the brittle grey whiskers.

Danny dropped his gaze to the ice- and salt-crusted sidewalk and for a moment was silent. How often had he wondered in the past week if the old man was just too lazy to work? Guilt poked at him, and he spoke quietly. "It's okay. We won't talk about it then. Look, I gotta get home before it gets too late. I got a doctor's appointment tomorrow. But—hey—after that, I'll try to stop by. Okay?"

The old man offered him a surprised nod and batted at his nose with the sleeve of his dirty jacket.

Danny waited until he'd slipped beyond the heavy wooden doors of the mission before turning away. He whistled the tune of his favourite rock song as he headed home.

I was thirsty and you gave me a drink. I was a stranger and you invited me in. Danny awoke the next morning to the same words running around in his mind. *Leave me alone! I don't want to think about some old guy hanging out in the streets*, Danny thought. *Why don't You send someone to help me? I'm scared about dying and all You do is keep telling me to go help some homeless bum!*

He'd asked Matt why those words kept running through his head. "Maybe God wants to use you to help this man," Matt had replied. "Or maybe He wants to teach you something." It wasn't the answer Danny wanted.

Danny had a violent reaction to his third chemo treatment. He woke up nauseated and scrambled to the bathroom, where he emptied himself of the previous night's meal. When the churning of his stomach finally died down he washed his face, brushed his teeth and pulled on a sweatshirt and jeans. He didn't feel like going out, but he didn't want to hang around the house either. Maybe if he went to see the homeless man one more time, God would leave him alone.

When his mother found him in the kitchen, she asked why he was packing a lunch on a Saturday. He told her about the homeless man.

A concerned look came over her face. "Danny, do you think you should be doing this—especially now? You can't afford to—you know—catch anything. It won't hurt for you to wait until you're better. That's what matters right now."

Danny frowned. "You're always telling me to do what Jesus would do. If I don't help him, nobody will," he mumbled, snatching up the lunch and letting the door close a bit louder than he should have.

The cold air hit him and he almost turned around. Dragging his feet, he kept on, following the inevitable trail to that patch of sidewalk.

What *would* Jesus do? He wouldn't help the guy out of guilt or obligation any more than He would just walk by. He'd love him.

"You want me to love him?" *But the greatest of these is love.* Danny sighed as more of Jesus' teachings drilled into his heart. "Okay, but this isn't going to be easy. I don't really feel like loving anyone right now." *But the greatest of these is love.* Danny forced a smile and approached the old man, who was huddled into the folds of his battered coat.

"Hey, I brought you something," Danny said.

The old man rolled his head around and fixed him with glassy eyes. A waft of sour breath hit Danny's face and he recoiled, turning his nose away. The old man was drunk. *What would Jesus do?* Dumb question.

Danny sat down and, pulling a sandwich from his backpack, broke a piece off and lifted it to the chapped lips, waiting for the old man to open his mouth. He repeated the action until the sandwich was gone; then pulled a small juice box from the bag. "Here, drink this. You need it." The old man drained the box and belched. Then he dropped his head to his chest and drifted off to sleep.

Shaking his head, Danny rose and returned home. *Another hour wasted.*

The winter ate at the days, small bitter chunks at a time, and most of the time the old man remained at his perch on the busy sidewalk.

When he felt up to it, Danny stopped and shared food and conversation. Some days the old man babbled incoherently, his breath strong with the smell of cheap cooking wine. Other days he just sat quietly and munched on the food, tears freezing to the silvered eyelashes. But sometimes the old man shared bits of his life and Danny sat mesmerized by the stories—stories he mulled over on the days when the chemotherapy made him too sick to leave the living room couch. It was on those days he wished he could do more for the old man.

"What about sharing Jesus with him?" his mother said. "You've got that New Testament Gramma gave you. Why not give him that?"

Danny punched the sofa pillow. "To be honest with you Mom, some days I find it hard reading the Bible myself. Why would he want to?"

"I didn't mean that you just hand it to him and leave it at that. Find some verses that mean something to you. Underline them. Dog ear the pages. That way you can share them with him. You never know unless you try." She smiled and returned to the dishes.

As Danny gathered strength over the next day, he picked John 3:16, Ephesians 2:8-9 and Romans 8:28, underlining them carefully in the small book. When he finally left the house, he whispered a plea as he walked. *Jesus, You know I'm not really good at this. I need Your help here. You want me to help this guy, so I'm asking You to show me how. Amen.*

Danny watched the old man as he handed him the small book.

"You know," the rough voice grated out the words, "I had someone give me one of these once and I just chucked it in the garbage can. I needed food and they gave me a book." Danny grew still. "A month ago, I might have thrown it back in your face. But now... I think I'll read it." He tucked it into the pocket of his coat and tipped his head back to look into the bright clear sky. "Boy, do you really think there's a God?"

Danny dropped down beside him and joined him in his search of the heavens. A sigh escaped as he thought about the question. "Yeah," he said. "I believe there's a God. Sometimes I kind of wonder what He's doing. Especially on the days when I'm puking into the toilet from the chemo. But the Bible says I'm supposed to trust Him. So I do."

The old man's face hardened and he looked away. "If He's so real and He cares, why does a good kid like you have to have cancer? Why did that little girl have to die?" He shook his head. "If He's there, He must not like us much."

Danny leaned back against the wall and turned to the old man. "When I first found out I had cancer, I was mad. I hated God." Danny paused for a minute. "But my Dad said I had to look at it as if it was him and me. Sometimes Dad tries to protect me from things that could be dangerous. Sometimes he lets me learn things the hard way. Sometimes he disciplines me for stuff. And sometimes he lets me try things that might be hard for me, so I'll find out things I need to know."

Danny halted briefly to see if the old man was still listening. "My dad also told me that God started out with a perfect world and we screwed it up. So He's been helping us deal with the consequences of that screw-up ever since. That book..." Danny nodded toward the pocket, "tells all about it. God doesn't cause cancer. But He's there to help me get through it. When I go through chemo, I remember that Jesus is there to help fix one more mess. And then I'm not scared anymore. I might not get better, but I just have to trust God like I trust my dad."

The old man ruminated over the answer and grunted as the boy rose to leave. "Okay. So I'll read your book. I'm not so sure it's all real. But I'll read it."

Danny offered a grin and headed home while the late afternoon traffic began to back up.

As he continued visiting the old man, Danny ignored his occasional bout of drunkenness. For his part, the old man never mentioned Danny's baldness. They talked. About life. About death. About Danny's faith. Danny began to realize he enjoyed the old man's friendship as much as the old man seemed to enjoy his.

April brought torrents of rain. Danny bought the old man an umbrella, which they shared during their brief meals together.

But just as the promise of spring whispered through the dirty grey streets, winter blew one last mighty breath upon the city. Freezing rain fell, power lines failed, cars slipped their way into ditches and each other, and most people stayed indoors.

Worried about the old man, Danny snatched his coat and slipped his way into the street. He was almost there when he heard the siren of an ambulance. He stopped to watch it race past. Seconds later, he saw a crowd gathered around the spot where the old man usually sat, and a car sprawled halfway across the curb.

Danny broke into a run, his small parcel of food flopping with each stride. He couldn't see the old man, but a policeman was talking to someone propped against the car hood, head in hands.

"Where is he?" Danny shouted. "Where's the old man?"

The officer looked up from his note pad. "You know him?"

Danny stopped and swallowed. "He's my friend."

"Do you know his name?"

Danny shook his head, ashamed that he'd never thought to ask. "Is he hurt bad?"

The policeman nodded and reached for his radio. "Tell you what. I'll get you to the hospital if you tell us what you know about him."

Danny nodded, watched the officer make the call, and then waited for a cruiser to arrive to take him to the hospital.

He knew Memorial Hospital well. It was where he had his treatments. Running through the emergency entrance doors, the second officer in tow, he approached the counter. "There was an old man brought in here. Hit by a car. I need to see him."

The nurse seated there continued to scribble on her chart. "Are you family?"

"Well—no. But I need to see him."

Pointing to a chair, she shook her head. "Sorry. I'll let you know when you can visit."

Firing off a short prayer, Danny sat, prepared for a long wait.

The policeman leaned on the counter and spoke in low tones to the nurse.

She looked up and pinned Danny with a surprised stare. "He did say something about a boy named Danny. You're Danny?"

Danny nodded.

"He hasn't stopped asking for you. Come with me."

Inside the emergency ward, the old man offered a tight smile through the pain as nurses bustled around him and machines hummed. "Knew you'd come. They say... say I got a lot of...," he coughed hard, "internal injuries."

Danny leaned close to hear the old man's hoarse whisper. "Want you to know, I been... been listening to what you said. I asked Jesus to bring you here. Figured if He did that... maybe He does care. Want you to know... I know Him now." Gripping the old man's hand, Danny cringed as a cough rattled through the heaving chest. "See you... some day... not too soon though..."

One of the machines began to blare out an alarm and a nurse called for help. Danny and the officer were ushered out into the hall.

Sitting in the waiting room, tears running down his face, Danny told the policeman everything he could remember about the old man. So little. So much.

A doctor approached, laid a gentle hand on Danny's shoulder. "I'm sorry, son."

Refusing the policeman's offer of a ride home, Danny rushed outside. His eyes blurred with tears, he staggered half a block before plopping down on a bench in the bus stop shelter. He sat there sobbing quietly, unaware of the cold or of the teen girl tucked into the shelter's corner watching him.

When he finally looked up, he caught her looking his way.

Her parka was torn, and her face was gaunt and dirty. Words came to him. *I was hungry and you fed me.* Wiping his jacket sleeve against tear-swollen eyes, he remembered the lunch bag he had shoved into his pocket. He offered her a small smile and said, "Have you eaten today?"

Padre, Can I Have a Word?

Non-fiction
Paul M. Beckingham

The moon hid behind the clouds on that early summer evening some years ago, tracing their silver outline against the deep blackness. Beneath the canopy of the trees all light was extinguished, so I could not discern the features of the duty Corporal beside me. He stood on guard in the Canadian Forces training area in Borden, Ontario, where we made our camp. I recognized him only by the sound of his voice, quiet, thoughtful and intense.

"I understand you served in Bosnia," I said. "How was it?"

"It was hell, Padre. I was blown up twice. Perhaps, one day, I can have a word with you about it, Padre."

"Sure," I said. "Why don't we take a walk right now? We can talk as we walk."

Under cover of darkness, we moved through the training area as this soldier, who I'd guess to be in his mid-twenties, began to tell me his story.

"I was driving an Iltis, a stripped-down jeep, at the head of a convoy. It was a dark night, just like tonight, and I was one of the duty drivers. It's a job that mostly Corporals get. Soon, it became pretty clear to me that we were passing through an enemy bivouac.[1] The trees formed a perfect harbour for armoured vehicles, and there was enough low vegetation to hide *houchies*[2] and tents."

"So what did you do?" I asked.

"I spoke to my crew commander in my vehicle. I told him my concerns and then I radioed back to *Niner*, the Officer in Command of the Unit."

"What did he say?" I inquired.

"Well, Padre, he was a young Captain with very little experience in command, and it was his first time in a theatre of operations. He told me to drive on."

"And did you?" I pressed.

"Yeah, but I radioed back and said, 'Look, Sir, this is a real obvious bivouac. There are traces of armoured tracks on this route in, and lots of coverage for tents and vehicles. I think they might still be occupying this area. I think we're in danger.'"

I felt the hair rising on the back of my neck. "What did he do?" I asked.

"He cussed me and told me to drive on. But I radioed back and told him that I needed to question his order. I felt certain that the enemy was close to us. I reminded him that in every bivouac there is only one safe route in and out. All the others are booby-trapped with explosives. But he just cussed me again and ordered me to drive on. He was really angry that time, because he didn't like my questioning his order."

"So what did you do?" I asked.

"Padre, I drove on. I had no choice. But it was about twenty seconds later... that it happened." He became quiet and thoughtful as his voice tailed off into silence.

"What happened?" I prompted.

"All hell broke loose! My vehicle hit a land mine, the front wheel on the driver's side was blown off, and my vehicle rolled into a ditch. I was thrown out into the undergrowth and my hearing was dull and everything echoed. Then, in the darkness, they started to fire on us with tracer bullets that glow in the dark. We came under direct fire. I managed to crawl back to the vehicle to find my weapon and I fired back."

He continued, "Eventually, all the firing stopped. The enemy made their getaway, leaving us to regroup in our remaining vehicles. Then we had to find our way out without hitting more land mines. It was very scary. I didn't want to be blown up again."

By now, this soldier was crying freely. I couldn't see his tears in the darkness, but I could hear his voice. He poured out his pain: the panic attacks, the post-traumatic stress disorders, the depression, anger, and suicidal feelings. He had lived through it all.

Just to hear his story was enough. Soldiers have few places where they can safely cry, few people who will listen. When a Padre listens, God shows up, somehow; He holds a soldier's pain, He gathers up his sorrow.

Sometimes, our churches are places where those with different kinds of battle scars seek healing. People who are honourably wounded, injured in the service of the King of Kings, need respite, help and understanding.

I wonder if our communities of faith are safe places for soldiers—of any sort—to cry. Maybe we need to learn how to walk a few paces with those in pain and let them talk freely in God's presence.

Sometimes, listening is enough. It says that God cares, too.

1. A temporary encampment.
2. One-person tarps for overnight shelter.

Shared Tears

Brian Austin

When wounds are deeper than words can heal;
When you've plumbed the pit of pain;
When you can't imagine the day will come
that you might smile again;
When you hurt with a bottomless depth of hurt,
more than you believed you could endure
and it seems that life has nothing left
and death's the only cure;

Then let me cry with you awhile,
share aching, silent tears.
Lean on me. Accept a hug.
Let me bear some of your fears.
I can't undo the hurt you feel
or take away your pain.
I can't bring back what you have lost
or make you whole again.
But if I'm wise enough to hold my tongue
and only share my tears,
'twill be a greater gift than wondrous words
with wisdom of the years.

When the night has dragged a century long
but you dread the coming day.
When your tears are wrung out, stale and dry
yet the pain won't go away.
When you're all alone in a private hell

with words of comfort a noisy din;
and you're empty, hollow, sick and numb;
just a deadening ache within;

Then let me cry with you awhile,
share aching, silent tears.
Lean on me. Accept a hug.
Let me bear some of your fears.
I can't undo the hurt you feel
or take away your pain.
I can't bring back what you have lost
or make you whole again.
But if I'm wise enough to hold my tongue
and only share my tears,
'twill be a greater gift than wondrous words
with wisdom of the years.
When one you love has let you down
and you're wounded through and through.
When they've gone for good without a word
and the healing's left to you.
When your living heart from beneath your breast
has been crushed and ripped apart;
When your eyes are dry, no tears left to cry,
just a wound where you had a heart;

Then let me cry with you awhile,
share aching, silent tears.
Lean on me. Accept a hug.
Let me bear some of your fears.
I can't undo the hurt you feel
or take away your pain.
I can't bring back what you have lost
or make you whole again.
But if I'm wise enough to hold my tongue

and only share my tears,
'twill be a greater gift than wondrous words
with wisdom of the years.

When everyone has a word to share
and their words are prob'ly true;
But your wounds seem too deep to heal
and it's all just noise to you;
When you're dead inside and you want to hide
but life demands that you play your role;
When the Love of God is lost in a fog;
Surviving seems a hopeless goal;

Then let me cry with you awhile,
share aching, silent tears.
Lean on me. Accept a hug.
Let me bear some of your fears.
I can't undo the hurt you feel
or take away your pain.
I can't bring back what you have lost
or make you whole again.
But if I'm wise enough to hold my tongue
and only share my tears,
'twill be a greater gift than wondrous words
with wisdom of the years.

This selection is adapted from *Laughter & Tears*, book and audio CD, copyright © 2005 Brian Austin (LittleBoxStudios/Word Alive).

On Writing with Passion and Integrity

Non-fiction
M. D. Meyer

Someone asked me the other day if I was "still working at the school." When I told them that I'd quit my job to write full-time, there was the inevitable question: "Any money in that?"

I had to admit that there isn't—or at least not much.
And narrowing the field to Christian writing only serves to further diminish my potential income.

"So it's kind of a hobby then?"

I had to smile. The image conjured up by the word "hobby" seemed far removed from my everyday writing experience.

But there is really no simple way to describe what I do or why I do it.

I write because I have to. It's like breathing.
It's a compulsion. An addiction.
It's a ministry. A gift.
A burden.

My research on the after-effects of Indian residential schools on Aboriginal Canadians tears at my soul. I ache to think about young children being taken from their parents and thrust into a foreign environment, forced to speak a new language, beaten and even molested, all in the name of Jesus.

And I agonize over the formidable task of telling their story,
knowing these children are now adults and many of their voices
have been silenced.
Do I dare to speak for them?

If I do speak, I know I first must listen.
Just sit and listen.
Not rush ahead and make assumptions,
But open my heart.
And listen until it hurts me too.

Immerse myself in their stories until I can feel…
the pain of an abused child,
the desperation of a prostitute,
the despair of an alcoholic.

Till I can know
or perhaps just imagine for a moment
the struggles of a young man with AIDS.

It's not what I *want* to do.
It's more like what I *have* to do.

Compelled by love.
His love for me.
My love for Him.
His love for a hurting world.

It would be a lie to say that I do it all alone.
That it is simply a talent that I was born with or earned.

I feel God's presence with me as I write.
Sometimes I think I am only a pen in His hands.
Or perhaps a microphone or an amplifier.
And he is the sound man, fine-tuning the dials.

I write what I have heard.
People read what I write and perhaps they hear, too.

I report the story of a man who was an alcoholic on the streets for more than 20 years. Jesus changed his life. Now he has been sober for more than 20 years. It is a milestone for him.

He dreams that his story, published in a newspaper, will help young people find hope in their lives, and that they too will be able to overcome alcohol.

I write a novel about a young woman who has begun a healing journey from child sexual abuse. She is a fictional character spun from a hundred stories told by a hundred people.

I dream of the day when others will read my book and feel hope. And find the courage to begin their own healing journeys.

Sometimes, well-meaning friends or colleagues suggest ways I can develop my writing career. They tell me I could be making money writing textbooks for schools or doing a parenting column for a local newspaper...

And occasionally I do try something for monetary gain. But it never really works for me.
When I feel no passion, I lack the commitment to strive for excellence.
I end up procrastinating on projects that haven't engaged my soul and my spirit.

If I don't feel passion, there is really no point.

I feel passionate about despair.
I feel passionate about hope.

Despair comes when no one hears. No one knows.
Hope comes when someone hears. When someone understands.

I see myself as a reporter.
Even when I write fiction.
Because either way, I am telling a story.
Of what I have seen and what I have heard.

Integrity—being true to yourself and what you believe.

I did stop writing once.
I gave up. Threw in the towel.
I was tired of swimming upstream.
Writing what no one wanted to read.
Fighting for a cause that no one had heard of.
Walking with only a candle lighting a path only I trod.

I convinced myself that I was justified in quitting.
The rewards were too few and too far between.
The recognition rare and so disproportionate to the cost.

I even shook my fist at God—my Maker, my Redeemer, my best
Friend.

I implied that He owed me something.
A book contract?
What next—a best-seller?
A whole row of best-sellers?

Is it really fame and fortune that I seek?

Well, I don't deny, it would be fun.
I'm human, after all.

But if fame and fortune elude me?

Is it enough for me to write just because I know He wants me to?
Is it enough for me to have His approval and His alone?
Is it enough for me to wait for the only reward that will
ever matter...
    When He says to me, "Well done."

Yes, it is enough.

Editors' Note: In 2004, Dorene won the God Uses Ink contest for unpublished writers sponsored by The Word Guild. First prize was free registration to the Write! Canada Christian writers' conference. Dorene and her husband made the four-day, 2,062-kilometre (1,281-mile) trip from northwestern Ontario to Guelph, Ontario by motorcycle, camping along the way. In 2007, Dorene attended her fourth Write! Canada with a Manitoba Arts Council travel grant. This time, she was a member of the faculty.

My Letter to the Editor

Non-fiction
N. J. Lindquist

When I was twelve years old, I decided to do something to help the people in my town who didn't seem to know God the way I did.

For as long as I could remember, God had been my best friend. As a young child, I had assumed everyone had the same kind of relationship with Him that I did. But as I got older, I realized there were differences, and I became puzzled. Had some people turned their backs on Him on purpose? Did they know what they were missing? Even my own parents didn't seem to understand that God wanted a relationship with them, and not just their attendance at a Sunday morning worship service.

At that time, we received three newspapers at our house: the daily *Winnipeg Tribune*, the bi-weekly *Brandon Sun*, and our local weekly, the *Souris Plaindealer*. I was familiar with the Letters to the Editor sections in each. After praying about it, I decided the easiest way for me to tell lots of people about God was to write a letter to the editor. I usually did okay in my essays for school, and the newspaper would reach more people than I could ever talk to on my own. I thought our local newspaper offered the best chance for me to get published. And while it was the smallest paper, there were 2,000 people in our town, plus many more in the surrounding countryside.

I worked on the letter, rewriting it several times, trying to keep it from being too long (I had counted the number of words in other letters) and trying to keep it from sounding as though I was putting people down. When I thought it was ready, I copied it in my best handwriting (we didn't own a typewriter).

But then it occurred to me that the letter might embarrass my parents. This was, after all, a very small town. My father was a businessman who owned Shaw's Clothing. The owner and editor of the *Plaindealer* was a good friend of my dad's.

Was there a way I could get the letter published without letting anyone know I wrote it? After all, I wasn't writing it to get attention for myself; I just wanted to tell people that God loved them.

I'd heard of authors using pseudonyms, so I decided to come up with one. I used my second name—Jane—which I thought was too plain. Ever since the actress Jayne Mansfield had become popular, I'd been adding a "y." For my last name, I decided to use my mother's maiden name. So I became Jayne MacDonald.

I don't know why I didn't just mail it. Stamps only cost eight cents in those days. But for some reason, I decided to drop it off myself. Of course, I had to get it into the newspaper office without being discovered. I put the letter in an envelope and addressed it to the editor, then took it to school with me. After school, I walked downtown as I frequently did. (In a town of 2,000 people, that isn't very far!) I went to my father's store, dropped off my books, and left again, keeping the letter out of sight.

I walked down to the newspaper office and hovered around the outside, peering through the window now and then, until I saw the woman at the reception desk get up and go into the back room. The instant she left, I whipped inside, threw the letter on the counter, and dove out of the office. My heart was racing 100 miles an hour. But as I walked back to our store, I relaxed. I had done my part. The letter was written and delivered. The rest was up to God.

For several days, I lived in dread that someone would say something to me. I expected the editor to tell my parents. Would they be angry with me for writing those words? Would my letter even be printed, or was it too "religious"? A week passed and I heard nothing. Then the new *Plaindealer* arrived. I opened it and looked in the Letters to the Editor section. There was my letter, exactly as I had written it.

For several more days, I was afraid someone might figure out I'd written the letter and say something to me. But no one ever did.

In case you're wondering what a 12-year-old might write, this is my letter, just as it was then.

Dear Sir:

Although I am not sure if you will use this letter, I sincerely hope you will, and that it will help some person to "see the light."

The "light" I refer to is God. I have been prompted to write this letter because I feel that there are millions of lost people who do not know that they have a friend, a Father, who cares for, and loves, them no matter who they are, what colour they are, or what they have done.

These people may be ignorant and lazy, or socially prominent. To him they are all alike. He loves them all. If only more people could realize this, our world would be a wonderful place in which to live.

Watching the Billy Graham crusade on television recently, I was thrilled to see hundreds of people streaming down onto a muddy field, in the rain, to acknowledge that they had at last found their Lord.

It was truly wonderful to know that their lives would now take on a new and glorious meaning.

I feel sorry for those empty people who do not know Christ. They have no one to confide in, no one to ask for forgiveness for their sins, no one to gather strength from. They do not know that there is a Lord who loves them so much that He sent His only Son to die so that they might live.

By saying that God forgives our sins, I do not mean that it is right to sin. Our Lord is deeply hurt when we yield to our temptations. But if we are truly sorry, He is glad to forgive us.

To me, God is a friend, a father, an advisor, and a rock on which I can lean in time of trouble. I deeply wish that more people could come to know God and to feel as safe and strong as I feel in his care.

Thank you.

Miss Jayne MacDonald

Years passed, and I completely forgot about my letter to the editor. For some reason I hadn't even saved a copy of it, or if I had, I lost it along the way.

By 1998, my mother, then in her late eighties, was living in a nursing home near us in Ontario. Multi-infarct dementia (loss of memory from a series of small strokes) had taken its toll, and a few of her belongings had recently gone missing, including a necklace she had worn for years. I was concerned she might lose something that was important, such as her birth certificate. So one day, while she was sleeping, I went through her purse to see if there was anything in it that needed to be put in a safe place.

In the back of her wallet was a small section for credit cards and photos, so I carefully took out the items, which primarily consisted of pictures of my family. But tucked away behind one of the photos was a newspaper clipping.

I expected to find an obituary, either that of my father, who had died in 1992, or another relative. Instead, folded and yellowed, I found my letter to the editor. Across the top was written, in my mother's handwriting, "Nancy wrote this."

She had saved that clipping for nearly 40 years, and yet she'd never said one word about it to me!

I'll never know if my letter to the editor played a role in her life, but I do know that after years of being puzzled and somewhat disparaging about my faith, she made a commitment to God while in her seventies. She affirmed it before her death in January 2000.

Finding that clipping in my mother's purse jolted me. For some time, in both my speaking and my writing, I'd been encouraging people to obey the desires of their hearts—no matter how crazy those dreams might seem. And I'd been urging them not to worry about the results—to leave that entirely up to God.

Discovering my long-ago letter hammered home the truth of what I'd been telling others. My heart needed that affirmation. It was both God's validation of my writing and speaking ministry, and further evidence of His faithfulness to me—and to all of His children.

This selection is adapted from the forthcoming book *LoveChild*, copyright © 2008 by N. J. Lindquist (That's Life! Communications/*www.lovechildministries.com*).

The Child on the Tracks

Non-fiction
Carmen Wittmeier

"It's not our problem that children in developing countries starve. If their parents are too lazy to take care of them, then they deserve to die!"

Silence—a rare thing indeed—came over my class of college English students. One or two met my eyes; others turned to peer curiously at their classmate, who sat in the third row with her chin up, her body rigid, her clothing impeccable.

Though a relatively new instructor at Langara College in Vancouver, British Columbia, I knew enough to avoid appearing shocked. Literature could lead to lively classroom discussion, and today's literary morsel, a controversial essay from *The New York Times Magazine* called "The Singer Solution to World Poverty,"[1] had definitely whetted my students' appetite for debate.

I always appreciated their candour, their passion, their willingness to voice what they really thought. Still, I was a product of my experience, and the month I had spent volunteering with World Vision in a Romanian orphanage two years earlier had left its mark. I could not let this statement go unchallenged.

"Is it possible that some parents lack the resources—the opportunity—to provide for their children?" I asked gently.

She shook her head. "People shouldn't have kids if they can't take care of them. It's irresponsible!"

"I wouldn't call impoverished parents lazy, exactly," another student offered. "Or irresponsible. The problem is that if we help them, they'll simply have more children, who will also end up starving. Isn't it more humane to let nature take its course?"

She was little more than a year old when she was found on the front steps of the orphanage. She had no name. No birth certificate. Though her skin revealed her gypsy heritage, she had no other identity. She was an abandoned child, a ward of the government.

And yet she lived fiercely. I could see her spark the moment I stepped through the door into the room of silent children. Anca,[2] now three, immediately scrambled to the front of her crib. Making whimpering noises deep in the back of her throat, she attempted to scale the bars of her crib to get to me. The moment she found her way into my arms, she smiled knowingly.

As if a switch had been turned on, every child in that room, some too small to stand, simultaneously lit up with a grin. Babies stared through the bars of their cribs, mesmerized, as Anca clung to me, her head tilted back in a long silent laugh. We spun around the room, two strangers in a dance.

In "The Singer Solution to World Poverty," Princeton University philosopher and ethicist Peter Singer tells the story of Bob and his Bugatti, a rare and valuable sports car into which he had invested his life's savings.

One day, having parked his Bugatti at the end of a railway siding, Bob walks up the track and into a crisis. Up ahead, he sees a child upon the rail, and a runaway train hurtling towards the tiny figure.

Bob has two choices. He can do nothing, allowing the train to follow its course and hit the child. Or he can pull a switch that will divert the train away from the child and into his prized car.

With his blonde hair and haunting brown eyes, Raphael was considered the most beautiful toddler in the home for abandoned children.

"Fermosa," a caregiver said to me, shaking her head as if in disbelief. "Beautiful."

More than anything, I admired how Raphi's angelic appearance concealed a genius for mischief and a fleetness of foot. He and his accomplice, a wild-haired imp named Soren, had the uncanny ability to climb onto—or into—all things forbidden. Woe to the volunteer who left a cupboard door unlocked or an exit unguarded! Raphi and Soren were always the chief instigators in "prison breaks," a term humorously applied whenever the orphans stampeded through a door that they had somehow pried open.

Raphi's mother visited him every chance she could, and her pride was evident. She spent every moment she could in the narrow hallway that served as a play area for the orphans, her eyes always on Raphael, her arms always open to her son.

A single mother, she worked long hours hawking newspapers in traffic, but they were not enough. Like so many other Romanian parents, she could not afford to provide for her son, to rescue him from an uncertain future.

Every time she left, Raphael would wander the halls looking for her.

Many students were shocked by the ending to Bob's story. Rather than sacrificing the Bugatti, Bob does nothing and the child subsequently dies.

"That's disgusting!"

"He should be locked up for the rest of his life!"

"Who would choose a car over a child?"

A few students would anticipate a moral ambush. Indeed, moments later, the outrage that had filled the classroom was replaced with an uncomfortable silence created by a single question.

Are we any different from Bob?

We have the resources to save children's lives, Singer argues. We know that there are children—too many of them to count—standing on the tracks. We each have a choice to make.

"It's not the same thing," one student said, pressing the heel of his hand to his forehead. "It can't be."

"It's hard on Mihai, always being with the other children," observed Tony, World Vision Romania's volunteer coordinator. "They're never alone, never apart. It's stressful for them."

Mihai was indeed having another meltdown, his third that day. He was the orphanage bruiser, a toddler who would physically remove all obstacles in his path—baby or otherwise. I once saw him pick up a plastic bowling pin. Before I could intervene, he had methodically thunked every baby around him on the head until a chorus of cries drowned out the television blaring in the background.

Despite his temper tantrums, Mihai was one of my favourites.

He was an unintentional comedian. When identical twins arrived one afternoon, Mihai faced them, gawking, his mind clearly unable to fathom how a toddler could replicate itself. He was equally astonished by his belly button. And one of my fondest memories involved this masculine little boy shredding a book with his mouth while wearing flowery shoes clearly intended for a girl.

Whenever I hoisted him on my shoulders, Mihai would sing in a deep, throaty voice. "Gida gida gida gida!" he would call out joyfully— his words for the sound the caregivers had made when tickling him as a baby.

My students were not the only ones shaken by Peter Singer's analogy.

For some time afterward, I struggled to come to grips with my responsibility for the children I could now see on the metaphorical tracks before me. Would I give up a dinner and movie with friends to feed a hungry child? Was it wrong to cater to my genetic predisposition for pumpkin spice lattés? Did I really need a new leather jacket to keep me warm, or was it evidence of an inherent selfishness?

But I sensed, too, that there was more to the picture.

Giving, I have since realized, is not the same thing as giving up—giving away. Dinner and a movie pale in comparison to the soul-nourishing experience of ensuring that a child will not go to bed hungry. No pumpkin spice latté, however frothy, is comparable to knowing that because of my actions, a child is now safe and warm. A new jacket is meaningless next to the wild joy I feel when a friend or acquaintance chooses to sponsor a child.

"I'm a child sponsor," one student informed her classmates. "Every year I see her grow. I receive a photo, and I know she's being clothed and fed. I'm not saying I'm a hero or anything, but I am changing the life of this one little girl."

Gabriella was the sort of orphan who could make a volunteer feel helpless one moment and ecstatic the next. Autistic, she was locked in her own world, unable to communicate through language or eye contact. When her needs, so different from those of the other orphans, went unmet, she clenched her fists, grimaced, and rocked, sometimes crying in frustration until her lips turned a pale shade of blue.

Of all the orphans, Gabriella struggled the most to make sense of the seemingly arbitrary rules that governed the adult world. Once, upon oversleeping and missing her snack, the little girl grabbed a volunteer by the hand. In vain she attempted to pull him to the lunchroom; in vain he tried to gesture that the food had been put away.

It took patience to break through her barriers. The volunteer before me had taught her to walk. I, in turn, formed a relationship by swinging her back and forth. Day after day she would seek me out, and I would swing her though the air. One day, a day I will never forget, Gabriella looked directly into my eyes and smiled.

I eventually gave up teaching, and in September 2007 I accepted a position with World Vision Canada. As a representative for Southern Alberta, I now stand before new audiences: students and teachers, church congregations and youth groups, businesses, and anyone else who longs to make a difference. It is my way of walking towards the children on the tracks, of trying to do what I can to pull them from the path of the train. It is my way of joining with others who refuse to make the choice Bob did.

On my last day at the orphanage, Gabriella knew that I would not be coming back. As I slipped through the door that would permanently separate me from the children who had shared their joy and grief so openly, I could see a sobbing Gabriella place her hands against the solid wooden barrier.

"I'm not really leaving you, Gabbie," I whispered, unable to fight back my own tears. *"I promise to do everything I can to help you. And if I can't bring you out of this place, I'll do everything in my power to make sure that other children don't suffer as you have."*

I believed, then, that I would save Gabriella. Now I know better: it was Gabriella, a child on the tracks, who saved me.

1. Peter Singer, "The Singer Solution to World Poverty," *The New York Times Magazine*, September 5, 1999, pp. 60-63. See http://www.nytimes.com/library/magazine/home/19990905mag-poverty-singer.html.
2. Names have been changed to protect the anonymity of the orphans with whom I worked.

The Stuckville Café

Fiction
Bonnie Grove

The town has a real name, but I call it Stuckville. Because, boy, oh, boy, I'm stuck here. Plunked down in the middle of nothing-to-write-home-about by a husband who wanted a change (so we moved here), then wanted a bigger change (so he left me). Now, I'm the sole proprietor of one rinky-dink café right across the street from the train tracks. I sell ice cream, espresso drinks and Mexican food. I know the combination sounds cock-eyed, but most everything about this town is cock-eyed.

Don't think there aren't times I think I should cut bait and run. But I suffer from the worst of human maladies—a double whammy of a total lack of a plan and an over-developed sense of responsibility. Like I said: stuck.

Gene's a regular. When I say "regular" I mean a constant presence. He's old, like dirt. Or so he says. One day he says, "Carol, I'm old." Me, diplomatic and tactful like I am, I say something like, "Oh, Gene, you're only as old as you feel," or some such gabber. He looks me square on and says, "Woman, I'm as old as dirt." And he pounds his cane on the floor. Now, I'm not old, but I've been around long enough to know that when an old man calls you "Woman," and bangs things on the floor, its best to just smile and nod.

Gene comes in twice a day, after lunch and just before supper. Sure, he likes the coffee, but he's actually coming to see me for medical treatments. Cancer has chewed away at his ear, and the doctors have taken most of the rest of it. They left a piece though, a ragged, festering gob of flesh that requires a salve to be applied three times a day. Unfortunately, Home Care only comes once a day, and because Gene is half blind, he can't see to apply it himself. So he walks the block and a half from his house across from the post office to my café twice a day. When the place is devoid of other customers, I apply cream to the stump of his ear with a Q-tip and tape new gauze to the wound.

One morning he presents his ear for my inspection and says, "What kind of a God lets an old man get cancer?"

I pull off the blood-encrusted tape and say, "The same one that let you get as old as dirt."

Gene grumbles, but I see a smile pull at the corners of his mouth.

He says, "Who says there's a God? You can't see Him. You can't know Him."

I squint at the oozing blob of flesh that used to be his ear. It looks bad. Worse than yesterday. "The Bible says you can know God if you are born again in the Spirit. 'The wind blows wherever it pleases,'" I quote. "'You hear its sound, but you can't tell where it comes from or where it's going. So it is with everyone born of the Spirit.'"

Gene pulls his eyebrows together until they form a V in the middle of his forehead. "Bible says that?"

I dab at his ear. It smells terrible. "Yeah, a guy named Jesus said that. Ever heard of Him?"

Gene smiles and nods like a bobble head.

"Hold still," I say, "Did the home care nurse say anything about the way your ear looks today?"

"Like what?"

"I don't know. When you see her tomorrow, you ask her about it, okay?"

Grumble.

Teresa comes to my shop several times a week. She normally orders a couple of burritos, a plate of nachos, and ice cream for dessert. Today she sits stirring herbal tea, the only thing she's ordered. I'm happy to be missing out on the money from her large orders 'cause Teresa is trying to lose weight.

She puts the spoon down on a napkin and takes a tentative sip. "My mother is coming this weekend. I'm dreading it."

It's quiet in the café, Teresa is the only customer. I sit at her table, absently wiping it with a damp cloth. "Why dreading?"

Teresa pulls a face, like she just ate a bug. "She hates me. She's always hated me."

The train across the road blows long "whuuuuunnnnnk, whuuuu-unnnnk" whistles, and scares us both out of our cotton socks. As the train screels and skreeks through town, Teresa and I smile patiently at each other. Only when the train has moved off a reasonable distance can we continue our conversation.

I prop my chin up with my right hand, elbow on the table. "That's a good reason to dread her arrival."

Teresa takes a long sip of tea. "Do you know what it's like to have your mother hate you?"

I think for moment. "Nope."

"It's horrible." She starts crying, quietly, small streams of tears leaking out of her eyes. She stabs at them with a finger. I get up and grab the box of tissues I keep behind the counter and place it on the table. She pulls one out and holds it to her eyes. "She's the reason I'm fat," Teresa says in a flattened voice. She rolls her eyes. "You think I sound stupid. Blaming my mother for my being fat."

I look her in the eye. "Eating makes you feel better."

The floodgates open. She grabs at the tissues and pushes a handful of them at her tears. "I'm bawling in public. What if someone comes in and sees me?"

I mime a Groucho Marx cigar and waggle my eyebrows at her. "Ya want me to tell you a joke?"

She smiles through her tears and sips the tea. She makes a long, loud slurping sound. Some of the tea sloshes down her shirt.

I grin. "You'll lose weight fast if you dump half of what you're putting in your mouth onto your clothes."

She starts to giggle, but tries to cover it by smacking her lips together. I slap my hand over my mouth, smothering a laugh. I take a sharp breath in and make a weird piggy sound with my nose.

The two of us dissolve into laughter, snorting and stomping like a couple of kids.

The door opens and a family of three walk in. I touch my face, which feels menopausal hot from laughing, and smile at the new arrivals.

Teresa turns in her chair and salutes them with her cup. "I highly recommend the tea."

They look confused, but the train whistle blows again and no one can explain anything.

It's three in the afternoon and the pipeline guys are jamming into the café. Twelve burly men, who smell of clay and metal, press their faces to the ice cream cooler.

A young guy looks up at me with Christmas tree eyes and says, "Can we order triples?"

"Yep."

A voice from behind the gaggle of men hollers. "Can they all be different flavours?"

I stand on my tip toes and shout into the crowd. "You bet."

Twelve grown men bellow "Woo hoo!" and begin ordering all at once.

I'm scooping a ball of Moose Tracks when I hear Debi's voice call me. "Surrounded by fawning men. What else is new?" She smiles at me over the heads of the men. She can do that. She's over six feet tall.

I strike a movie star pose. "Just my lot in life, I guess. Are you working this afternoon?" I ask, meaning the flower shop next door.

She joins me behind the freezer, grabs a scoop and says, "I work here now." She pokes a finger toward a short guy wearing safety goggles. "You want a waffle cone?"

I throw her a grateful smile and the triple scoop waffle cone I'm holding breaks in half and crashes to the floor with a dull sploot. I stare down at it, shaking my head. "Rats." I look up at the man in the hard hat who ordered it. He's grinning. "That's okay," he says. "I changed my mind anyway. I want Bear Claw instead of Cotton Candy."

The man in the hard hat is paying for the men's ice cream. "Thirteen triples."

I look at him. "Twelve."

He grins as he holds out the money. "Plus the one that hit the floor. We'll be back tomorrow."

Debi pops in on a break from her part-time job at the flower shop. The café is empty and I'm sitting at a table in the corner reading. Debi peers over the prep table. "Got nachos today?"

I put my book on the table, face down. "Sure."

I'm grating cheese and Debi sits at the table I just got up from. She picks up my book and flips the pages. "Whatcha reading?"

I fling chopped onion and red pepper onto the nachos. "It's about how God works with you when your life is messed up." I put the nachos in the microwave and push some buttons.

Debi sets the book down. "Should be a bestseller." She gets up, opens the fridge and pours salsa into a bowl. I snag the sour cream and the gooey hot nachos. We sit down and dive in.

"You know what?" Debi says. Her mouth is full so it comes out, "Woo now ut?"

"What?"

She wipes salsa off her chin with a napkin. "You keep wondering how on earth you ended up here—"

"In Stuckville," I say.

"Yeah, in Stuckville. But I thank God every day that you're here. Know why?" She jams three nacho chips in her mouth.

"Cuz you like my cooking?" I shove two chips in my mouth and a dollop of sour cream blops onto the table.

We chew loudly at each other, smiling. Debi is new to my life, but I feel like I've known her forever.

She's about to answer when the door opens and a "holy-smokes-get-a-load-of-this" guy walks in.

He's short, about five foot seven[1] with coal-black hair slicked back, and wearing what looks like an expensive black leather jacket. I get up from the table and smile at him. He flashes 32 blinding white teeth in return. He looks cool and handsome in a Fonzie sort of way. Except he doesn't ride a bike. I see his car out the window, a speeding bullet of a BMW. The top is down and the leather seats seem to purr in the sunlight. There is only one explanation for his presence in Stuckville: this guy is lost.

I smile. "What can I get you?"

He pulls off his sunglasses and his eyes, brown as Momma's gravy, look me up and down. "Your sign says you serve espresso. Is it any good?"

I think for a second. "I don't know."

He slides me another grin. "Well, make me one and I'll tell you." He sits at an empty table and begins rapping out a beat with his knuckles on the table. He glances at Debi and acknowledges her by cocking his thumb and finger, lone gunman style, at her and making a "click click" sound. Undaunted, Debi forms a gun with her fingers, points at him and says, "Kapow, right back at ya."

I start up the espresso machine. It's a honker of a stainless steel behemoth that can spew out up to four teensy cups of coffee at a time. It's so loud no one can be heard over its burbling and snorting. Still, Debi tries, bellowing something to him over the noise. He cups his ear with his hand and hollers, "Eh?" back at her.

I turn the machine off and Debi shouts, "Why are you here?" She slaps at her mouth, and then says in a normal voice, "Pardon my yelling. What brings you to town?"

I put the espresso on the table in front of him and he looks up at me. For a second our faces are close together. "Well," he says. "That remains to be seen." He smiles into my eyes and raises an eyebrow.

I back up fast until I make contact with the ice cream freezer. My stomach feels fluttery. I try to think back to the last time a man flirted with me. Ten years of memories fly by and I give up.

He's looking at me as he takes a sip of the coffee. "It's good. What's your name?"

"Uh, Carol. That's Debi." I point to her. They look at each other and exchange "Heys."

Like most people who spend more than ten minutes in my café, our new macho friend opens up like a can of worms. His name is James, but everyone, except his Mamma, calls him Jimmy. He's working in a nearby city overseeing the installation of video lottery terminals in a new casino. He tells us he's divorced from a "high maintenance" woman who colours her hair "bimbo blonde," wears too much makeup, and doesn't spend enough time with their two-year-old son. He worries about his son being in day care five days a week. He says he knows he isn't home enough, but his job involves lots of travelling. He worries what's going to happen to the kid.

He looks at me. "You married?"

Oh gee. How to answer? Technically, I'm married. But, since my husband is living with his pregnant girlfriend, I'm not holding out much hope for our future bliss together.

He frowns at me. "What? You don't know if you're married?"

I shrug. "Some questions are more complicated than they appear."

He finishes his coffee. "I gotta go. But I'll be back soon. I want an answer to my question."

I grab a dish towel and start twisting it. "Hey, listen, tough guy, it was nice to meet you. I'm sorry about your kid. What's his name?"

Hand on the door, he cocks his head. "Jonathan. I call him Jonny. Why?"

"I'll pray for him."

He smiles, but he's shaking his head. "Oh, man. You're a religious girl? I wouldn't have pegged ya for the type."

"We can be handy to have around."

He pushes the door open. "Yeah, that's what my Mamma says."

Teresa has lost ten pounds.[1] She comes by to tell me and to have a cup of raspberry jazz tea. "I need to thank you."

I lift an eyebrow. "What for?"

She shakes her head. "I don't know. You listened to me like you understood. It's not often that thin people listen to fat people."

I wave my hands in a no-way gesture. "Hey, inside this thin body is a couch potato yearning to get out. You're doing all the work. I'm just your herbal tea supplier."

She pushes her lips together hard. "Seriously, you did more than that." Her glance falls to the table. I watch her for a second and then I get it.

She's felt it. She knows I pray for her.

I feel tears well up in my eyes and I offer up serious gratitude to God for the cool ways He works to connect people together. My shoulder jerks in a tiny shrug. "I pray for people. It's what I do."

She doesn't look up. I see a tear hit the table. "I know. I think that's why I keep coming here."

Gene arrives earlier than usual. It's ten in the morning and I've just opened the café. He flops into a chair. "The nurse said it's fine. Looks terrible, but these things do, you know. They cut half my head off."

"You do remarkably well for a man with half a head."

He opens his mouth wide and slaps his knee. He's laughing. "She made me an appointment in the city on Tuesday."

I put the coffee pot down, walk over to the phone and dial. "Deb? Can you drive Gene to the city on Tuesday for a doctor's appointment?" I listen for a second, and then hang up.

Gene doesn't look up. "What'd she say?"

I pour fresh coffee and put it down in front of Gene. I take his hand and place it on the side of the cup. Gene's eyes aren't what they used to be. "She said if you start walking now, you should get there by Tuesday."

Gene throws his head back and laughs until it becomes a deep cough. He reaches into his back pocket, pulls out a hanky and hacks into it. I wonder how long it's been since the thing has seen the inside of a washing machine. When he's done bringing up a lung he puts the hanky away and I sop up the coffee he spilled over the table and floor. I pour him another. He takes out his salve and gauze. I glance at the clock. Oh, yeah. It's Saturday. Home Care comes late on Saturdays. Five in the afternoon instead of nine in the morning.

"Hey, Gene," I say. "I've been thinking about opening earlier on Saturdays. Ten is late. I'm missing out on customers. I think I'll open at nine next Saturday."

He stares at the floor. "Well, I'll come at nine. So you won't be lonely."

I pull at the tape on Gene's ear. "Good."

Jimmy is back. He sips espresso and grins at me. "Have you figured out if you're married or not?"

I stare at the floor, chewing the inside of my cheek. "I'm in the middle of a divorce."

He shrugs. "Is that all?"

I look up and smile, grateful for his nonchalance. I'm shy talking about my divorce. Most of the people in my church don't talk to me anymore, including the pastor. "That's all."

"What happened?"

"To my marriage? I don't know. He just… walked away."

Jimmy shakes his head. "He's an idiot."

I'm warmed by the insult.

He leans forward, his head low to the table and whispers, "Where's he at now?"

Something vague and spooky creeps up my spine. Something about the way he asked. I blink at him. "Somewhere in Michigan."

He seems to think about this. He sits back in his chair and is quiet for a moment. "Did he make you cry?"

Tears rush to my eyeballs. "Maybe a little."

He slams a fist on the table and I jump. Espresso sloshes onto the table. He pushes a napkin at it. "You tell me where he's at. Where in Michigan? What's his name?"

"Why are you asking?"

He looks me in the eye. "I know people in Michigan."

He knows people? He can't mean what I think he means. I grab a chair and sit down hard. I'm having a conversation I don't want to have.

He's watching me closely. He shrugs and sips his coffee. "Your call. It's a sin when a man makes a beautiful woman cry. That's all I'm saying."

I force a smile. "Sin? You're a religious guy? I wouldn't have pegged ya for it."

He leans toward me. "I don't know religion. But I know right and wrong. And walking out on someone like you—that's wrong.

"Thank you," I say, feeling oddly peaceful that he would look at me with such violent compassion. With such strange grace.

Debi is sitting across the table reading a calendar from a nearby university. "They have a good psychology department."

I'm reading material from a Bible college hundreds of miles away. I point at the university calendar. "I doubt I'd pass the entrance exam."

She taps the top of the paper I'm reading. "Why do you want to study psychology?"

I put the paper down. "I want to help people."

She laughs.

"What?"

She's still laughing, and shaking her head at me. "You don't think you're helping people?"

"I serve ice cream and coffee. I heat up burritos. Not exactly saving the world over here."

She cocks her head. "How come you're so dumb?"

"I want God to use me to help people. Ya know?"

She folds her hands on the table and sits tall in her chair in a "now-class-pay-attention" sort of way. "There's this guy, named Jesus. You may have heard of Him."

I stick out my tongue.

Debi ignores me. "He said, 'Whatever you did for the least of my brothers, you did for me.' Please note, He did not say, 'Whatever you did after you earned a degree and gained success in the world's eyes, you did for me.'"

I roll my eyes. "You gonna preach? You want me to pass the offering plate?"

She shrugs. "I'm just saying you don't have to go to school so God can use you. If you look around, you'll see He's already using you."

That's the way it is at the Stuckville Café. I never know what the day will bring. Or who'll walk through my door. And it's enough to keep me here. I open my café each day and find I am both the giver, and the receiver, of God's grace. It looks nothing like I thought it would.

1. Five feet, seven inches = 1.70 metres; 10 pounds = 4.54 kilograms.

The Clay and the Vine

Brian Austin

Make of me a vessel
that reveals the Master's hand;
Just ordinary clay transformed,
Living the life He planned.

> Graft me to the living vine,
> a wild branch though I be;
> The fruit of love & hope & peace…
> His likeness born in me.

Contributors

Janette Oke
www.janetteoke.com

Janette Oke is one of Canada's best-selling authors, and a pioneer in the field of inspirational fiction. Her first novel, a prairie love story titled *Love Comes Softly*, was published in 1979. This book was followed by more than 65 others. Her historical novels portray the lives of early North American settlers. The Alberta writer's books have sold more than 28 million copies and been translated into 14 languages.

Janette—who also writes children's stories and gift books—reaches both Christian and general markets, telling stories that transcend time and place. Her readers of all ages and walks of life can identify with the everyday events and emotions of her characters. Janette believes everyone goes through tough times, and that the key is to be prepared with a strong faith as the foundation from which decisions are made and difficult experiences are faced.

She has received numerous awards, including the Gold Medallion Award, The Christy Award of Excellence, the 1992 President's Award from the Evangelical Christian Publishers Association for her significant contribution to the category of Christian fiction, and in 1999 the Life Impact Award from the Christian Booksellers Association International. The Word Guild, Canada's largest association of writers and editors who are Christian, honoured Janette Oke's career achievement in 2004 with the Leslie K. Tarr Award for outstanding contribution to Christian writing and publishing in Canada.

Carolyn Arends

www.carolynarends.com

Carolyn Arends has released nine award-winning albums and is the author of two critically acclaimed books. She is in demand as a concert performer, public speaker, retreat facilitator, college instructor and columnist. Carolyn lives in Surrey, British Columbia with her husband, Mark, and their children, Benjamin and Bethany.

Wrestling With Angels (Harvest House/*Conversantlife.com*)
We've Been Waiting For You (Thomas Nelson)
Recordings: *Pollyanna's Attic, Christmas: An Irrational Season, Under the Gaze, We've Been Waiting For You* (all 2B Records); *Travelers* (Signpost Music); *Seize the Day and Other Stories* (Reunion Records)

Brian Austin

baustin@bmts.com

Brian Austin has more than 80 published articles and poems, as well as a collection of poetry titled *Laughter and Tears* in both book and audio CD format. Employed in a Bible bookstore, Brian also serves as a church librarian and on the board of directors of the Canadian Mental Health Association, Grey-Bruce Branch. He and his wife live near Durham, Ontario. They have three grown children and four grandchildren. His idea of a perfectly furnished room is floor-to-ceiling bookshelves, a comfortable chair and an excellent reading light.

Laughter & Tears Audio CD (LittleBoxStudios/Word Alive)
Laughter & Tears Trade Paperback Book (Word Alive)
I Barabbas Audio CD (LittleBoxStudios/Word Alive)

Paul M. Beckingham

http://walkingtowardshope.blogspot.com

Paul M. Beckingham has been able to travel to surprising places beyond his Vancouver, British Columbia home! Those diverse destinations deliver energy to his writing. Today, Paul's life unfolds in Canada; it once unravelled in Kenya. Africa beckoned him, but left him dying on the Limuru Road. A long recovery changed him forever.

Now Paul enjoys gentle walks, playing jazz trumpet and fireside moments to reclaim his broken dreams. Both his award-winning articles and his book have garnered national recognition. His exceptional writing carries readers on a personal soul safari, and they will reach with him towards new hope!

Walking Towards Hope: Experiencing Grace in a Time of Brokenness (Castle Quay)

Paul H. Boge
www.paulboge.com

Paul H. Boge is passionate about evangelism and encouraging believers in their faith in Jesus Christ. Paul is an award-winning novelist, the writer/director of the feature film *Among Thieves* (FireGate Films), and a practicing professional engineer. Paul is a public speaker in a variety of settings including church groups, and is actively involved with Mully Children's Family, a street children's rescue ministry in Kenya. He lives wherever his engineering projects and research for future novels and films take him. He calls Winnipeg, Manitoba home.

The Cities of Fortune (Castle Quay)
Father to the Fatherless: The Charles Mulli Story (BayRidge)
The Chicago Healer (Castle Quay)

Mark Buchanan
http://markbuchanan.net

Mark Buchanan is an award-winning author and pastor. He lives on Vancouver Island, British Columbia, with his wife and three children. Mark felt a call to write at age 12, and completed a degree in creative writing at the University of British Columbia. He currently is working on a novel.

Hidden in Plain Sight: The Secret of More
(Thomas Nelson)
The Rest of God: Restoring Your Soul by Restoring Sabbath (Thomas Nelson)
The Holy Wild: Trusting in the Character of God (Multnomah)
Things Unseen: Living in Light of Forever (Multnomah)
Your God is Too Safe: Rediscovering the Wonder of a God You Can't Control
(Multnomah)

Brad Burke, MD
www.bradburke.com

Brad Burke, MD, is a medical specialist, speaker and author who took a five-year sabbatical from practicing medicine to research and write the compelling book series *An MD Examines*. This four-book series is packed with creative illustrations and stories to share God's character through the eyes of a medical doctor. Brad has been a guest on several radio and TV shows including *100 Huntley Street* and Janet Parshall's syndicated show, *America*. Brad currently works and lives in the Windsor, Ontario/Detroit, Michigan area with his wife Erin.

An MD Examines: Is God Obsolete? (Cook)
An MD Examines: Why Doesn't God Stop Evil? (Cook)
An MD Examines: Does God Still Do Miracles? (Cook)
An MD Examines: Why Does God Allow Suffering? (Cook)

Donna Carter
www.straighttalk.ab.ca

Donna Carter has a unique ability to synthesize life experience into digestible lessons. She is sought after as a speaker in Canada and the United States because of her clarity, humour and the "light bulb moments" she triggers for women. Donna lives in Calgary, Alberta with her husband, Randy, and two daughters. The Carters founded *Straight Talk Ministries* in 1994, to pursue their passion of helping people find faith and apply it to everyday life. To learn more about Donna's life management course for spiritual seekers, visit 10smartthings.com. To book Donna for speaking engagements, visit her Web site.

10 Smart Things Women Can Do to Build a Better Life (Harvest House)
10 Smart Things Women Can Do to Build a Better Life: A Life Management Course for Women with No Previous Church Experience (Straight Talk Books)

Keith Clemons
www.clemonsbooks.com

Keith Clemons is the author of four novels. His first three titles, *If I Should Die, Above the Stars,* and *These Little Ones,* have accumulated a total of five awards, including The Word Guild's Canadian Christian Writing Awards Best Contemporary Novel in 2004, 2005 and 2007, respectively. Keith's suspenseful novels deal with current social issues that affect the church and society, such as child trafficking, euthanasia, the Hollywood film industry, our loss of religious freedom, and terrorism. He is a popular speaker and frequently appears on radio and television. He resides with his wife in Caledon, Ontario.

Mohammed's Moon (George Colton Publishing) Coming 2009
Angel in the Alley (George Colton Publishing)
These Little Ones (George Colton Publishing)
Above the Stars (George Colton Publishing)
If I Should Die (George Colton Publishing)

Donna Dawson (Donna Fawcett)
www.authordonnadawson.com

Donna Fawcett was brought up in a Christian home by godly parents. At age 27, she surrendered her life to Christ after realizing that religion and relationship with Christ were not the same. Donna and her husband live in rural southwestern Ontario, where she is actively involved in music ministry in her church. Using her military upbringing, her experience in home teaching and her love of horses, Donna writes faith suspense novels under her pen name, Donna Dawson, and both non-fiction for home-schooling families and faith romance novels under her own name, Donna Fawcett.

The Fires of Fury (Awe-Struck Books) Coming 2009
The Adam & Eve Project (Word Alive Press)
Redeemed (Word Alive Press)
Thriving in the Home School, by Donna Fawcett (Word Alive Press)

Angelina Fast-Vlaar

www.angelinafastvlaar.com
www.thevalleyofcancer.com

Best-selling author Angelina Fast-Vlaar, of St. Catharines, Ontario, has taught college-level psychology, worked as a counsellor, and led many Bible studies. Her book *Seven Angels for Seven Days* won The Word Guild's Best New Canadian Christian Author Award in 2004, and her articles and poetry have appeared in several magazines. The mother of five was widowed in 1987 and remarried in 1994. A popular inspirational speaker, Angelina draws on her wealth of experience to captivate and motivate her audiences. As a cancer survivor, she offers hope and encouragement via her "Valley of Cancer" Web site.

Seven Angels for Seven Days (Castle Quay)
The Valley of Cancer: A Journey of Comfort and Hope (Essence)

Grace Fox

www.gracefox.com

Grace Fox is a popular speaker at international women's events and a frequent radio and television guest on programs such as *100 Huntley Street* and *It's a New Day*. She publishes *Growing with Grace*, an inspirational monthly newsletter that encourages thousands worldwide, and a quarterly newsletter for Christian women in leadership.

Grace lives in Abbotsford, British Columbia, with her husband, Gene. They are the directors of International Messengers Canada Inc., a ministry that specializes in creative short-term and career overseas opportunities. They have three grown children, two of whom are married, and one grandchild.

Moving From Fear to Freedom: A Woman's Guide to Peace in Every Situation (Harvest House)
10-Minute Time Outs for You and Your Kids (Harvest House)
10-Minute Time Outs for Busy Women (Harvest House)
10-Minute Time Outs for Moms (Harvest House)

Jean Chamberlain Froese, MD
www.savethemothers.com

Jean Chamberlain Froese is an obstetrician and the founding executive director of Save the Mothers International. Now based in Uganda most of the time, for 10 years she has worked on behalf of mothers in several developing countries. When in Canada, she's based at McMaster University, Hamilton, Ontario (*jchamber@mcmaster.ca*).
Where Have All the Mothers Gone? Stories of Courage and Hope Among the World's Poorest Women (Epic Press)

Thomas Froese
www.thomasfroese.com

A 20 year-journalist, Thomas Froese writes provocative, humorous and maybe even enlightening columns for various Canadian newspapers from the Arab world, Africa, and, sometimes, beyond. He's gained a unique perspective on news, travel and life, and has received numerous honours for his work, which often explores spiritual and cultural themes.
Open Windows into Unknown Places: A Journalist's Dispatches from Arabia to Africa and Beyond (Epic Press) Coming 2008

W. Harold Fuller
www3.sympatico.ca/harold.fuller

W. Harold Fuller was born on Canada's west coast, served in the Canadian Navy on the east coast, studied missions and Bible on the prairies, edited Africa's largest circulation (at the time) monthly magazine, has ministered in six continents, and with his wife Lorna now resides in Stouffville, Ontario.

An award-winning author ("Jesus Wears a Stethoscope" is adapted from Harold's 12th book, *Sun Like Thunder*), Harold holds a diploma in journalism from the Newspaper Institute of America, an honorary doctorate in literature from Biola University, and the 1996 Leslie K. Tarr Award for career achievement and outstanding contribution to the field of Canadian Christian writing.

Sun Like Thunder: Following Jesus on Asia's Old Silk Road Today (SIM) Coming 2008; *Maxwell's Passion & Power* (Maxwell Foundation)
Global Crossroads, editor (World Evangelical Alliance)
People of the Mandate (Paternoster/Baker)
Celebrate the God Who Loves (SIM)

Bonnie Grove
www.bonniegrove.com

Bonnie Grove is an innovative thinker and writer. Passionate about people, she writes with clarity about empowerment, hope, strengths and the fullness of life found in Christ. Bonnie has training both in Christian counselling and secular psychology. She has developed and written several social programs currently in use throughout Alberta, and has published articles on parenting and family life. Bonnie lives with her husband, Steve, a pastor, and their two children in Saskatoon, Saskatchewan. Her first non-fiction Christian book is coming out later this year and she is currently at work on her first novel.

Living Out of Your Strengths (Beacon Hill Press) Coming 2008

Sheila Wray Gregoire
www.SheilaWrayGregoire.com

Sheila Wray Gregoire is a syndicated parenting columnist and a popular speaker. The author of four books with more on the way, she loves encouraging women to forget about the dust bunnies under their beds and keep their focus on Jesus. She also has a passion for family, and together with her husband, Keith, speaks at FamilyLife Canada marriage conferences around the nation.

You can usually find Sheila in Belleville, Ontario, where she home-schools her two daughters and knits. Preferably simultaneously.

How Big Is Your Umbrella? Weathering the Storms of Life (Kregel)

Reality Check (Essence)

Honey, I Don't Have a Headache Tonight: Help for Women Who Want to Feel More In the Mood (Kregel)

To Love, Honor and Vacuum: When You Feel More Like a Maid Than a Wife and a Mother (Kregel)

Deborah Gyapong

www.deborahgyapong.com

Photo by
ChristopherHumphrey
Photography.com

After finding God in a Boston, Massachusetts drug dealer's den, Deborah Gyapong moved to Nova Scotia in 1975 to live in a small commune on a dilapidated farm. The dream failed. So the newly single mother answered an ad for a job at a newspaper, and discovered her calling. From print she moved to radio, then to television. She spent 17 years at the Canadian Broadcasting Corporation (CBC), working mostly as a TV producer. Deborah now covers Canadian federal politics on Parliament Hill in Ottawa, Ontario, for religious newspapers. Her novel *The Defilers* won The Word Guild's 2005 Best New Canadian Christian Author Award.

The Defilers (Castle Quay)

Jane Harris

www.visionofcanada.com
http://visionofcanada.blogspot.com

Jane Harris's fascination with Canada's destiny led her to a career as a freelance journalist. Writing in both mainstream and Christian media, she digs into political and social issues that make Canada unique. She and her husband live in Lethbridge, Alberta.

Stars Appearing: The Galts' Vision of Canada
    (Volumes Publishing)

David Kitz

www.davidkitz.ca

David Kitz is an actor, award-winning author and a public school teacher. For more than 12 years, he served as an ordained pastor with the Foursquare Gospel Church of Canada. His love for drama and storytelling is evident to all who have seen his Bible-based performances. He has toured across Canada and the United States with a variety of one-man plays for both children and adults. Born and raised in Saskatchewan, David now lives in Ottawa, Ontario, with his wife Karen and their two adult sons, Tim and Joshua.

Psalms Alive! Coming 2008
Little Froggy Explores the BIG World (Essence)
The Soldier, the Terrorist & the Donkey King (Essence)

Marcia Lee Laycock

www.vinemarc.com

www.marcialaycock.blogspot.com

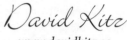

Marcia Lee Laycock is a pastor's wife in Blackfalds, Alberta and the mother of three girls. After first writing for her dolls in her parents' attic, she has become an award-winning writer and sought-after speaker/teacher. Her novel *One Smooth Stone* won The Word Guild's Best New Canadian Christian Author Award in 2006.

One Smooth Stone (Castle Quay)
Focused Reflections (Essence)

Keturah Leonforde

www.keturahleonforde.com

Based in Guelph, Ontario, Keturah Leonforde has one life mission—inspiring individuals, groups and organizations to achieve theirs! Whether as an award-winning author, worship leader, management consultant or career coach, Keturah's passion for igniting potential and facilitating positive transformation has been instrumental in motivating hundreds of clients to identify and pursue their God-given destiny.

Reflections from the Waiting Room: Insights for Thriving
When Life Puts You on Hold (Essence)

N. J. Lindquist

www.njlindquist.com

Photo by
Gofishredink.com

N. J. Lindquist is a motivational speaker, a columnist, and the author of two adult mysteries, five coming-of-age novels, three discipleship manuals for teens, and a Christmas play. Her overall focus is to encourage people to become all that God created them to be. The mother of four adult sons lives in Markham, Ontario. With the support of her husband, Les, she co-founded The Word Guild in 2002. N. J. has won numerous awards for her writing; she also received the 2006 Leading Women Award for Excellence in Communication and Media. N. J. currently is working on a spiritual memoir, *LoveChild*.

Glitter of Diamonds (MurderWillOut Mysteries)
Shaded Light (MurderWillOut Mysteries)
Circle of Friends series: *Best of Friends, Friends Like These, Friends in Need, More Than Friends* (That's Life! Communications)
In Time of Trouble (That's Life! Communications)
The New You (High Impact Ministries)
The Bridge: Student to Student Discipleship, Vols. 1 and 2 (High Impact Ministries)

M. D. Meyer

www.dorenemeyer.com

Photo by
JayGaune.com

M. D. Meyer is the award-winning author of a series of books set in a fictional First Nations community. Her books touch on such issues as recovery from child sexual abuse, residential school syndrome and alcohol abuse. With published credits that also encompass journalism, poetry and playwriting, Dorene teaches workshops and classes for aspiring writers in all genres. She lives in Norway House, northern Manitoba.

Deep Waters (Art Bookbindery)
Get Lost! (Art Bookbindery)
Colin's Choice (Essence)

Photo by Sue Careless

Wendy Elaine Nelles

www.wendynelles.com

Wendy Elaine Nelles is an award-winning journalist, writer, editor and speaker with wide-ranging experience in the corporate, not-for-profit and publishing sectors. Her news articles, features and profiles have appeared on the front pages of Canadian Christian publications. She holds an MA in Communications with high honour from Wheaton College, Illinois. Her work has impacted many of Canada's writers and editors who are Christian, through co-founding The Word Guild in 2002 and directing many writing awards programs and writers' conferences. The Toronto resident has served on the leadership team of Canada's largest Christian writers' conference, Write! Canada, for 20 consecutive years. Wendy was honoured nationally with the Leading Women Award for Excellence in Communications and Media in 2006.

Denyse O'Leary

http://post-darwinist.blogspot.com
http://mindfulhack.blogspot.com

Photo by Sue Careless

Denyse O'Leary is a Toronto-based journalist and blogger who is the author of three books on faith and science issues, including her latest, *The Spiritual Brain: A Neuroscientist's Case for the Existence of the Soul*, (co-authored with Montreal neuroscientist Mario Beauregard), and another on the intelligent design controversy. She has taught writing, editing, and business practice for writers and editors for many years. Denyse is the winner of numerous awards for her articles, columns and books; frequently appears as a media commentator; and is a columnist for the newspapers *Christian Week* and *Maranatha News*.

The Spiritual Brain: A Neuroscientist's Case for the Existence of the Soul with
   co-author Mario Beauregard (HarperOne)
*By Design or by Chance? The Growing Controversy on the Origins of Life in the
   Universe* (Augsburg Fortress)
Faith@Science: Why Science Needs Faith in the Twenty-First Century
   (J. Gordon Shillingford)

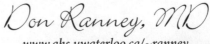

Don Ranney, MD

www.ahs.uwaterloo.ca/~ranney

Don Ranney, MD, went to India in 1969 to help leprosy sufferers through reconstructive surgery. He also trained five surgeons, wrote two medical books and published 14 scientific papers. Later he established the School of Anatomy at the University of Waterloo, Waterloo, Ontario, and wrote 98 more scientific papers. Currently, Don helps accident-injured people through orthopaedic assessments.

When Cobras Laugh, with co-author Ray Wiseman (Capstone Fiction)
Chronic Musculoskeletal Injuries in the Workplace (WB Saunders)

Diane Roblin-Lee

bydesignmedia.ca
dianeroblinlee.com
www.journalbydesign.blogspot.com
www.miraclesbydesign.blogspot.com

Diane Roblin-Lee's first book, *My Father's Child*, was deemed a classic by television host David Mainse. In her remarkably transparent style, Diane engages hearts, encouraging readers to find life, lessons and leading through their own challenges.

Photo by
Gofishredink.com

Living in Ontario, she has been a writer, TV host (*Nite Lite* and *Raiders of the Lost*), occasional co-host of *100 Huntley Street*, speaker, publisher, mother and grandmother. Her history of The Peoples Church, *Into all the World*, with a foreword by Dr. Billy Graham, won The Word Guild's first-place award in the special book category. Through her company, byDesign Media, Diane also designs books (including the interior of *Hot Apple Cider*) and print media.

The Forgotten Key to Christian Marriage, with Rev. Gordon Williams
    (byDesign Media) Coming 2008
To My Family—My Life (Castle Quay)
Spirit-Led Days: Day by Day with the Holy Spirit, with Rev. Gordon Williams
    (Castle Quay)
Like a Rushing Mighty Wind, with Rev. Gordon Williams (Praise Productions)

Eleanor Shepherd
http://eleanorshepherd.blogspot.com/

Truly Canadian, Eleanor Shepherd was born in St. John's, Newfoundland; by age 10, she was living in Vancouver, British Columbia. Bilingualism came with a move to France in 1987. She hosted a radio talk show with other pastors in Paris from 1998 to 2002. She has more than 85 articles published in Canada and France, with some also appearing in the U.S.A., Belgium, Switzerland and New Zealand. They furnished material for her teaching on integrated mission in Africa. Eleanor contributes regularly to *Woman Alive* magazine and *Salvationist.ca*. She served nearly 30 years as an ordained officer of The Salvation Army.

Why Families? A Series of Seven Inductive Bible Studies on the Family, with co-author Glen Shepherd (The Salvation Army)

Ray Wiseman
www.ray.wiseman.ca

Ray Wiseman of Fergus, Ontario, began writing seriously in the early 1980s, following careers in electronics and ministry in Canada and South Africa. He has written eight books and nearly 1,000 editorials, newspaper features and columns. Ray teaches writing and critiques manuscripts for new authors.

When Cobras Laugh, with co-author Don Ranney, MD (Capstone Fiction)
Write! Better: A Writing Tip for Every Week of the Year (WordWise)
Exploring God's Route 66: An Introduction to the Bible (WordWise)
A Difficult Passage: From Prairie Poverty to Heights Beyond (WordWise)

Carmen Wittmeier
www.carmenwittmeier.blogspot.com

Carmen Wittmeier completed her MA in English at the University of Alberta in 1999. She taught college courses, edited novels and wrote fiction before joining World Vision Canada in 2007. She resides in Calgary, Alberta, with Rod, her husband of one year, and Woodstock, her cockatiel of 26 years.

Affirming the Birth Mother's Journey: A Peer Counselor's Guide to Adoption Counseling (Trafford)

Eric E. Wright

www.countrywindow.ca

Eric E. Wright, author of six books, has 44 years of experience as a missionary, seminary professor, pastor and writer. He lives with his wife, Mary Helen, in the eastern Ontario countryside where his new devotional collection, *Down a Country Road*, is set. He edits the *Fellowship Baptist LINK* magazine.

Down a Country Road: 52 Seasonal Readings From Out Where the Sky Springs Free (Day One Publishers) Coming 2008

The Lightning File: A Josh Radley Suspense Novel (Hidden Brook Press)

Revolutionary Forgiveness: Developing a Forgiving Lifestyle (Evangelical Press)

Through a Country Window: Inspiring Stories from Out Where the Sky Springs Free (Essence)

Church—No Spectator Sport: In Search of Spiritual Gifts (Evangelical Press)

Ron Wyse

www.marriageupgrade.com

Canadian-born Ron Wyse brings to his reflections 20 years in a cross-cultural marriage, life on three continents, and extensive training in Scripture as well as in counselling. Ron served eight years as a missionary with the Africa Evangelical Fellowship. While teaching Biblical studies in Zimbabwe, Ron did his doctoral work in Proverbs and counselling, and earned a Doctor Divinitatis (DD) degree at the University of Pretoria, South Africa. Ron also taught in Hong Kong, the birthplace of his wife, Sarah. They now make their home with their two teens in Markham, Ontario.

Beyond Survival: Marriage and the Quest for Paradise (VMI Publishers)

Acknowledgements

We're delighted to have been able to showcase the writing of these terrific authors in *Hot Apple Cider: Words to Stir the Heart and Warm the Soul.*

Of course, we didn't do it alone! So we need to thank a few people.

First of all, we want to thank the 30 authors who had faith in this venture, many of whom committed to being part of the undertaking before all the details were known.

Our sincere thanks go to Janette Oke, who so generously wrote the foreword, and to all of the leaders who read advance copies of the book and wholeheartedly endorsed it.

We appreciate the expertise of Ingrid Paulson of Ingrid Paulson Design, who designed the book cover; and the creativity of Diane Roblin-Lee of byDesign Media, who did the interior design and layout. To Cameron Wybrow, PhD, our main proofreader, and to Alan Yoshioka, PhD, who assisted with proofreading, we offer our thanks for their keen observations.

We wish to thank World Vision Canada, a Christian relief, development and advocacy organization  dedicated to working with children, families and communities to overcome poverty and injustice. Most particularly, Eric Spath, manager of speakers and events, forged the partnership with The Word Guild that made this groundbreaking project possible. The

Girls Night Out (GNO) is managed under the planning and guidance of World Vision Canada and its ministry partners.

www.gnolive.com

Word Guild is making 30,000 copies of *Hot Apple Cider* available for World Vision Canada to distribute as gifts to women who attend Girls Night Out events— evenings of fun, faith and fellowship hosted by churches across Canada that help World Vision inspire sponsors to contribute to its ministry of caring for children orphaned by AIDS in Africa.

We also extend our sincere thanks to the more than 325 members of The Word Guild throughout Canada, who have enthusiastically supported and promoted this book; and to the 60-plus members of The Word Guild's prayer team, who have prayed for this book since its

THE **word** GUILD

Connecting, developing and promoting Canadian writers and editors who are Christian.

www.thewordguild.com

inception. We especially thank The Word Guild's leadership team, in particular Sandra Reimer and Denise Rumble, for their vision, passion and commitment.

If you are a Canadian writer or editor—whether a raw beginner or a much-published professional—we encourage you to find out more about this collaborative community at *www.thewordguild.com*. The Word Guild sponsors conferences, writing contests and awards, a national e-mail discussion group, and other opportunities for learning and networking. They also welcome as affiliate members people working in related fields, such as publishers, book retailers and librarians, as well as avid readers who want to show their interest and support, and non-Canadian writers and editors.

We express our gratitude to Les Lindquist, N. J.'s husband and partner, who has provided advice, support and encouragement for everything we have done.

Most importantly, we wish to thank our God for His grace, guidance and wisdom in the unexpected faith adventure of founding and leading The Word Guild for the past six years, and in the creation and production of this book.

Our prayer is that you will find encouragement, hope and faith through the words on these pages—all of which are inspired by the One who is the Word: "In the beginning was the Word, and the Word was with God, and the Word was God" (John 1:1).

N. J. Lindquist
Wendy Elaine Nelles
Editors of *Hot Apple Cider*
Co-Founders, The Word Guild

For more information about *Hot Apple Cider* and its authors, or to comment about this book, see *www.hotapplecider.ca*.